Pyrrhus of Epirus

Pyrrhus of Epirus

Jeff Champion

Pen & Sword
MILITARY

First published in Great Britain in 2009 and reprinted in this format in 2016 by
PEN & SWORD MILITARY
an imprint of
Pen & Sword Books Ltd
47 Church Street
Barnsley
South Yorkshire
S70 2AS

ISBN 978 1 47388 664 3

Typeset in 11/12pt Ehrhardt MT by
Pen & Sword Books Ltd, Barnsley

Printed and bound in England
By CPI Group (UK) Ltd, Croydon, CR0 4YY

Pen & Sword Books Ltd incorporates the Imprints of Pen & Sword Aviation,
Pen & Sword Maritime, Pen & Sword Military, Pen & Sword Atlas, Pen & Sword Politics,
Pen & Sword Discovery, Pen & Sword Archaeology, Pen & Sword Family History,
Wharncliffe Local History, Wharncliffe True Crime, Wharncliffe Transport,
Pen & Sword Select, Pen & Sword Military Classics, Leo Cooper, The Praetorian Press,
Claymore Press, Remember When, Seaforth Publishing and Frontline Publishing

For a complete list of Pen & Sword titles please contact
PEN & SWORD BOOKS LIMITED
47 Church Street, Barnsley, South Yorkshire, S70 2AS, England
E-mail: enquiries@pen-and-sword.co.uk
Website: www.pen-and-sword.co.uk

Contents

PREFACE

'It is pretty generally stated by authors, that no king, either of that or the former age, was to be compared to Pyrrhus; and that there has seldom been seen, either among princes, or other illustrious men, a man of more upright life or of stricter justice; and that he had such knowledge of the military art, that though he fought against such great princes as Lysimachus, Demetrius, and Antigonus, he was never conquered. In his wars too with the Illyrians, Sicilians, Romans, and Carthaginians, he never came off inferior, but generally victorious.'
- Justin, 25.5

Pyrrhus, king of Epirus, was born in 319 and would die in battle in 272. He would spend many of his early years in exile, totally reliant on the patronage of foreign kings. Yet, during his life, Epirus would rise from what was considered a barbarous backwater of the Greek and Macedonian world, to a major power. At times during his reign, although never all at once, he would expand his rule to include Macedonia, Thessaly, much of central and southern Greece, Sicily and southern Italy almost to the gates of Rome. He would be the first of the Hellenistic kings to fight the Romans and the only one to defeat them in a major battle. After his death Epirus would again return to the position of a minor kingdom.

To properly understand this rapid rise and fall his career must be placed within its historical context. His life would span the period of history known as the 'age of the Successors'. The great contemporary historian of the era, Hieronymus of Cardia, would end his history of the period at the point of Pyrrhus' death. The Successors were those generals of Alexander the Great, who would, to quote Plutarch, 'carve up his empire like the carcass of some great slaughtered beast.'[1] Alexander had justified his conquest and rule over the Persian Empire as 'spear-won land'. This concept is best summed up in his reply to Darius before the battle of Gaugamela, 'go tell your king that what he has lost and what he still possesses both remain the prizes of war. It is war that will determine the boundaries of our respective kingdoms.'[2] The Successors would justify their rule by the same ideology. It was a period when individuals with sufficient talent, ruthlessness and luck, could rapidly win large kingdoms and even more quickly lose them. Single events such as battles, rebellions and assassinations, could overnight destroy one dynasty and create a new one. This was the world that Pyrrhus was born into and it is in this context that his mercurial career must be viewed.

It is as a military leader, however, that Pyrrhus was mostly remembered by the ancient historians. There is an often repeated anecdote that records a supposed conversation between the great Carthaginian general Hannibal and his Roman conqueror Scipio Africanus.[3] Scipio asked Hannibal who he considered to be the greatest general of all time. In the usual Roman manner he no doubt expected Hannibal to name him. Hannibal instead replied that he considered 'Alexander to have been the mightiest of generals, and next to him Pyrrhus, and third himself.' A different version of the story has Hannibal stating 'that the foremost of all generals in experience and ability was Pyrrhus.' This conversation, most likely, never occurred. Its constant repetition does, however, show the high regard in which Pyrrhus' generalship was held by the ancient writers. The basis of this renown probably rests on the reputation he achieved by his two great victories in battle over the Romans at Heraclea and Asculum. His reputation may also have persisted through his writings on military theory and practice. Although these works are now totally lost, they were still being read by his enemies, the Romans, over two centuries after his death. Despite the high degree of interest in Pyrrhus' career, no attempt has been made to produce a biography in English since the publication of Petros Garoufalias' second edition of his work *Pyrrhus, King of Epirus* in 1979. The purpose of writing this book was to provide an easily accessible narrative history of Pyrrhus' life and campaigns. The first problem for anyone attempting such a work is the relative shortage of ancient sources. Although there were a number of contemporary historians for the period, and Pyrrhus reputedly wrote his own memoirs, all of their works have been lost except for a few surviving fragments. The only continuous narrative of Pyrrhus' life that survives is Plutarch's biography. Although invaluable this work has it limitations, for as Plutarch readily admits he was a biographer not a historian. Plutarch confesses that:

> It is not Histories that I am writing, but Lives; and in the most illustrious deeds there is not always a manifestation of virtue or vice, no, a slight thing like a phrase or a jest often makes a greater revelation of character than battles when thousands fall, or the greatest armaments, or sieges of cities.[4]

Such a method produces obvious shortcomings for any military history based primarily on Plutarch's writings. Fortunately, his work is able to be supplemented by a number of other historians whose works include sections dealing with Pyrrhus' life and campaigns.

Given the limited nature of the ancient sources, much of what I have written is open to alternative interpretations. I have, however, written what I believe to be the most likely version of events. This work is not aimed at an academic audience. I have, therefore, generally limited my endnotes to the attribution of direct quotations or to give the sources of any statistics. Anyone seriously interested in the historiographic problems concerning Pyrrhus' life should consult Garoufalias' work and its voluminous endnotes.

Although this book is primarily a narrative history, any course of historical events cannot be understood in isolation. There will be, therefore, a number of short discourses on topics that are relevant to the general historical context of the period. Topics covered will include: the military developments of both the Greeks and Romans in the period immediately before Pyrrhus' reign; short histories of Rome's expansion into southern Italy and the conflicts between the Greeks and Carthaginians in Sicily; the character of Hellenistic kingship and the nature of the relationships between the Greek cities and the kings. This last theme is important in understanding the eventual failure of Pyrrhus' expeditions to both Italy and Sicily. As shall be seen, the Greeks of Italy and Sicily probably would have taken exception to the first part of Justin's statement. The first chapter will mainly be concerned with giving the background to the wars of the Successors and how Epirus, and more particularly the Epirot royal family, were drawn into these events.

All dates in this work are BC unless otherwise noted. I have used the Latinised version of most names, believing them to be more familiar to most readers. Modern place names have generally been placed in brackets after the first use of the ancient name.

The bibliography consists of those modern works that I have found most useful in the composition of this work. For the works of the ancient authors I have given the translation that I used.

Sections of this work derive from a research project that I was engaged upon while a student at the University of Western Australia. I would like to take this opportunity to thank the staff of the Department of Classics and Ancient History at U.W.A. for their continuing, friendly and always learned assistance.

I would also like to acknowledge the assistance of Andrew, Geoff, Julie and Vince for their help in their many and varied ways. Finally, I would like to thank my wife Janine, without whose encouragement and assistance this work would not have been commenced or completed.

List of Plates:

List of Maps

Greece and Macedonia in the Third Century BC

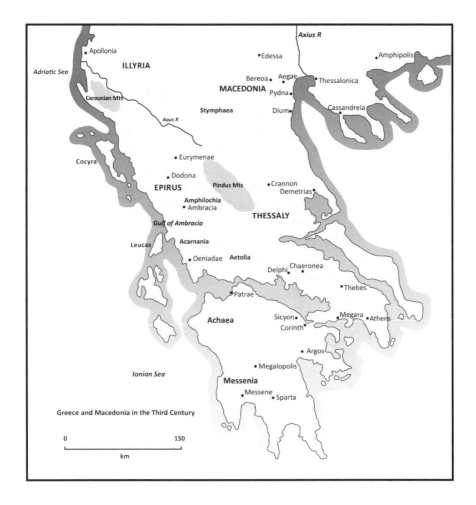

Italy in the Fourth Century BC

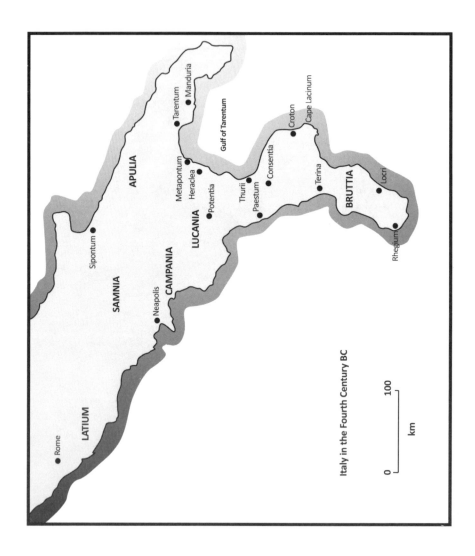

Italy in the Fourth Century BC

Italy in the Third Century BC, showing Pyrrhus' campaign of 280 BC

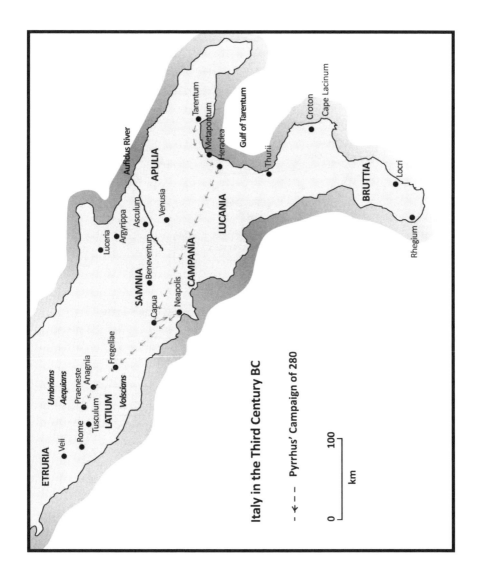

Italy in the Third Century BC

- ← - - Pyrrhus' Campaign of 280

The Battle of Heraclea

Battle of Heraclea: Opening Moves

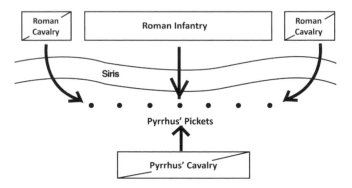

Battle of Heraclea: Possible course of final stages of the battle.

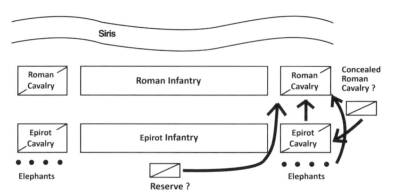

The Battle of Asculum, second day

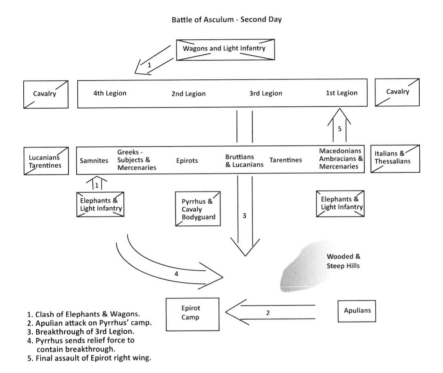

Battle of Asculum - Second Day

1. Clash of Elephants & Wagons.
2. Apulian attack on Pyrrhus' camp.
3. Breakthrough of 3rd Legion.
4. Pyrrhus sends relief force to
   contain breakthrough.
5. Final assault of Epirot right wing.

Pyrrhus' Sicilian Campaign of 278-276 BC

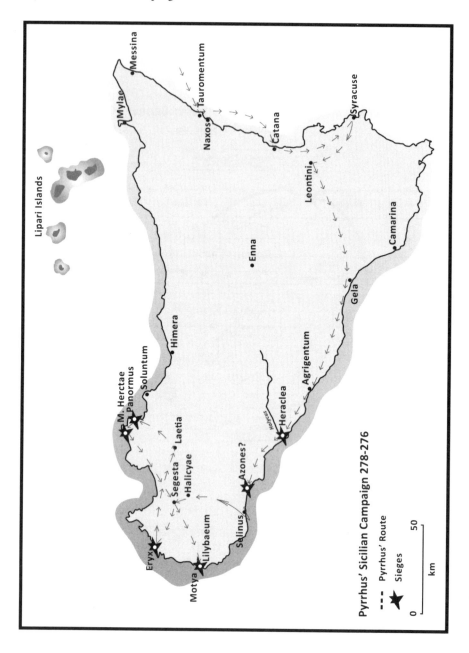

Pyrrhus' Sicilian Campaign 278-276

--- Pyrrhus' Route
★ Sieges

0   50
km

Possible Reconstruction of the Battle of Beneventum

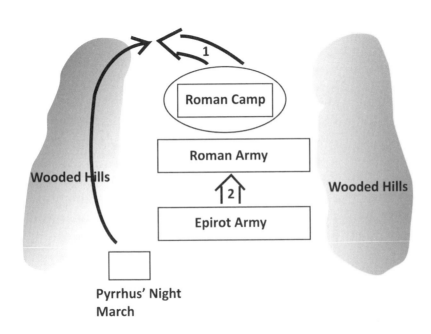

1 Roman attack on Pyrrhus' flanking force.

2 Attack of main Epirot Army.

Pyrrhus' Peloponnesian Campaign of 272 BC

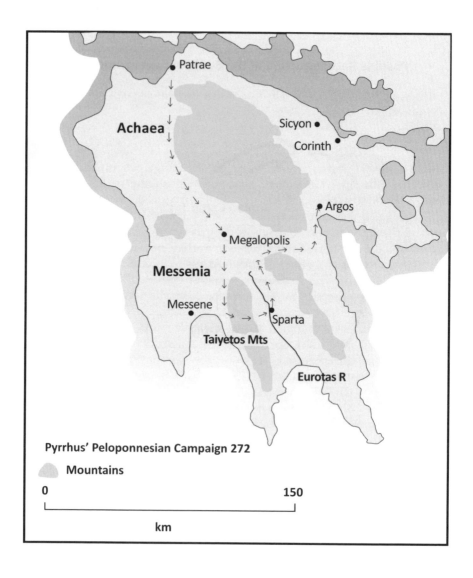

Chapter I
Epirus

'barbarian Chaonians, who belong to a nation that has no king'
- Thucydides, 2.80

The historical region of Epirus was regarded by the geographer Strabo as extending from the Ceraunian Mountains in southern Albania to the Ambracian Gulf in Greece. Its eastern boundary was defined by the Pindus Mountains that form the spine of mainland Greece.[1] It was bordered to the west by the Adriatic and Ionian seas. Epirus is a rugged and mountainous region. To the north lived the Illyrians, a warlike, non-Greek people, feared for their slave raids and piracy. To the east was Macedonia and Thessaly. To the south lived the Acarnanians. The Greek name Epirus signifies 'mainland' or 'continent', to distinguish it from the Ionian islands off the Epirot coast.

Epirus has been occupied since Neolithic times, when hunters and shepherds inhabited the region and constructed large burial mounds, tumuli, to bury their leaders. The grave goods found in these tumuli have many characteristics similar to those later used by the Mycenean Greeks. This suggests a possible ancestral link between Epirus and the Mycenean civilisation, probably beginning in what is now modern Albania.[2]

In Archaic times Epirus was most famous for the oracle at Dodona. It was the oldest of the Greek oracles according to Herodotus, and is mentioned in Homer's *Iliad*.[3] The original site dates to pre-Hellenic times. Herodotus tells the story of two kidnapped women who escaped from Egypt by turning themselves into doves and flying away. These escapees founded the sanctuary. A priestess gave the oracles by interpreting the rustling of the wind in the oak trees and the sounds of copper vessels being struck. The prow of Jason's ship the *Argo* supposedly had the gift of prophecy, as it had been carved by Athena from an oak tree that had been taken from the wood beside the sanctuary at Dodona. As an oracle Dodona was second in prestige only to Delphi.

The original Mycenean Greek inhabitants were either driven out or overwhelmed by the invasions of the Dorian tribes at the end of the second millennium (*circa* 1100-1000). By the early first millennium Epirus was occupied by fourteen tribes. The three most powerful were said to be: the Chaonians in the north, the Molossians in the centre and the Thesprotians in the south. Of these only the Molossians are recorded as having a continuing monarchy. The Epirots do not appear to have lived in, or around, walled cities, unlike many of the Greeks. Instead they inhabited small villages and were a mainly pastoral people. There is no evidence of walled cities in Epirus prior to the fourth century.[4] As such they were treated with disdain by more urbanised eastern and southern Greeks. The fifth century Athenian historian Thucydides repeatedly refers to them as barbarians.[5] The literal meaning of this would mean that they did not in fact speak Greek. It is more likely, however, that Thucydides is referring to their pastoral way of life, and lack of an urban - based political culture, rather than their language. Hammond has argued convincingly that the Epirots were a Greek-speaking people.[6]

The history of Epirus down to the fourth century is mostly obscured by myth. The most common tradition is that the kingship of the Molossians was founded by Neoptolemus, who was called Pyrrhus in his youth, and was the only son of Achilles, the great hero of the Trojan War. Neoptolemus was brought to Troy following the prophecy of the captured Trojan seer, Helenus. He gained a reputation as the most savage of the Greek heroes, murdering the Trojan King Priam, his daughter, Polyxena, and Hector's son, Astyanax. After the sack of Troy he took Hector's widow, Andromache, as his concubine. As the result of another oracle of Helenus, he did not return to his homeland of Thessaly but sailed instead to Epirus, accompanied by both Andromache and Helenus. He had no legitimate children by his wife Hermione, but Andromache bore him three sons, named Molossus, Pielus and Pergamus. Neoptolemus' violent past eventually caught up with him and he was murdered at Delphi, reputedly by Hermione's previous husband Orestes. Helenus then married Andromache, assumed the throne and became guardian of Neoptolemus' sons. On his death Molossus became king. It was, however, from his brother Pielus that the later kings traced their ancestry.

The Epirots then sink into obscurity until the reign of the Molossian King Tharrhypas (*circa* 430-390), who supposedly introduced Greek customs, writing and humane laws. Tharrhypas was followed by his son Alcetas. He was, in turn, succeeded by his son Neoptolemus, who died in 360. Neoptolemus' son Alexander was then only about ten years old, and his uncle Arybbas succeeded to the throne in his place. Such an accession was common amongst Hellenistic kings. A minor could not be expected to carry out the duties of king, one of which was leading the army into battle. These arrangements did, however, often lead to dynastic conflict and even civil war between the two contending branches of the family. Pausanias claims that the Molossians had always had a single throne and it was the sons of Alcetas that first quarrelled over the kingship.[7]

The new king, Arrybas, strengthened his position by making treaty with Philip II, the king of Macedonia, who had also usurped his nephew to become king. To confirm the alliance Arrybas married his niece, Neoptolemus' daughter, Olympias, to Philip in 357. Alexander was sent away to Macedonia to receive a Greek education. The latter move backfired on Arrybas as Philip pretended love for the youth and seduced him. Philip then invaded Epirus in 343, and installed his brother-in-law Alexander on the throne. As a reward for his intervention Philip was granted the eastern regions of Epirus. Philip had, in effect, secured his western border by setting up a client regime in Epirus. Arrybas fled to exile in Athens. These marriage intrigues would lead to the fate of the Epirot and Macedonian royal families becoming intertwined for most of the next century.

Little detail is known of the early years of Alexander's reign. It is generally accepted, however, that it was he who united the tribes of Epirus into an alliance, with the Molossian king as the military commander.[8] In 337 he openly defied Philip by granting asylum to his sister, who had fled following Philip's marriage to Cleopatra. At the wedding feast Philip had brawled with his and Olympias' son, Alexander (the Great). This Alexander fled with his mother, leaving her in Epirus, while he sought refuge in Illyria. While in exile in Epirus, Olympias appears to have plotted the assassination of her husband, Philip. He, however, won back Alexander of Epirus's alliance by betrothing him to his daughter by Olympias, Alexander's niece, also named Cleopatra. Fortunately for Olympias, Philip was murdered before Alexander felt obliged to send her back to Macedonia. Olympias later returned to Macedonia, following the ascension of her son Alexander, and wreaked a terrible revenge on her rivals. She roasted to death Cleopatra and her new son over a brazier, on the same day her brother Alexander of Epirus was married to his Cleopatra.[9]

The southern Italian, Greek city of Tarentum invited Alexander to assist them in their wars against the growing power of the Italian tribes. Tarentum was founded in 706 by exiled Spartan settlers. The original colonists were the sons of Spartan women and men who were not full Spartan citizens. Such unions were only allowed due to the heavy losses the Spartans suffered during their wars to conquer the Messenians. Following the war these marriages were no longer tolerated and the children were driven into exile. The city, situated on a harbour in Apulia, was named after Taras, a son of Poseidon. Tarentum soon became the leading Greek city among those of southern Italy. The Greek expansion was later checked by the resistance of the neighbouring Italian tribes, the Bruttians, Lucanians and Apulians. In

472, and again in 466, the Italians defeated coalitions of the Greek cities led by the Tarentines. Losses amongst the nobility in these two battles were so great that in Tarentum the monarchy was overthrown and a democracy introduced.

The failure of the Greek cities to defeat the Italian tribes prevented their expansion inland and they soon began to dwindle in power. Strabo states that the Tarentines had once been a military power, but now had to rely on foreign assistance. This he claims was as a result of the citizens becoming decadent due to increasing wealth and luxury.[10] Although there may be some truth in these accusations, it is more likely that the Tarentines sought military aid from abroad because they were no longer strong enough to find allies amongst the other Greek cities of southern Italy, with whom they had long standing rivalries. Their continued defeats at the hands of the Italians had damaged their claims to military leadership and their ability to force the other Greek cities into an alliance.

This inability to form alliances with their neighbours, usually centuries-old adversaries, was an ongoing problem for the fractious Greek cities when faced with powerful foreign invaders. The successful defence against the Persians in 480/79 should be seen as the exception rather than the rule. Even then, a number of Greek cities had either stood aloof or allied themselves with the Persians. In 343 Tarentum was forced to appeal to Sparta for assistance in yet another war against the Bruttians and Lucanians. The Spartan king Archidamus III answered the appeal and landed with an army. In 342 he too was defeated by the Italians at the battle of Manduria. The Tarentines were now forced to search for a new ally.

Justin gives Alexander's motives for accepting the invitation:

> As if, in a division of the world, the east had fallen by lot to Alexander, the son of his sister Olympias, and the west to himself, and as if he was likely to have not less to do in Italy, Africa, and Sicily, than Alexander in Asia and Persia.[11]

As will be discussed later, the desire to be seen as a successful general, both for the prestige and the expansion of one's realm, was an integral part of Hellenistic kingship. Epirus was hemmed in to the east and south by the power of the Macedonians, and to the north by the Illyrians. Expansion to the west would have appeared an attractive option to Alexander and the newly-emerging power of the Epirots. Before setting out for Italy, Alexander had received a prophecy from Dodona, warning him to beware of the river of Acheron and the city of Pandosia, for this was where he would meet his death. Places of both names were located in Epirus and this omen had, reportedly, encouraged him to cross over into Italy.

In 334 Alexander crossed the Adriatic into Italy with a fleet of fifteen warships and a greater number of cavalry transports and supply ships.[13] The sources do not tell us the size of his force, although given the size of the fleet it must have numbered many thousands. His allies the Tarentines had previously been able to raise 30,000 infantry and 4,000 cavalry, but, if Strabo is to be believed, both numbers and morale had declined. The campaign commenced with a successful invasion of Apulia to the north. Alexander's forces took the port of Sipontum and forced the Apulians to come to terms. He then turned southwest, marching towards the toe of Italy, into the territory of the Lucanians and Bruttians. He recaptured the city of Heraclea, a colony of Tarentum, and took a number of other cities, including Potentia from the Lucanians, and Consentia and Terina from the Bruttians. In 332 he defeated an alliance of the Lucanians and Samnites at the Battle of Paestum. Following these victories Alexander is reputed to have established friendly relations with Rome.

His successes caused, however, a breach with his allies the Tarentines. Strabo states that this was due to their ingratitude but it is more plausibly the result of conflicting goals. Alexander was probably seeking to increase the power of the Epirots by establishing a long-term, binding coalition, with himself as commander-in-chief. In contrast, the Tarentines probably wanted a short-term alliance, in order to win a military victory and relieve the pressure from the advancing Italian tribes. As an independent state, and as a democracy, they would not have desired a permanent alliance involving their subjection to the hegemony of a foreign king.

Alexander then sought to re-establish his position by allying himself with some of the other Greek cities of the region. In order to get back at the Tarentines he attempted, somewhat vindictively, to shift one of the Tarentines' more prestigious festivals from their colony of Heraclea to their rival city, Thurii. This split allowed the Bruttians and Lucanians to regather their strength, make new alliances and go over to the offensive. The newly-formed Italian alliance attacked Alexander's army. Livy gives a graphic description of Alexander's last battle and death:

> He had, meanwhile, occupied a permanent position on three hills not far from the city of Pandosia, which is close to the frontiers of the Lucanians and Brutti. From this point he made incursions into every part of the enemy's territory, and on these expeditions he had as a bodyguard some two hundred Lucanian refugees, in whose fidelity he placed confidence, but who, like most of their countrymen, were given to changing their minds as their fortunes changed. Continuous rains had inundated the whole country and prevented the three divisions of the army from mutually supporting each other, the level ground between the hills being impassable. While they were in this condition two out of the three divisions were suddenly attacked in the

king's absence and overwhelmed. After annihilating them the enemy invested the third hill, where the king was present in person. The Lucanian refugees managed to communicate with their countrymen, and promised, if a safe return were guaranteed to them, to place the king in their hands alive or dead. Alexander, with a picked body of troops, cut his way, with splendid courage, through the enemy, and meeting the Lucanian general slew him after a hand-to-hand fight. Then getting together those of his men who were scattered in flight, he rode towards the ruins of a bridge, which had been carried away by the floods, and came to a river. Whilst his men were fording it with very uncertain footing, a soldier, almost spent by his exertions and his fears, cursed the river for its unlucky name, and said, 'Rightly are you called Acheros!' When these words fell on his ear the king at once recalled to mind the oracular warning, and stopped, doubtful whether to cross or not. Sotimus, one of his personal attendants, asked him why he hesitated at such a critical moment and drew his attention to the suspicious movements of the Lucanian refugees who were evidently meditating treachery. The king looked back and saw them coming on in a compact body; he at once drew his sword and spurred his horse through the middle of the river. He had already reached the shallow water on the other side when one of the refugees some distance away transfixed him with a javelin. He fell from his horse, and his lifeless body with the weapon sticking in it was carried down by the current to that part of the bank where the enemy were stationed. There it was horribly mutilated. After cutting it through the middle they sent one half to Consentia and kept the other to make sport of. While they were pelting it at a distance with darts and stones a solitary woman ventured among the rabble who were showing such incredible brutality and implored them to desist. She told them amid her tears that her husband and children were held prisoners by the enemy and she hoped to ransom them with the king's body, however much it might have been disfigured. This put an end to the outrages. What was left of the limbs was cremated at Consentia by the reverential care of this one woman, and the bones were sent back to Metapontum; from there they were carried to Cleopatra, the king's wife, and Olympias, the latter of whom was the mother, the former the sister of Alexander the Great.[13]

Justin has a less dramatic and more believable version of events after Alexander's death, simply stating that his body was ransomed and buried by the Thuriians at public expense. The prophecy of Dodona had been realized, for as Livy puts it, 'as often happens, in trying to avoid his fate he rushed upon it.'[14] Alexander's death briefly ended the ambition of the Epirot kings to extend their power to the west. Pyrrhus would later renew it. The more immediate result of Alexander's campaigns was to force the Tarentines into an alliance with the Samnites, leading to their eventual confrontation with Rome.

Alexander was succeeded by his three-year-old son Neoptolemus, with his mother Cleopatra acting as regent. At some stage she was joined by her mother Olympias, who appears to have acted as co-regent, or even supplanted her daughter. In a letter to the Athenians written in 330, she claimed that 'Molossia was hers'.[15] From Epirus Olympias continued her feud with Antipater, Alexander the Great's commander in Macedonia. She was joined is this campaign by her daughter Cleopatra. When Alexander returned to Babylon from India in 325 he was informed of the instability and turmoil caused by the intrigues of his mother and sister. Their campaign against Antipater did succeed. In 324 Alexander ordered his replacement and summoned him to Babylon. Antipater wisely prevaricated and his position was saved by Alexander's death in 323.

Alexander the Great's death tore apart the political situation in the entire Greek and Macedonian world. He had created an empire stretching from the Peloponnesus to the Indian border, but had died without an obvious heir, creating a huge power vacuum. Power within Macedonian society was centred on the person of the monarch. The king was the state, issuing decrees and concluding treaties in his own name. He might consult with his 'companions' before taking action but the final decision was his alone, in a manner not dissimilar to that described in the Homeric *Iliad*. Ultimately, the only avenues of appeal or dissent available to other members of Macedonian society were riot, rebellion, conspiracy and/or assassination. In all these cases the question of the continued existence of the monarchy was never in dispute, the conflict being rather who should rightfully exercise the traditional powers of the king. The monarchal system was deeply rooted within Macedonian society and as an institution was never questioned, even in times, such as this, of extreme crisis.

Alexander's generals immediately began squabbling over who should succeed him. After bitter argument and some fighting they came to an agreement. Alexander's mentally disabled half-brother, Arrhidaeus, would become King Philip III. If Alexander's Persian pregnant wife gave birth to a son, as she did later that year to Alexander IV, he would become joint king. When, as in this situation, the king was a minor, or otherwise incapable of ruling in his own right, a regent was appointed to rule in his name. The assembled Macedonian nobles appointed Perdiccas, Alexander's second-in-command, to this position. The question of who should be regent, and wield the royal powers, would be the main cause of the early wars of the Successors. The Epirots, as a neighbour of the Macedonians, and entangled with the Macedonian royal family by marriage, would be drawn into these conflicts.

The Greek cities took advantage of Alexander's death to revolt from Macedonian control in the so-called Lamian War of 323-2. Olympias tried to strengthen her position against Antipater by supporting the Greeks. As Neoptolemus was too young to lead the Epirots in battle, she recalled the exiled king, Arrybas. Arrybas is recorded as fighting in the Lamian war in 322. It was possibly at this time that the family secured a friendship with the Thessalian general, Menon, who had earned much renown during the war. Arrybas' son, Aeacides, married Menon's daughter, Phthia. From this union Pyrrhus was born in 319. Arrybas died shortly after and was succeeded as joint king by Aeacides. As a young man Aeacides was heavily under the influence of Olympias. He would remain steadfastly loyal to her cause. Antipater eventually won the Lamian War, defeating the Greeks at the Battle of Crannon in September 322, and re-imposed Macedonian control over Greece.

Meanwhile, Perdiccas had completed a successful campaign against the tribes of Asia Minor. At first the two Macedonian commanders attempted to secure their joint supremacy through a marriage alliance. Perdiccas agreed to take Antipater's daughter Nicaea as his bride, and recognised him as supreme commander in Europe. Diodorus claims that Perdiccas' victories then convinced him to grasp for even greater power, perhaps the throne itself.[16] He now began to negotiate marriage with Cleopatra. Perdiccas also attempted to prevent a marriage between Philip Arrhidaeus and Philip II's granddaughter, Eurydice. A bungled attempt to intercept Eurydice led to the death of her mother, Cynane. The army revolted in disgust and forced Perdiccas to allow the marriage. Perdiccas' machinations, and his arrogance, led to a growing suspicion of his ultimate ambitions amongst the other commanders. War now broke out between Perdiccas and a coalition of Antipater, Antigonus the One-eyed, the satrap of Phrygia, and Ptolemy, the governor of Egypt. The latter two would play important roles in Pyrrhus' life during his exile from Epirus from 302 until 297.

Antigonus fled to Antipater in Macedonia. Upon his arrival Antipater broke off his post-Lamian War campaign against the Aetolians and made plans to move against Perdiccas. Antipater crossed into Asia with a large army, sometime in the spring or summer of 321, leaving Polyperchon, one of Alexander the Great's bodyguards, in charge of Macedonia. Perdiccas responded to this threat by sending Eumenes, Alexander's former secretary, to confront Antipater, while he lead the main part of his army against Ptolemy in Egypt. Eumenes defeated a detached part of Antipater's army. Before news of this victory reached Egypt, Perdiccas' own commanders murdered him. He had suffered an initial defeat and heavy losses at the hands of Ptolemy, while trying to cross the Nile.

At another assembly of the army Antipater was made regent. He continued, unsuccessfully, to campaign against Eumenes in Asia. In 319 Antipater returned to Europe with the two kings. Later that year he died and the Macedonian nobility selected Polyperchon to be the new regent. Antigonus, Ptolemy and Antipater's son, Cassander, swiftly formed a new coalition to overthrow Polyperchon's regency. A new round of fighting between the Successors then broke out. Olympias, in an effort to increase her own power through her grandson, Alexander IV, would become a major antagonist in this war, and involve the Epirots in the fighting.

Sometime during this period (the exact timing is impossible to determine) further political developments occurred in Epirus. In the late fifth century the Epirots had been individual tribes with their own armed forces, commanders and magistrates. During Alexander of Epirus' reign they are described as the 'Molossians and their allies', most likely a military alliance lead by the Molossian king. From the epigraphic and numismatic evidence we now hear for the first time of the Epirot Alliance (APEIROTAN). The exact nature of this alliance is not certain, but it was most likely a loose confederation with powers dealing with military matters, taxation and coinage. The individual tribes continued to have control over their own internal affairs, but the king of the Molossians remained as the commander-in-chief of the combined Epirot army.[17] The exact reasons for this change are not clear. One possible explanation is a strengthening of the position of the other tribes in relation to the Molossians during this period of dynastic instability.

Faced by the revolt of his governors, Polyperchon sought to form his own alliance. He wrote to Eumenes and Olympias for assistance. Eumenes agreed to support him, but advised Olympias to remain in Epirus and wait on events before committing herself. Polyperchon's campaigns in Greece, during 318, against the forces and allies of Cassander, were a dismal failure. Eurydice, wife of Philip III, hearing that Olympias was planning to return to Macedonia, now launched her own coup. She dismissed Polyperchon and made herself regent. Eurydice also allied herself with Cassander, who, as Antipater's son, had inherited his father's hatred of Olympias. A courier was sent to Cassander begging him to march on Macedonia as soon as possible. Meanwhile, Eurydice attempted to win over the Macedonians with bribes and great promises.

For once Polyperchon acted with decision. He allied himself with Aeacides and the combined army marched back into Macedonia. The two forces clashed at Euia, a town just beyond the Macedonian western frontier. Both sides were prepared to decide the issue with a single battle. When, however, the Macedonians were drawn up for battle, their respect for Olympias, as mother of their beloved Alexander, overcame them. They deserted to Polyperchon and took Philip prisoner. Eurydice escaped the field but was quickly captured.

Olympias now returned to Macedonia in triumph. As she had done on her previous return, however, Olympias used the opportunity to mete out violent retribution to her enemies. Eurydice and Philip were imprisoned in appalling conditions and brutally maltreated. Olympias, believing correctly that her lack of restraint was losing her support, had Philip stabbed to death by some Thracian mercenaries. Eurydice was given a choice of method of suicide. Olympias sent her hemlock, a noose and a sword. She chose to hang herself with her own girdle, praying that Olympias would meet 'a death worthy of her cruelty'. Olympias now turned her vengeance towards the sons of Antipater. She executed Nicanor and violated the tomb of Iollas, reputed to be Alexander's assassin. Next she selected and slaughtered a hundred prominent Macedonian friends of Cassander. As Diodorus claims, 'by glutting her rage with such atrocities, she soon caused many of the Macedonians to hate her ruthlessness.'[18]

In 317 Cassander, learning of Olympias' declining support, saw his opportunity. He ruthlessly abandoned his Greek allies in order to march immediately on Macedonia. The Aetolians, allies of Olympias, occupied the pass at Thermopylae, barring the land route into Macedonia, but Cassander bypassed them by sea. His rapid movements surprised his divided enemies. He sent part of his army to delay Polyperchon, who was on the Thessalian border, waiting in vain to confront him. Cassander then moved against Olympias and drove her back into the city of Pydna. He laid siege to the city by land and sea, and won over many of Polyperchon's troops with bribes. King Aeacides marched from Epirus to relieve the siege, but Cassander sent yet another force to occupy the western passes into Macedonia. A large part of the Epirot army were reportedly brought against their will and mutinied. Aeacides released the mutineers, but as a result his army was then too small to achieve anything.

With no hope of relief the besieged force began to starve, some even resorting to cannibalism to survive. First the non–combatants died, then the garrison began to desert. In the spring of 316 Olympias surrendered on the condition that Cassander guarantee her personal safety. All of Macedonia quickly fell under Cassander's control. Cassander continued to fear Olympias' still-considerable influence. He attempted to persuade her to go into exile but she refused, trusting in her prestige amongst the Macedonians to ensure her safety.

Despite his former promise, Cassander summoned the people to an assembly in order to judge her. He ensured the result by stacking the assembly with the parents of those whom she had killed. They put on mourning apparel and denounced her cruelties. Olympias was condemned, but the soldiers sent to execute her refused to carry out the verdict. They were again overwhelmed with the recollection of her former royal dignity, and with her connection to so many of their kings. Cassander solved this problem by again summoning the relatives of the murdered, who eagerly stoned her to death. Cassander was now supreme in Macedonia and would rule the kingdom for the following two decades, first as regent and then as king.

Meanwhile, back in Epirus, the deserters from Aeacides rebelled against their absent king. They condemned him to exile and made an alliance with Cassander. Diodorus claims that this was the first time ever that the Epirots had overthrown their king, and that all previous monarchs had died upon their throne.[19] All of the remaining close relatives of King Neoptolemus had now been driven out of Epirus, with Aeacides in exile, Cleopatra a prisoner of Antigonus in Asia, and Olympias under siege in Pydna. Cassander was able to take advantage of the situation. He sent one of his generals, Lyciscus, to command the Epirot forces and act as regent for the still-underage king. These steps effectively turned Epirus into a puppet kingdom of Macedonia.

The rebels captured and executed many of the supporters of Aeacides in Epirus, and actively hunted the three-year-old Prince Pyrrhus. Pyrrhus' bodyguards managed to escape with the prince, his servants and nurses. Slowed by their entourage, Pyrrhus' bodyguards turned to confront their pursuers. They entrusted the prince to the care of three young soldiers, giving them orders to flee to the town of Megara, just over the border in Macedonia. The town may have been one of those that Epirus had been forced to surrender, and Pyrrhus' family may have had supporters among the residents. The bodyguards managed to fight off the pursuers and later rejoined Pyrrhus.

The trials of the fugitives were not yet over. They next found their way blocked by a flooded stream. Unable to communicate with the people on the other side, due to the noise of the torrent, they managed to send them a message by attaching it either to a brooch, or a javelin, and hurling it across the stream. Eventually the party crossed the river to safety. Plutarch relates the appealing tale that the first man to take Pyrrhus ashore was named after his legendary ancestor, Achilles.[20]

Not being safe in Cassander's Macedonia, the fugitives continued on to the court of Glaucias, king of the Illyrians. At first the king was not sure what to do with the fugitives, being afraid of Cassander. According to one account, Pyrrhus then crossed the floor, took hold of the king's robe, pulled himself up and grasped Glaucias knees while sobbing. This was the traditional position of a supplicant and Glaucias, taking this as a sign from heaven, was moved to pity. He gave refuge to Pyrrhus, giving him to his wife to bring up with his own children. Despite continued threats and offers of bribes from Cassander he refused to surrender the boy to his enemies.

As charming as these anecdotes are, one should be careful when tapping them for historical information. Although the description of Glaucias being won over by a sign from heaven is possible, even likely in that superstitious age, it is also possible that a political decision based on the current situation was made. Glaucias may have, more rationally, decided that a claimant to the Epirot throne was of more value than Cassander's good will. The Illyrians and Macedonians were traditional enemies, and any goodwill obtained from the Macedonians would likely be short lived.

Since Aeacides' exile from Epirus a new round of fighting between the Successors had broken out in 315. Antigonus had allied himself with Polyperchon against an alliance of Cassander, Ptolemy and Lysimachus, a former bodyguard of Alexander and now the governor of Thrace. The fighting between Cassander's and Antigonus' forces in southern Greece during 315/4 had been confused, with offensive and counter-offensive being launched, but it had generally gone in Antigonus' favour. To offset this Cassander had considerable success in western Greece. He had defeated Pyrrhus' guardian, Glaucias, in battle and captured the important Adriatic port of Apollonia.

By 313 Antigonus was poised to invade Thrace and continue his offensive against Cassander in southern and central Greece. Aeacides, who until then had been campaigning with his old ally Polyperchon, took advantage of Cassander's difficulties and returned to Epirus. He appears to have regained popularity and quickly gathered a large army. Perhaps the Epirots had tired of Macedonian domination, made obvious by the presence of a foreign governor.

Meanwhile, Cassander had sent his brother Philip with an army to Acarnania, on Epirus' southern border, with orders to attack Aetolia. Aeacides had advanced into Acarnania hoping to unite with the Aetolians. Philip launched an immediate attack before the two potential allies could join together. A battle was fought and Philip won an overwhelming victory, inflicting many casualties and capturing fifty leading supporters of Aeacides. These he sent as prisoners to Macedonia. Aeacides rallied the survivors and succeeded in joining the Aetolians. Despite this, Philip renewed the offensive, and a few days later at a battle fought at Oeniadae in Acarnania, he again defeated the Epirot king. Aeacides was wounded in the battle, and died shortly afterwards.

The following year, 312, the Epirots elevated Aeacides' brother, Alcetas, to the kingship. Alcetas had previously been banished by his father, Arrybas, due to his uncontrollable temper. Lyciscus, who had either been replaced as governor, or more likely driven out of Epirus, invaded from Acarnania. Alcetas does not appear to have been universally popular; Pausanias describes him as acting like a madman, and Diodorus speaks of the affairs of the kingdom being in disorder.[21] The king advanced towards the Macedonians with a small force, while he sent his sons, Alexander and Teucer, to levy more troops. Confronted by Lyciscus' much larger force, the Epirot army deserted. Alcetas fled to the town of Eurymenae, where the Macedonians besieged him. Alexander brought up reinforcements for his father and a battle ensued. The Epirots were victorious, although casualties were heavy on both sides. The Macedonians, in turn, were now reinforced, and in a second battle they routed the Epirots and sacked Eurymenae. Alcetas and his sons fled to another stronghold.

Cassander, not having heard of the victory, rushed to Epirus. He established peace and an alliance with Alcetas. Cassander then moved against Apollonia, which had allied with the Illyrians and driven out his garrison. The Apollonians defeated him in battle, driving him out of western Greece and liberating many of the cities Cassander had previously taken in 314. The people of Epirus, tired of Alcetas' harsh treatment, rose up and murdered him and his sons. The campaigns of late 312, and the murder of Alcetas, had seriously undermined Cassander's formerly-strong position in western Greece and Epirus.

The next year, 311, would see a peace made between Cassander and his allies, and Antigonus. This would seal the fate of Alexander IV, who would shortly after be murdered. Over the next few years the Successors would gradually assume the title of king. In 310 Cassander was again forced to campaign to the west of his kingdom, giving military assistance to his ally, the king of Paeonians, against the Illyrians. Another member of the Epirot royal family died in 308, when Antigonus finally tired of Cleopatra's intrigues and had her murdered. In 307, the low-level conflict that had been simmering between the Successors since 311 again broke out into full-scale warfare. Antigonus sent his son Demetrius to invade Greece. He quickly took Athens and Megara and Cassander's position was again under direct threat. These events created the circumstances to allow Pyrrhus' supporters to attempt to bring him back from Illyria and to place him upon the throne of Epirus.

Chapter II

Exile

'He was adept at turning to his own advantage the favour of his superiors, just as he was inclined to look down upon his inferiors.' - Plutarch, *Pyrrhus*, 4

In 307, after eight years of exile, Pyrrhus finally returned to Epirus. Glaucias, king of the Illyrians and Pyrrhus' protector, invaded Epirus and placed his protégé upon the throne. Pyrrhus' was then only eleven, but his cousin and king, Neoptolemus, was now in his mid-twenties. The sources do not tell us whether the two shared power as joint kings, or if Neoptolemus was driven into exile. The latter appears more likely, as Justin states the Epirots, 'turning their hatred into pity, brought him back, when he was eleven years old, into the kingdom, appointing him guardians to keep the throne for him till he became of age.'[1] Either way, following Glaucias' invasion, Epirus must have become a client state of the Illyrians, as it had earlier been of the Macedonians.

The events of the next five years in Epirus are not recorded. Meanwhile, the war in Greece had finally turned against Demetrius and in favour of Cassander. Antigonus, under attack from Seleucus, king in Syria, and from Lysimachus, ordered Demetrius to bring his army over from Greece and into Asia. Cassander took advantage of the situation to again invade and take possession of Thessaly.

By the time Pyrrhus had reached the age of seventeen years he looked firmly seated upon the throne. He left Epirus to travel to the wedding of one of the sons of Glaucias. During his absence the Molossians rose in rebellion, drove out his friends, plundered his property, and placed Neoptolemus upon the throne as sole ruler. His adoptive father, Glaucias, was unable to come to his assistance as he was currently under attack by pirates. Whether he was driven out for being a dependent of the Illyrian king, or was overthrown by a rebellion of the lower classes as his uncle Alcetas had been, cannot be determined. He was well-known in antiquity for his arrogant attitude towards his social inferiors. Either way, the overthrow would have been supported by Cassander. Whatever the reason, Pyrrhus had been driven out of Epirus for a second time. He fled to seek refuge with Demetrius, who had earlier married his sister, Deidameia, in 303.

Pyrrhus arrived at the court of Demetrius in Greece in 302. He travelled with him to join Antigonus in Asia. Antigonus and Demetrius were two of the foremost generals of the Successor period. Demetrius in particular was an expert in the rapidly-evolving science of siege-craft, and famous for his construction of massive siege-towers. Under the two kings Pyrrhus' education in the arts of generalship would certainly have been further advanced. He is recorded as being a keen student of military matters. Antigonus is reputed to have said that Pyrrhus would be the greatest general of his time, if he lived long enough. This was, most likely, a tribute to both his theoretic knowledge of military affairs and his personal courage. Pyrrhus was present when Antigonus finally confronted his foes at the Battle of Ipsus, fought somewhere in Phrygia in 301. Although Pyrrhus may have fought in the constant skirmishing along the Epirot border with various raiders, this was to be his first experience of a major battle. He was only eighteen, and there is no record of Epirus being at war during his first reign.

Ipsus was one the largest and most important battles during the wars of the Successors. On one side was Antigonus with an army of 70,000 infantry, 10,000 cavalry and seventy-five elephants. Opposed to him was an army commanded by Lysimachus and Seleucus, numbering 64,000 infantry, 15,000 cavalry, reputedly 400 elephants and 120 scythed chariots.[2] Antigonus, as was a common ploy among the Successor generals, massed most of his cavalry on his right wing. His phalanx of heavy infantry occupied the centre and his left was held by a smaller holding force of cavalry. The elephants were spread out evenly along his front. Antigonus' plan was to attack rapidly on the right with his strike force of cavalry, engage the slightly smaller enemy infantry phalanx in the centre and to delay on his left. The victorious right wing horse, commanded by Demetrius, were then to return to the field and attack the exposed flank of the enemy infantry.

This stratagem was orthodox but perhaps too obvious. It was the same tactics that had won Alexander victories at Issus and Gaugamela. Antigonus had used the same plan in his victories over Eumenes, at the battles of Paraitacene and Gabiene, fifteen years earlier. Both of these victories, however, had been hard fought and costly. When Demetrius tried similar tactics five years later at Gaza, albeit with a strong left wing, against the more experienced Ptolemy and Seleucus, he had been soundly defeated.

The dispositions of the enemy are less clear. They appear to have divided their superior numbers of cavalry evenly on both wings and, as was the norm, massed their infantry in the centre. Some of their elephants were spread along in front of their battle line, but a large number, crucially, were held in reserve. The disposition of their chariots is unknown, but they are not recorded as playing any significant role in the battle. Spectacular as such weapons were, no Hellenistic army had any trouble in dealing with them, as Alexander had shown at Gaugamela. Alexander's light-infantry had shot down the majority of the chariots, and the remainder had been channeled harmlessly through gaps deliberately opened in the ranks of the Macedonians.

Immediately the battle began, Demetrius lead a successful attack on the enemy cavalry and quickly put them to flight. He then, however, failed to keep his own troops in hand. Plutarch now describes the crucial point of the battle, as Demetrius:

> Followed the pursuit, in the pride and exultation of success, so eagerly, and so unwisely far, that it fatally lost him the day. For when, perceiving his error, he would have come in to the assistance of his own infantry, he was not able, as the enemy with their elephants had cut off his retreat.[3]

Seleucus had manoeuvred his elephant reserve, perhaps 300 animals, to block Demetrius' return to the battlefield and prevent his planned charge against the vulnerable flank and rear of the allied phalanx. His troops' horses would not approach the elephants due to their fear of their smell and the noise. An increasingly anxious Demetrius could not find a way round this mobile roadblock.

The allies were now in a better position to exploit the situation, having superior numbers of cavalry on the field. They sent their light cavalry, both bow and javelin-armed, to surround and harass Antigonus' infantry. They fired missiles into the close-packed ranks of Antigonus' phalanx and threatened to charge against their exposed right flank. Antigonus' phalanx, now faced by infantry attacks to its front and threats to its exposed rear and flanks, began to panic. Soon whole units deserted, further exposing the remainder to attack. Loss of formation was fatal to the tight-packed infantry ranks of the Hellenistic armies. To the last, the eighty-year-old Antigonus bravely tried to rally his troops. He looked desperately for the return of his son, who, even then, could have saved the battle.

Plutarch dramatically describes the climax of the battle:

> But the old king Antigonus still kept his post, and when a strong body of the enemies drew up to charge him, and one of those about him cried out to him, 'Sir, they are coming upon you', he only replied, 'What else should they do? But Demetrius will come to my rescue.' And in this hope he persisted to the last, looking out on every side for his son's approach, until he was overwhelmed by a cloud of javelins and fell.[4]

Just what Pyrrhus' role in the battle was the sources do not relate, except that, though still a youth, he routed the enemy opposed to him, and made a brilliant display of valour among the combatants. Courage in battle would be an ongoing feature throughout Pyrrhus' life. Ipsus may very well have been Pyrrhus' first experience of battle and he appears to have acquitted himself bravely. During the fighting, the expected place for a young aristocrat would have been in the cavalry, alongside his brother-in-law Demetrius. This would account for him routing the enemy, and he certainly escaped with Demetrius after the battle. If so, Pyrrhus would have experienced both the exhilaration of a successful mounted attack, and the impotence of cavalry when faced by elephants. This latter lesson he appears to have taken to heart. Frontinus describes him as using elephants in order to throw the Roman cavalry into disorder when fighting against them in Italy.[5]

Antigonus' defeat and death at Ipsus destroyed his empire in Asia, which was divided between the victors, Seleucus, Cassander and Lysimachus. 'And took each his portion, adding thus to the provinces which the victors already had, those of the vanquished kings.'[6] Demetrius sailed for Greece, accompanied by Pyrrhus. He was enraged, however, to find that most of his previous allies had turned against him:

> An embassy from Athens met him with a request to keep away from the city, on the ground that the people had passed a vote to admit none of the kings ... his wrath drove him beyond all proper bounds ... that the Athenians should disappoint his hopes and play him false, and that their apparent goodwill should prove on trial to be false and empty, was painful to him.[7]

Prior to this, Demetrius had consistently followed his father's policy of leaving the Greek cities ungarrisoned. Following these supposed betrayals Demetrius switched to the less popular, but more reliable, expedient of placing garrisons in those cities he still controlled. Both his son Antigonus Gonatas, and Pyrrhus, would learn from Demetrius' experience and adopt his new, harsher policy. Demetrius left Pyrrhus as commander of what was left of his allies in Greece and sailed to make war on Lysimachus in Thrace and Asia.

Sometime later, in 298 or 297, Demetrius made peace with Ptolemy. As part of the terms of the treaty he sent his and Deidameia's son Alexander, along with his uncle Pyrrhus, to Ptolemy as hostages. Pyrrhus impressed the Egyptian court with his strength and prowess, both in hunting and in military exercises. His years in exile appear to have made him skilful at ingratiating himself with his patrons. At the time Ptolemy's most influential wife was Berenice, and Pyrrhus went out of his way to win her goodwill. His efforts were rewarded when he was married to Berenice's daughter, Ptolemy's stepdaughter Antigone. Ptolemy, no doubt, saw the exiled king as a useful asset in the ever-changing alliances of the Successors. Nor, as a descendant of Achilles and a cousin of Alexander the Great, would Pyrrhus have been an unsuitable groom.

In 297, Ptolemy decided to assist Pyrrhus' return to Epirus, and provided him with both men and money. Ptolemy was almost certainly taking advantage of the situation in Europe following the death of Cassander in that year. With Neoptolemus' patron dead, Ptolemy took the opportunity, as others had done before, to place his own man on the Epirot throne, and give himself a useful ally on the Greek mainland. Given the history of enmity between Cassander's and Pyrrhus' families, the new Macedonian king, Philip IV, and Pyrrhus were unlikely to be amicable neighbours. In addition, Ptolemy's alliance with Demetrius had broken down. Pyrrhus' sister had died in 299 or 298 and there was no longer any close family relationship between him and Demetrius. He could now be used against his former brother-in-law. Pyrrhus probably returned to Greece with the same fleet that Ptolemy sent to Athens to attempt to break Demetrius siege of the city.

Pyrrhus' return to Epirus was reported to be popular, as Neoptolemus had become hated due to his harsh and arbitrary rule. Fearing that Neoptolemus might call on support from his allies in Macedonia, Pyrrhus came to terms with him. They agreed to share the royal power. Now that both were adults, however, such an arrangement could not be expected to last. Both kings, probably correctly, began to suspect that the other was plotting against him.

Things came to a head during a religious ceremony in Molossia, where the kings exchanged oaths with the Epirot people. Here the kings promised to rule according to the laws and the people to support the kingdom according to the same laws. Plutarch then relates a tale of seduction, conspiracy and murder; sordid, but common enough among the Hellenistic kings. Following the oaths and sacrifices the two kings, and their supporters, exchanged gifts. One of Pyrrhus' companions, Myrtilus, asked for the king to pass on a certain present of oxen to him. He was deeply offended by Pyrrhus' refusal. Gelon, one of Neoptolemus' supporters, invited Myrtilus to dine with him, and seduced the younger man. Gelon then tried to convince Myrtilus to betray Pyrrhus and assassinate him with poison. Myrtilus pretended to agree but secretly informed Pyrrhus of the plot. Gelon then compounded his error by boasting of his plot to his friends. This was overheard by the wife of one Pyrrhus' servants. Given corroborating evidence of Neoptolemus' conspiracy, Pyrrhus felt justified to act. He invited his fellow king to dinner and murdered him. The act does not appear to have been unpopular, as 'the chief men among the Epirots were devoted to himself and were eager to see him rid himself of Neoptolemus; also that they wished him not to content himself with having a small share of the kingdom, but to follow his natural bent and attempt greater things'.[8]

Pyrrhus appears to have had considerable support among the Epirot nobility, both for the assassination and for his ambitious plans for the expansion of the kingdom. He was now sole king and would remain firmly on the Epirot throne for the next twenty-four years.

Another of the Successors to take advantage of Cassander's death was Demetrius. In 294 he broke off his Asian campaigns and returned to Greece. He was able to retake Athens, despite Ptolemy's interference, by besieging it and starving it into submission. For the next six years Demetrius and Pyrrhus would be constant opponents. Demetrius was one of those larger-than-life characters that the era of the Successors made possible. Like Pyrrhus, Demetrius' career was one of constant changes of fortune. He was the heir to Antigonus' empire, but this was largely lost at Ipsus. He recovered to seize the throne of Macedonia, only to lose it to a rebellion of his own subjects. He was renowned for abandoning himself to luxury and revelry whenever possible, but never let this interfere when decisive action was necessary. He was one of the greatest generals of his age, yet is unjustly remembered for his defeats at Gaza and Ipsus. Demetrius was nicknamed 'Poliorcetes', 'taker of cities', but again is remembered for the failure of his most famous siege at Rhodes. He did, however, succeed in the taking of a number of cities, including the considerable feat of twice capturing Athens.

It is, perhaps, now the time to describe how the sources portray Pyrrhus. Plutarch gives us a physical description of Pyrrhus: 'In the aspect of his countenance Pyrrhus had more of the terror than of the majesty of kingly power. He had not many teeth, but his upper jaw was one continuous bone, on which the usual intervals between the teeth were indicated by slight depressions.'[9]

He is described as having a terrifying rather than noble appearance. Surviving busts of Pyrrhus would support the description of him as not a handsome man. He was, however, as has been related above, strong and fit. Pyrrhus dental condition may have been an extreme example of the disorder of fusion of the teeth. This may be genetic in nature, and given the propensity of royal families to marry their close relatives, such inherited complaints are not unexpected. More likely, however, is that his condition was a more common one, calcification of the teeth. A thick layer of hard calcium can build up on the teeth, obscuring the gaps, and making it appear as if the person has only one tooth.

In an age when womanising and drunkenness were common among the nobility, Pyrrhus was noted for being 'decent and prudent in his way of life'.[10] He was also known for a love of animals. One anecdote records him rescuing, and adopting, a starving dog that had guarded its master's dead body for three days. After Pyrrhus' death, his pet eagle was supposed to have starved itself to death, and a pet dog to have jumped upon his funeral pyre, due to their love for their master.

The anecdotes that survive do not show any great depth of learning on Pyrrhus' part, other than what relates to military matters. There are few of the quotes from the poets that abound in the lives of the other kings, with the exception of Homer. This is not particularly exceptional, as all Greek aristocrats were expected to learn Homer by rote. Pyrrhus was not, however, totally uneducated, as he reputedly composed his memoirs and a number of military treatises, which were still being read by the Romans and Greeks centuries later. It is more that his interests appear narrow. This lack of imagination is perhaps best displayed by his response to a question concerning who was a better flute player. Pyrrhus replied that Polyperchon was a good general. Plutarch claims that Pyrrhus was always, 'studying and meditating upon military matters, regarding them as the most kingly branch of learning, the rest he regarded as mere accomplishments and held them in no esteem' and 'implying that it became a king to investigate and understand such matters only'.[11] This lack of interest in other arts, particularly those of diplomacy when dealing with allies, would cost Pyrrhus dearly during his reign.

This concentration on military matters and lack of other interests supposedly lead to boredom when forced to live in peace and reign over his people. He reputedly found 'it tedious to the point of nausea if he were not inflicting mischief on others or suffering it at others' hands, and like his purported ancestor Achilles could not endure idleness, as it: "ate his heart away. Remaining there, and pined for war-cry and battle."[12]

This restless spirit would also cost Pyrrhus dearly. He would prove himself capable of winning victories, but not of consolidating his gains before he began looking for a new campaign of conquest.

Plutarch also relates two of the myths concerning the king's apparent ability to cure problems of the spleen:

> He would sacrifice a white cock, and, while the patient lay flat upon his back, would press gently with his right foot against the spleen. Nor was any one so obscure or poor as not to get this healing service from him if he asked it. The king would also accept the cock after he had sacrificed it, and this reward was most pleasing to him. It is said, further, that the great toe of his right foot had a divine virtue, so that after the rest of his body had been consumed, this was found to be untouched and unharmed by the fire.[13]

Pyrrhus miraculous abilities to heal are not unique. The belief that the ability to cure by the 'laying on of hands' by those with divine powers, such as kings, emperors and priests was widespread in the ancient world. The kings of England were ceremoniously 'laying on hands' as late as the end of the seventeenth century. These myths should be seen in the wider context of the beginning of the granting of divine powers to the royal rulers in the Hellenistic world. It began with Alexander's eastern campaign, and most likely his visit to the Egyptian oracle at Siwah. By the end of his reign Alexander appears to have demanded divine honours from the Greek cities. At first such beliefs and demands were treated with distaste and even derision. The Athenian orator Hepereides saw it as hubris and an attack on traditional religious institutions. The more earthy Macedonian infantry made mockery of his belief to be the son of Zeus. During one mutiny they told him, 'in bitter jest, that on his next campaign he could take his father with him.'[14] Yet within a generation the Athenians had voted to honour Antigonus and his son Demetrius as saviour gods, and shortly after the Rhodians granted the same divine status to Ptolemy.

The overall picture that emerges of Pyrrhus is of an individual of burning ambition, and almost totally absorbed by fighting and military matters. He was reputed to be kind towards his close friends, capable of charming his superiors, but aloof and arrogant to his social inferiors. Great care must always be taken though when attempting to assess the character of individuals based on the anecdotes related by the ancient authors. This applies even more so in Pyrrhus' case, as most of this material comes from one source, Plutarch's biography. Caution must be used when such anecdotes are tapped for historical information, as writers in the Roman period employed such anecdotes to highlight the supposed character of their subject. The assessment of their accuracy and reliability by the authors was often less important than their content.

This stricture applies even more so when reading Plutarch, as he was writing biographies not history. For Plutarch a chance remark or joke may tell more about his subject's character than any of his exploits. Plutarch's selection of evidence is further distorted by his method of pairing lives, which influenced his choice of material. His choice to include or to omit actions depended on whether they fit his preconceived views on the characters of his subjects. The themes of his biographies were often determined early in the work and highlighted in the comparison between the lives. Unfortunately, the comparison between Pyrrhus and Marius has been lost, but some of the comments on his character can be seen to mirror those of Pyrrhus. 'For since he was naturally virile and fond of war, and since he received a training in military rather than in civil life, his temper was fierce when he came to exercise authority.' Perhaps even more pointedly for the overall summation of both lives:

Unmindful and thoughtless persons who let all that occurs to them slip away from them as time passes on. Retaining and preserving nothing, they lose the enjoyment of their present prosperity by fancying something better to come. Yet they reject their present success, as though it did not concern them, and do nothing but dream of future uncertainties.[15]

The possibility that Plutarch exaggerated these traits in Pyrrhus in order to match those of Marius, or the reverse, must be kept in mind.

With himself firmly on the throne, Pyrrhus began to consider many ambitious schemes, in particular the expansion of his kingdom at the expense of his neighbours. It is not certain what the exact powers of the Epirot king were, other than that he was certainly the commander-in-chief of the armed forces, but this was his most important role. The evidence of the exchange of oaths with the people, and the overthrow of Alcetas due to his harsh rule, implies that the king did have civil functions as well as military ones. Although Hellenistic kings did have important law-making and judicial functions, they were above all war leaders. Armed conquest played an important role in the legitimization of their leadership.

Military success, particularly since the death of Alexander the Great, was crucial for personal prestige and the right to rule. But military conquest was not simply a means of establishing prestige; it was also a method of accumulating more lands. The control and exploitation of agricultural land was still the major source of wealth throughout the Hellenistic world. Successful campaigning might bring huge amounts of pillage. For example, Ptolemy III in the 'Third Syrian War' of 246/5 acquired 40,000 talents of booty, a figure to be compared to the annual revenue of Ptolemy II of 14,800 talents. The enormous wealth plundered by Alexander was still fresh in the minds of the Successors. Alexander's conquest of Asia is recorded as having brought in 120,000 talents from the capture of Persepolis alone.[16] Although such figures are spectacular, this was a one-off, unreliable source of funds. The conquest of new territories was the only reliable method of increasing a ruler's revenue base. Without money an army could not be raised nor maintained. According to Caesar, 'there were two things that procured, protected and increased power - soldiers and money - and these depended on each other ... and if one of the two was lacking the other would fall.'[17] To put it succinctly, the bigger the kingdom, the bigger the revenue base, the bigger the army.

It has often been argued that the main cause of the wars after 315 was the desire of Antigonus to make a bid for supreme power and to unite the empire of Alexander the Great under his own leadership. This ambition is compared to the supposedly more modest and regional ambitions of the other Successors, particularly Ptolemy and Cassander. Such arguments appear to ignore the actions of both. They had, at different times, invaded Cilicia and Lycia, and campaigned in Greece, attempting to win over the cities controlled by both their enemies and former allies. The struggles to carve up the realms of Antigonus and Cassander after their deaths do not show any tendency to purely-regional interests on behalf of any of the surviving dynasts. The very nature of Macedonian leadership and Hellenistic kingship demanded that all the major participants must aim for the dominant position or risk being destroyed.

Pyrrhus would now become a keen participant in these struggles. Plutarch describes the supposedly-grandiose extent of his expansionist goals, claiming that after annexing all of Italy, he desired to conquer Sicily, Carthage, Libya, Macedonia and all of Greece. At least Pyrrhus' grandiose schemes had a limit. The poet Alkaios of Messene claims that after conquering the land and the sea Philip V planned to march on Olympus itself.[18] A more realistic appraisal might well be that all the Successors aimed at dominating the entire Macedonian and Greek world, and anyone else over whom they could impose themselves. To claim otherwise would appear to mistake necessity for policy.

In common with the other Successors, Pyrrhus would attempt to expand his kingdom by military force. The instrument he would use was the Epirot army. Thucydides describes the fifth-century Epirot army as a typical tribal levy; disorganized, brave when things were going their way, but easily discouraged. 'The Chaonians, filled with self-confidence, and having the highest reputation for courage ... rushed on with the rest of the barbarians', but 'a panic seizing the Chaonians ... they were seen to give way.'[19] This was the Greek stereotype of the barbarian warrior. At some time over the next century the Epirot army, no doubt influenced by its Macedonian neighbour, underwent a radical transformation.

The fourth century was a period of great military transformation and re-armament by the Greeks. The Theban commanders Pelopidas and Epaminondas had revolutionized tactics by increasing the depth of the heavy infantry (hoplite) phalanx up to fifty deep and the use of the oblique approach, attacking on one wing while refusing the other. Using these tactics, they had smashed the power of the Spartans with their overwhelming victory at Leuctra (371), and fought a bloody draw at the second Battle of Mantinea (362). They had also developed the battlefield use of cavalry, which had previously been used mainly to cover the advance of the infantry and protect their flanks. At the Battle of Cynoscephalae (364), Pelopidas used his cavalry as a strike force against the flanks of the enemy hoplite phalanx. At Mantinea, Epaminondas ordered his mounted troops to attack the flanks and rear of the enemy hoplites.

The Athenian general Iphicrates had also experimented with infantry equipment, rearming his light troops with a 4m spear, longer than the traditional 3m spear of the hoplite, to augment their smaller shields, and allow them to fight effectively as close-order foot. This combination of a longer spear and smaller shield is most likely to have been the prototype for the introduction of the Macedonian pike-armed infantry. Philip had been a hostage in Thebes during this time and would certainly have known of the Theban developments. He was also a friend of the family of Iphicrates.

At some time during Philip's reign he undertook a thorough re-organization and re-arming of the Macedonian army. Traditionally, the Macedonian infantry had been seen as almost militarily useless, and the kings had often taken to the field leading only cavalry forces. Philip was able to reform them into a disciplined force, armed with a smaller shield than that of the traditional Greek hoplite, and a longer, 5.5m long pike (*sarissa*), wielded in both hands. It has been claimed that these changes took place under Alexander's reign rather than Philip's. The evidence of two sources demonstrates, however, that it is almost certain that Philip was the instigator. The contemporary historian Theothrastus gives us the length of the pike during Philip's time and Polyaenus, describing the training of his infantry, states that 'Philip accustomed the Macedonians to constant exercise, as well in peace, as in actual service: so that he would frequently make them march three hundred furlongs, carrying with them their helmets, shields, greaves, and *sarissa*'.[20] It would seem to be incomprehensible that Philip would train his infantry with a weapon they did not use.

The exact timing of Philip's reforms is more difficult to ascertain. The traditional view is that he did it almost as soon as he claimed the kingship in 359. The key passage is in Diodorus, which describes that one of the first acts of Philip's reign was to improve the 'organization of his forces, and, having equipped the men suitably with weapons of war, he held constant manoeuvres of the men under arms and competitive drives. Indeed, he devised the compact order and the equipment of the phalanx'.[21]

Unfortunately, Diodorus does not mention the introduction of the pike. The word he uses to describe the infantry, *puknotes*, was used by earlier writers to describe the more traditional hoplite and by later writers when referring to pikemen. Nowhere in the reign of Philip do the sources describe the Macedonian infantry using the *sarissa*. At the battle against the Phocians in 353, the Macedonian phalanx is described as fighting from afar with javelins. Archaeological research has found evidence of pike spearheads at the Battle of Chaeronea in 338 and none at the siege of Olynthus in 349. This has lead to speculation that Philip's initial reform merely converted the Macedonian infantry to the traditional spear-armed hoplite, and a later re-armament took place between 349 and 338.

It is known that when necessary, usually when assaulting cities or fighting in difficult ground, the Macedonian infantry would fight with javelins rather than their more unwieldy pikes. At the battle against the Phocians in 353 the Macedonians were attacking steep, rocky hills in just such a situation. The question of Olynthus is more problematic. Although much of the fighting took place near the city walls, Diodorus records two battles being fought outside of the city.[22] Perhaps no Macedonian foot were involved in the fighting, as Philip is renowned for preferring to use mercenaries whenever possible, in order to preserve his more valuable Macedonians. On balance it would appear that the more common view is the simplest and inherently more likely. Having one period of re-armament at the start of Philip's reign and another ten or more years later appears unnecessarily complicated. The lack of any detailed account of the use of the pike in combat during Philip's campaigns is probably the result of the paucity of any detailed account of Philip's battles in our sources.

The introduction of the longer weapon changed the nature of infantry fighting. The traditional hoplite fight had involved combat at very close quarters, literally shield to shield. As well as stabbing with their spears, the opposing hoplites would push and shove with their shields. If one side did not break it could degenerate into biting, kicking and punching. Fighting with a pike was quite different. The length of the *sarissa* allowed five spear points to extend beyond the first rank. Closing to chest-to-chest combat was now impossible. If both sides were so armed they would stand apart and fence with their pikes.

The length of the new weapon gave a considerable tactical advantage to the pike phalanx over infantry who were not so armed, as they could not close to a range where their weapons were effective. This led to all sorts of methods being used to overcome the wall of spears. One was to hack at the pikes with swords. Another, more extreme method was to grasp the spearheads by hand and to try to render them useless. One commander ordered his first line troops 'not to use their weapons, but with both hands to seize the enemy's spears, and hold them fast. ... by this manoeuvre of Cleonymus, the long and formidable *sarissa* was rendered useless and became rather an encumbrance, than a dangerous weapon.'[23]

This tactic was, perhaps, only successful as it took place in a breach in a wall and the Macedonia phalanx was, possibly, unable to form up in depth. Plutarch describes a more normal battlefield situation:

> For the Romans tried to thrust aside the long spears of their enemies with their swords, or to crowd them back with their shields, or to seize and put them by with their very hands; while the Macedonians, holding them firmly advanced with both hands, and piercing those who fell upon them, armour and all, since neither shield nor breastplate could resist the force of the Macedonian long spear.[24]

Philip also re-organized and re-armed the Macedonian cavalry. Traditionally, Greek cavalry had been armed with a helmet, breastplate and javelins. Their main method of combat was to fight from afar by throwing their javelins. This suited their main roles as raiders, scouts and a screen for the infantry phalanx. Their increasing use as a strike force during the mid-to-late fourth century rendered this form of armament less appropriate. Philip re-equipped his cavalry with a longer, 4m lance, and trained them to fight in a wedge formation. These reforms were possibly modelled on the Thracian cavalry Philip had fought, and been wounded by, in 339. Whatever the inspiration for the changes, the newly-equipped cavalry were far more devastating in the charge, greatly enhancing their role as shock troops.

At some point the Epirot army was reformed in the Macedonian manner. Pyrrhus' infantry in Italy are described as being drilled, fighting in close order and armed with the pike, and the cavalry as using lances. The exact date of the re-organization is not known. There are two likely initiators of these reforms. The first is Alexander, following his return to Epirus in 343 and before his departure to Italy in 334. The second is Pyrrhus after his return from Egypt in 297. Both had been exposed to the Macedonian military system during their exiles. Alexander does, however, seem to be the more likely candidate, as he had greater time and opportunity to carry out the necessary changes. The victories of the Epirots in Italy under Alexander, and the willingness of the Epirots to fight, and at times defeat, the Macedonian armies of Antipater, Polyperchon and Cassander suggests a level of military sophistication greater than that described by Thucydides.

The numbers of the Epirot army at the start of Pyrrhus' reign are more difficult to establish. The first figures given in the sources detail those for Pyrrhus' invasion of Italy in 280. The army consisted of 20,000 heavy infantry, 3,000 cavalry and 2,500 light infantry, as well as an advance guard of 3,000 troops. These figures, however, include mercenaries, 5,000 Macedonian infantry, and troops from Thessaly and Ambracia, which were not a part of Epirus at the start of Pyrrhus' reign. If the Macedonians, and a reasonable approximation of the others, were subtracted, a figure of between 10,000 and 15,000 for the Epirot component would appear reasonable.

This would not, however, be the total of Epirus' forces, as Pyrrhus would have left a sufficient force behind to defend Epirus and his Greek holdings. The only yardstick available for approximating the size of such a force is Alexander's invasion of the Persian Empire, where he took slightly more than half the available Macedonian army. If Pyrrhus left a similar proportion of soldiers at home, then the total numbers of troops available to him at the start of his reign was, most likely, in the range of 20,000 to 25,000. Even the lower number would make the Epirot army a match for any of the individual

Greek states, but would not be a threat to a united Macedonia. In contrast to these figures, Garouflias estimates that Pyrrhus' army totalled only 15,000, but this would appear to be too conservative.[25] Whatever the exact size of his army, Pyrrhus was able to embark confidently on his campaign of expansion with, by contemporary standards, a large, up-to-date, disciplined and effective army.

Chapter III

Macedonia

'we see that kings have no reason to find fault with popular bodies for changing sides as suits their interests; for in doing this they are but imitating the kings themselves, who are their teachers in unfaithfulness and treachery, and think him most advantaged who least observes justice.' - Plutarch, *Pyrrhus*, 12

Pyrrhus' next opportunity for expansion came with the fraternal conflict for the Macedonian throne that followed Cassander's death in 297. Cassander was succeeded by his son Philip IV, but he too died of natural causes the following year. The next eldest brother, Antipater, should then have inherited the kingdom. His youngest brother Alexander was, however, the favourite of their mother Thessalonice, another daughter of Philip II. She connived to have the kingdom divided between the two brothers. Antipater received the eastern portion and Alexander the western, with the border to be the River Axius.

Antipater was, quite justifiably, not satisfied with this arrangement. In 294 he murdered his mother, seized the whole of the country and drove his brother into exile. This deed scandalized everyone, as the ancient Greeks considered matricide to be one of the most terrible of crimes. As Justin put it, 'no reason can be alleged sufficient to justify the crime'.[1] Alexander, in turn, sent messages to both Demetrius and Pyrrhus, seeking assistance. Demetrius was unable to respond immediately as he was campaigning against Sparta in the Peloponnesus. Pyrrhus, seeing the possibility to take advantage of the brothers' conflict, was able to arrive in Macedonia first. In return for his alliance he demanded that he receive the cities of Stymphaea and Parauaea in Macedonia, and the Greek regions of Ambracia, Acarnania, and Amphilochia. Alexander, in his desperation, gave way to these demands, and Pyrrhus secured his newly-acquired territories with garrisons. The city of Ambracia later became the Epirot capitol, as it was the first truly Greek city to be included in the kingdom. Over the course of his reign Pyrrhus would spend much time and money on enlarging and beautifying the city. Pyrrhus then conquered the rest of Macedonia from Antipater and handed it over to Alexander.

Antipater attempted to counter Alexander's move by appealing to his father-in-law, Lysimachus, for assistance. Lysimachus was a former bodyguard of Alexander the Great. Following the king's death he had been made governor of Thrace and began his rule with a notable victory over the Thracians. During the wars of the Successors he had been a consistent opponent of Antigonus and loyal ally of Cassander. Following the victory at Ipsus he seized a large part of Antigonus' kingdom, and was now one of the most powerful of the kings. He had a deep, personal hatred of Demetrius, who had publicly insulted his manhood by referring to him as a treasurer, a position traditionally held by a eunuch. Demetrius had further insulted him by deriding the virtue of Lysimachus' first wife and inferring that her children were not really fathered by her husband. Lysimachus was eager to give aid to Antipater, but could not come in person. He was fully occupied with a campaign in Asia Minor, annexing the remaining possessions of his nemesis, Demetrius. Lysimachus relied instead on his cunning. He attempted the stratagem of sending Pyrrhus a forged letter. This stated that his patron, Ptolemy, urged him to give up his expedition in return for a payment of 300 talents from Antipater. As soon as Pyrrhus opened the letter he perceived it to be a forgery, for the letter did not have the customary greeting, 'the father, to the son, health and happiness,' but instead, 'King Ptolemy, to King Pyrrhus, health and happiness.'[2]

Pyrrhus condemned Lysimachus for the fraud, but unwilling to confront the superior might of Lysimachus, made the desired peace. Lysimachus apparently advised his son-in-law to come to terms with his brother, rather than allow his father's enemy, Pyrrhus, to dominate Macedonia. Lysimachus, no doubt, also feared that a divided Macedonia would allow Demetrius the opportunity to intervene in Macedonia. Future events would show him to be correct in his fears. At Lysimachus' urging, Pyrrhus and the two kings met to ratify the treaty with sacrificial oaths. The ceremony, however, provided Pyrrhus with a chance to avoid taking the vow. One of the three sacrificial animals, a ram, prematurely dropped dead, causing much laughter. Pyrrhus' priest conveniently declared this to be a bad omen, and that the gods had predicted the death of one of the three kings. Pyrrhus was, therefore, able to avoid taking the oath and being bound by the treaty. Having won a large amount of territory, he withdrew back to Epirus.

Meanwhile, Demetrius, having failed to take Sparta, had finally responded to Alexander's entreaty. He marched his forces to Macedonia and met the prince at the town of Dium, on the border between Thessaly and Macedonia. Alexander, with the conflict apparently settled, was now more afraid of his would-be ally than his brother. He received him respectfully, but told him that he no longer required his assistance. As was normal in such situations suspicions arose, with both apparently plotting to murder the other. Demetrius, as he was on his way to dine with Alexander, was informed that there was a plot against his life and that he would be murdered during the banquet. The more experienced and wily Demetrius was not in the least disconcerted and quickly made his own plans. Taking his time, he gave orders to his commanders to keep his troops under arms. He then entered the dining room with his guards and the officers of his household, who were, wisely, much more numerous than those of Alexander. Alexander's supporters, intimidated by the size of his retinue, dared not attack Demetrius, who made excuses and left early. Next day, Demetrius prepared to depart, claiming that he was called away by some new emergency, and asked Alexander to excuse him.

Alexander, relieved that Demetrius was finally withdrawing, unwisely believed that he had no hostile intentions and accompanied him into Thessaly. Perhaps, with the withdrawal of Pyrrhus, he did not feel safe from his brother. Both were still, however, in the usual way of Hellenistic kings, plotting each other's murder. Demetrius struck first. Following a feast his bodyguards cut Alexander to pieces, along with those bodyguards who attempted to assist him. One of the latter is reported to have said, as he was dying, 'Demetrius is but one day ahead of us'.[3]

In the traditional manner Demetrius called an assembly of the Macedonian army in order to defend himself against any charges of murder, and to claim the Macedonian throne for himself. Justin records the accusations that Demetrius made to the assembly: that Alexander had attempted to murder him and he was only acting in self-defence; that he, Demetrius, was the more legitimate king of Macedonia, as his father had been a follower of King Philip and of Alexander the Great, and afterwards the rightful regent of the children of Alexander; that Antipater, Cassander, and his sons had always been unjust as the rulers of the kingdom; that Cassander had been the destroyer of the king's family, sparing neither women nor children, and not resting till he had destroyed the whole of the royal house; that as he could not exact vengeance for these crimes from Cassander himself, he had inflicted it on his child; and that Philip and Alexander, if the dead have any knowledge of human affairs, would wish that the avengers of these murders should sit on the throne of Macedonia. Demetrius' speech appears to have won the Macedonians over and the assembly acclaimed him king.[4]

None of the other kings were in a position to oppose Demetrius. Lysimachus was still absent in Asia Minor. Antipater fled to his father-in-law, Lysimachus. Much of Pyrrhus' early work had been unravelled, and by the end of 294 the dangerous Demetrius firmly held the Macedonian throne. With his conquest of Macedonia secure, Demetrius now controlled a strong empire that included the entire Greek peninsula, with the exceptions of Epirus, Sparta and Messenia.

Although it is possible that Justin reports accurately what Demetrius said to the assembly, the sentiments expressed probably also represent those of Justin himself. There is a hostile tradition towards Cassander found in the works of the later writers, Pausanias, Plutarch and Justin. They believed, almost certainly unjustly, that he was the murderer of Alexander the Great. All wrote during the early part of the Roman Empire when the official view of Alexander had changed. Beginning with Augustus, and carried even further by Domitian, Trajan and Hadrian, the emperors emphasized their status as the elect of Jupiter. Alexander was now viewed as the popular prototype of the divine conqueror and enlightened autocrat, with a broad imperial vision. With this official view of Alexander in fashion, it is not surprising that the man accused of his regicide would be seen as the victim of divine vengeance.

The period of composition of these three fits nicely with this assertion: Justin's work is an epitome of Trogus, who wrote during Augustus' reign; Plutarch wrote around the turn of the first century AD and Pausanias shortly after, when the pro-Alexander view of history had already taken deep root. Cassander is said to have been eaten alive by worms while dying, a fate shared by others who were seen as deserving of divine vengeance. Josephus describes Herod the Great as having his genitals attacked by worms on his deathbed, the result of 'God inflicting just punishment on him for his lawless deeds'.[5] Others to suffer a similar fate were Herod Antipater and Sulla. The nature of Cassander's death, and the murders of his sons, was seen by the writers under the empire as divine justice for the family's supposed responsibility for the destruction of Alexander's family.

Pyrrhus and Demetrius now shared a common border but their ambition and greed for power, the natural diseases of Hellenistic dynasties, made them dangerous and suspicious neighbours. Their family ties no longer existed, as Deidameia had died some years before. The garrisons in the Macedonian cities Pyrrhus had taken from Alexander also created tension between the two. Pyrrhus now took steps to secure his kingdom against Demetrius. He strengthened the fortifications of his new capitol Ambracia.

At about this time, most likely in 295, Pyrrhus' first wife Antigone died, possibly in childbirth. The dates of this event, and his subsequent marriages, cannot be dated exactly but rather inferred from hints within the sources. Antigone's son had been named Ptolemy in honour of the Egyptian king. Pyrrhus' second son, Alexander, was fifteen at the time of the Italian expedition in 280, and therefore must have been born in 295/4. Pyrrhus did not take any further wives until Antigone had died, so 295 is the latest possible date for her death. This supposition is supported by Ptolemy being old enough to command an expedition in 277. Following the death of Antigone, Pyrrhus then embarked on a series of marriages, all for political reasons and designed to strengthen his kingdom. This was a normal practice for Hellenistic kings. Lannassa, his second wife, was the daughter of Agathocles of Syracuse, and brought him the island of Corcyra as a dowry. The next was with Bircenna, the daughter of Bardylis, one of the Illyrian kings, the union designed to secure his northern border. The last marriage was with the daughter of the king of the Paeonians, and was aimed at creating a threat to Demetrius' northern border. The sources record Pyrrhus as having three sons, in order of birth, Ptolemy, Alexander, son of Lanassa, and Helenus, son of Bircenna. Multiple sons by different mothers often produced great dynastic conflict, especially as the king aged. Such clashes would help lead to the downfall of Lysimachus, plague Ptolemy of Egypt, cause the assassination of Seleucus and lead to civil war after his death. Pyrrhus is supposed to have foreseen these problems. When asked by one of his sons who should inherit the throne he replied, 'to the one of you who keeps his sword the sharpest.'[6] This was the famous curse of Oedipus, that thrones should be won by the sword and not by order of birth. Although rivalry between surviving brothers did not affect the Epirot house on Pyrrhus' death, it would be an ongoing blight on the other Successor kingdoms.

Now that Demetrius had become king of Macedonia, the Greek cities, as usual, chaffed at being under the command of a foreign ruler. The first to revolt were the Boeotians in 293, who received support from both the Aetolians and the Spartans. Demetrius quickly crushed this challenge and accepted the surrender of the Boeotians. The next year, Demetrius took advantage of the capture of Lysimachus during a campaign against a Thracian tribe, the Getae, and attacked his possessions. Encouraged by his absence, the Boeotians revolted again. Demetrius was forced to break off his campaign and return to Greece, where he laid siege to the Boeotian city of Thebes. Pyrrhus, with his kingdom now secure, took advantage of Demetrius' difficulties and invaded Thessaly along with his Aetolian allies. The Aetolians during this period are recorded as raising armies of 7-12,000 men.[7] Along with Pyrrhus' Epirots, the invading army probably totalled close to 30,000 troops. Demetrius responded immediately. Leaving the conduct of the siege to his son Antigonus, known as Gonatas, he marched against the Epirots. The size of Demetrius army is not recorded, but with the forces of Macedonia and most of Greece to call upon, it would have been much larger than that of the enemy. Pyrrhus, obviously not confident enough to face the full might of Demetrius, precipitately withdrew. Demetrius placed a garrison of 10,000 infantry and 1,000 cavalry in Thessaly, commanded by reputedly his best general, Pantauchus, and then returned to the siege. Demetrius took Thebes the following year.

While he was back in Epirus, Pyrrhus suffered a further setback. His wife Lanassa, daughter of Agathocles, deserted him. She claimed that she, the daughter of a Greek king, could no longer bear to share her home with barbarian women. She fled to Corcyra and offered herself to Demetrius. Always one to seize the opportunity of a conquest, both political and sexual, Demetrius sailed with his fleet to Corcyra and took possession of both the island and Lanassa. On the way home he also seized the island of Leucas. Pyrrhus, with no fleet to call upon, was impotent to stop him. Demetrius was just as restless and ambitious as Pyrrhus. He now planned to invade Epirus, probably hoping to remove this threat to his western frontier forever. In 289 Demetrius invaded Pyrrhus' allies the Aetolians, hoping to neutralize them before he invaded Epirus. Demetrius advanced into northern Aetolia from Thessaly, ravaging the countryside as he went. The outmatched Aetolians adopted their usual strategy, refusing battle and retreating back into the hills. Demetrius left Pantauchus with a force to occupy Aetolia and proceeded to move through the mountain passes to invade Epirot Ambracia. Pyrrhus, learning of Demetrius' attack, quickly gathered what forces he could and advanced rapidly to assist his allies. As speed was crucial Pyrrhus probably took the coastal route. The two armies, now on different roads, passed by one another, not an uncommon occurrence given the limited reconnaissance and communications capabilities of pre-industrial armies. Demetrius invaded Epirus and plundered the countryside.

Meanwhile, Pyrrhus encountered Demetrius' general Pantauchus and forced him to fight a battle. Pyrrhus, presuming he had the bulk of the Epirot army with him, perhaps 20,000 men, would probably have heavily outnumbered the detached force of the enemy. Pantauchus' force was, most likely, similar in size to that which he had commanded in Thessaly, about 11,000 troops. The fighting was heavy, and during the battle the two commanders sought out each other. Pantauchus challenged Pyrrhus to individual combat. Pyrrhus, supposedly wishing to emulate his ancestor Achilles in glory, accepted. After hurling spears at one another the two came to sword blows. Pyrrhus was wounded but in return twice wounded his opponent, in the thigh and neck. Pantauchus' bodyguards carried him away. The Epirots, exalted by the exploits of their king and inspired by his valour, overran and cut to pieces the phalanx of the Macedonians. They killed many in the pursuit, and took 5,000 prisoners. The anecdote of the individual challenge is a set piece that would not have been out of place in the pages of Homer, two heroes throwing spears at each other and coming to close-quarter blows. Although there is no good reason to doubt that the incident happened, given that such encounters were common enough in the battles of the Successors, the details should be treated with some scepticism. After learning the result of the battle Demetrius ended his pillaging of Epirus and withdrew back into Macedonia.

This was Pyrrhus' first victory in battle and won for him great admiration, both for his generalship and for his courage. The Epirots, flushed with victory, bestowed the surname of 'Eagle' upon him. This nickname would remain with him for the rest of his life. Pyrrhus' victory had saved both his kingdom and his allies' lands. His defeat of a Macedonian army, and his demonstrated courage in battle, had given him the most important asset for a Hellenistic king, a reputation as a brave and successful general. Plutarch claims that the Macedonians bore no malice towards Pyrrhus, but held him in great esteem and made unflattering comparisons between him and their own king, Demetrius. This he claims was the beginning of the end for Demetrius' rule over the Macedonians, as they saw in Pyrrhus 'that of all the kings, it was in Pyrrhus only that they saw a lively image of Alexander's valour; whereas the other princes, especially Demetrius, imitated him only in a theatrical manner, by affecting a lofty bearing and majestic air.'[8] Such a claim was largely rhetorical on Plutarch's part, always conscious to parallel Demetrius with his paired life of the dissolute Marc Anthony. In reality Demetrius, for courage at least, is better compared with Pyrrhus. On Plutarch's own testimony he had led from the front during his numerous sieges, and twice been wounded. At the Battle of Salamis he had fought courageously while his three bodyguards had been cut down around him.[9]

Despite his victory, the loss of his wife and Corcyra and the pillaging of Epirus must have led to resentment on Pyrrhus' part. Learning that Demetrius was dangerously ill, Pyrrhus took his revenge and invaded Macedonia in 289. His original intention was merely to plunder the countryside, but with Demetrius unable to lead the defence he met no opposition. Pyrrhus had penetrated as far as the old capitol of Aegae before Demetrius was able to raise himself from his sick bed. Again Pyrrhus was unable to stand against the strength of the Macedonian army led by its king. Pyrrhus fled, losing part of his army to the attacks of the pursuing enemy. Twice within four years Pyrrhus had tried to attack Demetrius' possessions while Demetrius was initially unable to oppose him, but both times had been easily repulsed when faced by the full force of the Macedonian army. Demetrius, however, was now planning an invasion of Asia to recover his father's domains, and had no desire for renewed conflict on his western border. The two kings came to terms and made peace. The details of the peace are not recorded but most likely they were recognition of the *status quo*. Demetrius would recognize Pyrrhus' holdings in Macedonia, and Pyrrhus would accept the loss of Corcyra and Leucas.

Demetrius had prepared for his invasion of Asia by reputedly raising a force of 110,000 troops and 500 warships.[10] Even if the numbers are exaggerated, this was clearly an immense force. Perhaps the numbers record the sum total of all Demetrius' forces, including those garrisoning his Greek subjects. Faced by such overwhelming might, the other kings, Ptolemy, Lysimachus and Seleucus, allied together against him, just as they had against his father. This time, however, they would attack their rival king in Macedonia itself.

The three kings also sent letters and embassies to Pyrrhus. They pointed out that this would be the ideal time for Pyrrhus to confront Demetrius, while he was under attack from them all. To remain neutral in such a situation would lead to no gain for Pyrrhus. If Demetrius won he could overwhelm Pyrrhus at any time in the future. If the three kings won and Pyrrhus was not a part of the alliance he would receive none of the spoils of victory. Pyrrhus' personal enmity towards Demetrius and his gratitude towards Ptolemy probably played a part in his decision. More important, however, was the chance to conquer easily part, or all, of Macedonia while Demetrius was under attack from all fronts. Pyrrhus decided to ally with the other kings. As a product of these negotiations, Lysimachus put to death Cassander's last remaining son Antipater. A rival claimant to the throne would have proved embarrassing, because, as events would show, Lysimachus planned to seize Macedonia for himself. His death would also have been welcomed by Pyrrhus for much the same reasons.

In 288, the kings attacked. Ptolemy sailed against Demetrius' Greek allies with a great fleet. Lysimachus attacked upper Macedonia from Thrace. Pyrrhus waited in Epirus until Demetrius had gone north to confront Lysimachus. As soon as the Macedonian army was entangled with Lysimachus, he reneged on his agreement with Demetrius and invaded from the south. This clearly came as a shock to Demetrius as Pyrrhus advanced through western and southern Macedonia without any opposition. According to Plutarch, Pyrrhus had a dream where a sick Alexander the Great called to him and promised to give him aid. Supposedly encouraged by his dream, Pyrrhus took the town of Beroea, the traditional birthplace of the Antigonid dynasty.[11] He then continued to overrun the rest of the country. Meanwhile, Demetrius' northern campaign had begun well. He had defeated Lysimachus' army in battle near the important town of Amphipolis. His army, however, soon learned that Pyrrhus was overrunning their homeland unopposed. The Macedonian soldiers turned on Demetrius. His grandiose schemes and autocratic, oppressive rule had become unpopular in Macedonia. His army was in uproar and he feared that many would desert to his rival Macedonian king, Lysimachus.

Learning that Pyrrhus had betrayed him and had seized his ancestral home, Demetrius decided to lead his army against Pyrrhus. He believed that his rebellious troops would more willingly fight against a foreign invader than against Lysimachus, a veteran of Alexander's campaigns. The desire to punish his betrayer must have also been a motive. Demetrius had underestimated his unpopularity. His troops were so tired of him they were willing to desert to anybody, in order to rid themselves of Demetrius. The Macedonians had, supposedly, always admired Pyrrhus' valour and the clemency he had earlier shown to his Macedonian prisoners. Pyrrhus sent agents into the enemy camp to encourage the tumult and spread favourable propaganda. Small groups began to desert and then the whole army rebelled. Finally, a delegation confronted Demetrius and told him that they were tired of fighting to maintain his luxury. They advised him to escape while he could. Demetrius wisely took their advice and fled to the coastal city of Cassandreia. Meanwhile, Pyrrhus had entered the Macedonian camp and quelled the looting and rioting. The Macedonians deserted to Pyrrhus *en masse* and proclaimed him to be their king.

Demetrius' overthrow was rapid and spectacular. The primary role of military leadership in Hellenistic kingship has already been discussed, but by any standards Demetrius' six-year rule must be judged as having been militarily successful. He had re-imposed Macedonian domination over southern Greece, easily fought off Pyrrhus' invasions, and successfully raided both Epirus and Thrace. Clearly something more was expected of a king in addition to a history of successful conquests. From the ceremony at Dodona it is clear that some sort of social contract existed between the Epirots and their king. Although any exchange of oaths between the Macedonian king and his people is not recorded, that such a contract existed is implied by Arrian, who quotes Callisthenes, a member of Alexander's court, as claiming that the Macedonian kings had 'long ruled not by force but by law.'[12] The other main attributes expected of a king appear to be to act as a just law-giver, and to enrich one's followers and subjects by gifts and donations. Demetrius is recorded as being difficult to approach for his subjects, and being harsh and discourteous. In one famous anecdote he threw their petitions into a river, and in another he told an old Macedonian woman that he had no time to hear her petition. She retorted by screaming at him, 'then don't be king.' Demetrius' ostentatious tastes offended the Macedonians and they, supposedly, 'were tired of waging war in support of his luxurious way of living.' Most likely they believed that more of his wealth should have been distributed to themselves. In the end, they tired of his perceived aloofness and selfishness and overthrew him, helping themselves to his wealth by 'pillaging and tearing down his tent, and fought with one another for the spoils.'[13]

Pyrrhus' complete triumph was short-lived, however, as Lysimachus soon marched down to join him. Until then he had been delayed besieging Amphipolis, but following Demetrius' overthrow his garrison commander betrayed the city to Lysimachus. He claimed that the removal of Demetrius had been brought about by the actions of them both, and demanded his share of the spoils. Pyrrhus did not feel certain of the loyalty of the fickle Macedonians and agreed to Lysimachus' demands. The two kings divided Macedonia between them, setting the boundary at the River Axius.

Demetrius, despite his many failings, was never one to let adversity overpower him. He retreated into Greece where his son Antigonus had been commanding his garrisons and defending against Ptolemy's attacks. Demetrius quickly rebuilt his forces and won over Thebes. The Athenians, meanwhile, had renounced their alliance with him and overthrown his puppet government. They were, however, surprised and scared by his rapid return to a position of strength. Demetrius, enraged to be deserted by the Athenians for a second time, marched against them and laid siege to the city. He had previously re-captured Athens in 295. The Athenians called on Pyrrhus to assist them. Before he could arrive, Demetrius withdrew, as he was too weak to both maintain the siege and confront Pyrrhus at the same time. The Athenians showed their gratitude by erecting a bust to Pyrrhus and allowed him to enter the city and sacrifice to Athena. They did, however, refuse to allow his army to enter. Pyrrhus made the most of the situation and told the Athenians he was pleased with their goodwill and gave them advice to never again let a king enter the city. Despite this show of superficial friendship, Pyrrhus was, no doubt, disappointed that he could not garrison Athens himself.

Pyrrhus and Demetrius once more made peace but, as with all the prior agreements, it did not last. Demetrius soon departed for Asia, in order to attack the empire of Lysimachus. In 286 Pyrrhus, at the request of Lysimachus, attacked Thessaly and Demetrius' garrisons in Greece. Plutarch claims that this was to keep his fractious Macedonians busy and thereby less likely to rebel.[14] Pyrrhus himself was not one to be content to live in peace. The chance of easy conquest would have been a strong inducement for the ever ambitious and restless Pyrrhus. He quickly defeated Antigonus, who ceded Thessaly in order to make peace. Pyrrhus' Greek empire was now at its zenith. He controlled an enlarged Epirus, Thessaly and half of Macedonia. As was so often the case during the period of the Successors, however, great success was often quickly followed by rapid collapse.

A year later Demetrius was defeated and captured by Seleucus. The removal of Demetrius, however, now freed the hands of Lysimachus. The two had been inveterate enemies, both political and personal. Lysimachus, in his hatred for Demetrius, is accused of offering Seleucus a bribe to either hand him over, or to execute him. To the latter's credit he refused. He merely held him prisoner and allowed him to drink himself into an early grave. Demetrius died in 283, much to the relief of all the other kings. The expansionist nature of Hellenistic kingship has already been discussed but Plutarch, describing this period, puts it far more eloquently:

For how men to whose rapacity neither sea nor mountain nor uninhabitable desert sets a limit,†men to whose inordinate desires the boundaries which separate Europe and Asia put no stop, can remain content with what they have and do one another no wrong when they are in close touch, it is impossible to say. No, they are perpetually at war, because plots and jealousies are parts of their natures, and they treat the two words, war and peace, like current coins, using whichever happens to be for their advantage, regardless of justice; for surely they are better men when they wage war openly than when they give the names of justice and friendship to the times of inactivity and leisure which interrupt their work of injustice.[15]

The alliance between Lysimachus and Pyrrhus had always been based on self interest and the philosophy that, 'my enemy's enemy is my friend'. With Demetrius now removed from the scene, Pyrrhus rightly judged that Lysimachus would now turn on him. Lysimachus began his campaign by isolating Pyrrhus from his traditional allies. He married Arsinoe, the sister of the new Egyptian king Ptolemy II. He also made large donations of money to the Aetolians, ostensibly for the foundations of new cities. Searching around for new allies, Pyrrhus approached his recent enemy, Antigonus. Antigonus, no doubt, believed that if Pyrrhus was overthrown he would himself become Lysimachus' next target. Neither was strong enough to stand up against the might of Lysimachus alone, so they buried their differences and made an alliance based on the same doctrine.

Lysimachus invaded Pyrrhus' share of Macedonia in 284. In 301 at Ipsus he had been able to field in excess of 40,000 troops. Since then he had acquired most of western Asia Minor and half of Macedonia. With these combined assets, his army in 284 could easily have numbered more than 70,000 men. Pyrrhus' combined Epirot and Macedonian forces may have totalled 40,000 troops at best. Unable to match Lysimachus' numbers, Pyrrhus retreated to Aegae, in northern Macedonia, where he was joined by the forces of Antigonus.

Upon his arrival at Aegae, Lysimachus decided not to risk battle, but to use his Macedonian heritage and links to Alexander to undermine the Epirot king. First he captured Pyrrhus' supply trains, causing hunger within his camp. Then he appealed to the patriotism of the leading Macedonians. He castigated them for choosing a foreign lord, one whose ancestors had, supposedly, been subject to the Macedonians. Lysimachus' propaganda campaign won many over and they turned against Pyrrhus. Without being able to rely on his Macedonian troops Pyrrhus was unable to face the overwhelming forces of Lysimachus, and he prudently withdrew back into Epirus. Within three years, Pyrrhus had lost Macedonia precisely as he had won it, by the treachery of the Macedonians. Plutarch sums up the irony of the situation by observing that the kings cannot expect loyalty from their subjects when they show none to each other. They were simply imitating the behaviour of their rulers by following their own interests.[16] Lysimachus followed up his defeat of Pyrrhus by invading and ravaging Epirus during the following year in 283. During this invasion Lysimachus was accused of plundering and desecrating the tombs of the Epirot kings. Pausanius claims that the accusation is not true and is the result of propaganda from the historian Hieronymus of Cardia, a member of Antigonus' court. He accuses Hieronymus of hating Lysimachus for destroying his native city of Cardia and of being a 'king-hater in his writings, except for Antigonus who he unjustly favours'.[17]

Pausanius also claims that Lysimachus was unopposed in this raid as 'Pyrrhus was roaming around as usual'.[18] Just where Pyrrhus was can only be inferred from the sources. It appears that after his loss of Macedonia he attempted to enlarge his kingdom at the expense of his northern Illyrian neighbours. His former guardian Glaucias had already died. Justin tells of a successful war against the Illyrians. Frontinus records the following stratagem:

> Pyrrhus, king of Epirus, in his war against the Illyrians, aimed to reduce their capital, but despairing of this, began to attack the other towns, and succeeded in making the enemy disperse to protect their other cities, since they had confidence in the apparently adequate fortification of the capital. When he had accomplished this, he recalled his own forces and captured the town, now left without defenders.[19]

Pyrrhus, at some time, also captured the city of Apollonia, in Illyrian territory, as Pliny records him as devising the grandiose scheme of building a bridge from there to Italy, 'intending to have a passage over on foot.'[20] The Frontinus' passage above may refer to the capture of Apollonia. Although such a scheme seems fantastic, the era of the Successors was one of grandiose construction projects. Demetrius had planned to build a canal across the Isthmus of Corinth, and Seleucus another to link the Black and Caspian seas. Pyrrhus also retook Corcyra at some point. The most likely time for these campaigns is the period between the years 283 and 281.

Through these conquests Pyrrhus had again enlarged his kingdom. It now spread from Apollonia in the north to Corcyra in the south. It included all of Epirus proper plus all the Greek regions Pyrrhus had annexed during his reign, except Thessaly. Garoufalias estimates that the population of this 'Greater Epirus' was between 483,000 and 505,000.[21] The usual range of estimates for the population of Athens at the outbreak of the Peloponnesian War in 431 is between 250,000 and 300,000 people. Thucydides documents that at his time Athens could field 29,000 hoplites and 1,200 cavalry.[22] Although Athens at its height was a much wealthier state than Epirus, it can be seen that the earlier estimate of the Epirot army as around 25,000 is by no means excessive, and quite possibly too conservative.

While Pyrrhus was busily enlarging his kingdom the final clash of the generals of Alexander the Great was taking place in Asia. It came about due to the intrigues within Lysimachus' own family. During the wars he had sealed an alliance with Ptolemy of Egypt by marrying his sister Arsinoe. She began to conspire against Lysimachus' oldest son Agathocles, the product of a previous marriage. Arsinoe hoped to gain the succession for her own sons. In this plot she was joined by her brother, Ptolemy Ceraunus (Thunderbolt). He had been disowned and driven into exile by his own father, Ptolemy I. Agathocles was extremely popular in Asia where he had been his father's governor for many years. Arsinoe was able to use his popularity against him, accusing him of conspiring with Seleucus to set up his own kingdom. Demetrius' accusations over Agathocles' paternity had earlier enraged Lysimachus, but may have sewn seeds of doubt in the old man's mind. Arsinoe convinced her paranoid, 80-year-old husband that Agathocles was planning to overthrow him. Lysimachus had Agathocles executed. This was a huge miscalculation. Many of the cities of Asia revolted, and most of Lysimachus' most trusted friends deserted, fearing that they would be Arsinoe's next victims. Agathocles' wife, Lysandra, and Ptolemy Ceraunus, who also appears to have fallen out with his sister, fled to Seleucus in Babylonia. Lysandra entreated him to come to her assistance and place her son on the throne of Lysimachus. This was too good an offer for Seleucus to refuse. With Lysimachus weakened, Seleucus had an excuse to intervene in Thrace and Macedonia. He could also attack in Egypt in favour of Ptolemy Ceraunus. Ptolemy had died in 282 and been succeeded by his son Ptolemy II. The Ptolemies and the Seleucids had a long-running dispute over the control of Phoenicia (Lebanon) and Coele-Syria (Israel/Palestine), which Ptolemy had annexed during the Ipsus campaign. Seleucus had believed both to be rightfully his, but in gratitude for Ptolemy's help early in his reign he had taken no action. With Ptolemy dead, however, it would become an ongoing cause of war between the two dynasties for the next century. Although the refugees would provide the excuse, Seleucus, no doubt, saw an opportunity to seize both kingdoms on his own behalf. In the winter of 282/281, he invaded Lysimachus' Asian possessions. In February 281 the armies of the 77-year-old Seleucus and the 80-year-old Lysimachus clashed at Corupedion, near Sardes in Lydia. Seleucus won the battle and Lysimachus was killed in combat. Reputedly his body was guarded by his faithful dog for several days until found on the battlefield. Lysimachus' kingdom, riven by internal rivalries, collapsed like a house of cards. Seleucus marched into Europe, where, it appeared, nothing could prevent him from adding Thrace and Macedonia to his empire. During the march, Ptolemy Ceraunus treacherously assassinated him. With no obvious other candidate present the army declared Ptolemy king. He then improved his position by forcing his half-sister Arsinoe, the widow of Lysimachus, to marry him. After the ceremony he killed Arsinoe's two younger sons. Ptolemy had successfully seized the throne of Macedonia, and the European domains of Lysimachus, for himself.

The only other possible claimant to the Macedonian throne was Pyrrhus. He would, however, decide on an alternative plan: the invasion of Italy.

Chapter IV

Italy

'the Tarentines ... were inclined to let him do their fighting for them while they remained at home in the enjoyment of their baths and social festivities, he closed up the gymnasia and the public walks, where, as they strolled about, they fought out their country's battles in talk.' - Plutarch, *Pyrrhus*, 16

'The Romans, to speak generally, rely on force in all their enterprises.' - Polybius, 1.37

The Tarentine invitation to Pyrrhus was a result of the continuing decline in their power to resist the Italian tribes since the death of Alexander of Epirus in 331. The Greek cities of the south were still suffering from the continuous attacks of the neighbouring Lucanians and Bruttians. In 303 the Tarentines were at war with both the Lucanians, and the newly-emerging Italian power, the Romans. At first the Tarentines had taken a benign attitude to Rome's expansion as they were attacking the Tarentine's Italian enemies. As the Romans advanced further south and began to encroach into what the Tarentines considered to be their sphere of influence this attitude changed.

The Tarentines were now too weak to confront their opponents on their own, and again they approached their founding city, Sparta, for assistance. They requested that Cleonymus, a noted general, be sent to take command. Previously, Cleonymus had been passed over as king in Sparta because of his violent nature and tyrannical behaviour. The Tarentines sent money and ships to the Spartans, who despatched Cleonymus, along with 5,000 mercenaries, to Italy. After arriving in Italy he raised a further 22,000 troops from Tarentum.[1] Now a power to be reckoned with, he won the support of most of the other Greek cities and the Apulians. The Lucanians, alarmed at the size of his force, made peace and established an alliance with the Tarentines. Cleonymus, in co-operation with his new allies, captured the Greek city of Metapontum.

Flushed with his success, Cleonymus' behaviour now reverted to its true nature. From one city alone, he is supposed to have demanded 200 virgins as hostages and also extorted 600 talents in cash, an enormous sum. Turning his back on his Spartan upbringing, he is reputed to have satisfied his lecherous appetites on the virgins and wasted the money on a luxurious lifestyle.

Rather than make war on the Romans he made plans to invade Sicily. Meanwhile, he sailed to Corcyra, captured it, exacted tribute and placed a garrison within the city. He also raided the coast of Illyria. Cleonymus planned to use the island as a base to create a kingdom within Greece. The Tarentines, tired of his behaviour and his failure to fight their Italian enemies, rebelled against him. Cleonymus returned to Italy and captured and plundered a number of Italian, most likely Apulian, towns.

The next year he captured and sacked the Greek city of Thurii on the eastern coast of the Bay of Tarentum. The Romans, with their Italian allies, made a night attack on his encampment, inflicting heavy casualties. At the same time a storm arose and destroyed twenty of his ships. Cleonymus then decided to retreat back to Corcyra. Livy claims that he was actually defeated in the battle and driven back onto his ships.[2] From here on Cleonymus continued to ravage the eastern coast of Italy. He attacked Patavium, a city of a Celtic tribe, the Veneti, in northern Italy. The Celts (or Gauls as the Romans knew them) defeated the invading force and inflicted heavy losses on his fleet while it was trapped in the shallow waters of a river. Cleonymus was once again forced to retreat back to Corcyra.

Cleonymus' intervention had temporarily reduced the pressure on the Tarentines, but had alienated many of the neighbouring cities. Tarentum was forced to make peace with Rome and the two cities entered into a maritime treaty. The full terms of this treaty are not recorded, but most likely the Romans recognized the Tarentine hegemony over the Greek cities around the Bay of Tarentum. In return the Tarentines recognized the Roman conquests in Apulia and Samnia. One clause is certain: that the Romans agreed not to send ships east of the Cape of Lacinum (Capo Noto) and into the Bay of Tarentum.[3] Despite this agreement, it was the rapidly increasing power of Rome that would now become the Tarentine's biggest threat.

The founding of Rome is very much embroiled in myth. The traditional date celebrated by the Romans was 21 April, 753. This date fits with traces found by archaeologists of early settlements on the Palatine Hill dating back to the mid-eighth century. Rome was just one of a number of Latin-speaking cities that occupied a fertile plain on the central western coast of Italy, known as Latium. Such areas in Italy were rare, the main three being Latium, Etruria to the north and Campania to the south. This made Latium a highly-desirable area to the hill tribes who surrounded the plain. For much of their early history, Rome and the other Latin cities were under constant attack from these people. During the seventh century the northern

Etruscans conquered both the Latin plain and Campania. Rome was made subject to Etruscans kings. In 510 the Romans rebelled against their last Etruscan king, but it was not until 506 that, allied with other Latin cities, they won their independence. The victorious Latin cities then formed the Latin League.

Rome would spend most of the next century constantly at war with her neighbours. By the end of the fifth century she had come to dominate the other Latin cities, although in theory they were independent allies. In 396 she finally conquered her constant enemy, the southern-most Etruscan city of Veii, and annexed a large area west of the River Tiber. The decisive victory was in part due to other attacks that had weakened the Etruscans. A new enemy, the Gauls, had completely overrun the basin of the Po. From this base they were constantly crossing the Apennines and invading Etruria itself. The Etruscans had also been driven out of most of their possessions in Campania, a region south of Rome, by the Samnites, a group of tribes occupying the central Italian hills.

The Celtic invaders soon turned against Rome. In 390 they captured the city, and either sacked it or demanded a huge ransom. Much of this event is swathed in legend, such as the tale of the Gallic chief Brennus tossing his sword onto the scale with the words '*vae victis*' ('woe to the vanquished'). What is clear is that the Gauls, having swept devastatingly over Etruria, poured into Rome, pillaged it, and then retreated back to the north. The Etruscans never fully recovered from these attacks, while the Romans were severely weakened. Other Italian tribes, the Aequians and Volscians, joined by some of Rome's Latin allies, seized the moment to make a last desperate effort to break her power. The revolt was crushed and the Latins were made even more subject to Roman control than before. The other major Latin city, Tusculum, was absorbed into Roman territory, with her people receiving full Roman citizenship in 380. Rome now dominated all of Latium and a substantial section of Etruria. Despite this, some of the Latins made one last effort to overthrow Rome's domination and allied themselves with the Gauls. The Etruscans, taking advantage of the situation also attacked Rome. Yet again the Romans prevailed. By 351 the Gauls had been defeated and the Etruscans were forced to accept a forty-year treaty.

Soon after, in 348, Carthage recognized Rome as a power to be reckoned with and made a treaty with her, perhaps the first between the two states, or possibly a renewal of an earlier treaty made in 509, the first year of the Republic. Carthage undertook to respect all Latin territory and coastal towns as a Roman sphere of influence. The agreement also granted Roman traders admission to the ports of Carthaginian dominions in Africa, Sardinia, Sicily, and to Carthage itself. Carthaginian merchants were to have similar access to Rome. Roman ships of war were allowed access to these ports in wars against third parties. The Romans were excluded from settling in Sardinia and Africa. Carthage was granted freedom of military action in Italian territory outside of Roman control.[4] The important effect of the treaty was to bind Rome not to oppose Carthaginian attacks on the Greek cities in the south of Italy and Sicily.

The almost continual campaigning from the Republic's foundation had made Rome an extremely militaristic society. The calling up of the Roman army in the spring had become an annual event. It has been calculated that in the eighty-six years following 327, Rome was only at peace for four or five of these.[5] According to Thucydides, the Athenians espoused that 'of the men we know, that by a necessary law of their nature they rule wherever they can ... we found it existing before us and it shall exist forever after us.'[6] This belief, that the strong would always rule the weak, applied just as much to relations between Rome and the Italian cities as to those of the Greeks.

The fifth and fourth centuries saw a constant struggle within Rome between the aristocratic patricians and the poorer class, the plebeians, with the latter winning a number of concessions. Roman politics, nonetheless, was still dominated by the aristocratic Senate and the two annually-elected magistrates, the consuls. The main role of the consuls was to command the Roman armies in war. In order to attain a consulship a young aristocrat had to win election to a number of minor offices. Successful military service was essential in the race for these positions. In order to even run, the candidate must have served in the military for at least ten years. To have any chance of success a candidate must also possess sufficient glory (*gloria*) and fame (*laus*). The major method of earning these attributes was in war. In such a martial society, Roman aristocrats had strong reasons for allowing disputes with their neighbours to grow into war. Polybius claims that the Romans always relied on force of arms (*bia*) to solve problems with their neighbours.[7]

Following the defeat of the Gauls and final subjugation of the Latin League, Rome now turned its martial energy to the task of conquering the entire Italian peninsula. Many earlier historians have argued that Rome's wars were all defensive in nature and that it acquired its empire by accident. This ignores the fact that nearly all her campaigns would now be fought on enemy territory. A successful campaign would see the defeated enemy forced into alliance with Rome, and Latin colonies placed within its territory. These would act as loyal, strategic fortresses for Rome in case of any rebellion. For the Romans peace appears to have been possible only following a victory in war, anything else was merely a short-term armistice. Polybius states that from their victory over the Gauls, in 386, the Romans deliberately embarked on a series of expansionist wars against their neighbours. At some stage during these wars they came to see all of Italy as being rightfully their own country.[8]

The next period of Roman expansion would be dominated by a series of wars with the Samnites, starting in 363 and not ending until 290. The Samnites were intent on overrunning the rich farmlands of Campania. The Campanians appealed for help from the Romans. The First Samnite War was brief, lasting from 343 to 341. It was ended by yet another revolt of Rome's Latin allies lasting between 340–338. Rome's victory over the Latins further tightened her grip upon them. Some of the cities were incorporated into Rome, while others were granted the civil but not the political rights of Roman citizenship. The Latin League was dissolved, and all the Latin cities were banned from forming separate alliances with each other, or any external power.

The Second Samnite War began in 323 and continued for twenty years until 303. The main cause was the Romans placing two Latin colonies in Samnite territory, in breach of the earlier treaty. At first the Roman arms were so successful that in 321 the Samnites sued for peace. As was their usual practice, the Romans offered terms that were so severe that they were rejected, and the war went on. The war then swung in the Samnite's favour and at the Battle of the Caudine Forks (321) they won a significant victory over the Romans. The Romans were forced to give up their spears and march under them, a sign of the ultimate battlefield humiliation. Six hundred nobles had to be handed over as hostages, the colonies abandoned, and the Romans agree to a five-year treaty. During this five-year respite, the Romans took the opportunity to strengthen their military position. They attacked the Apulians and Lucanians to the east and south of Samnia, forcing some into alliance. These victories all but surrounded the Samnites with Roman allies and colonies.

The war recommenced in 316, and the Samnites again defeated the Romans at the Battle of Lautulae. In 311 the Etruscans joined the war, when a forty-year-long peace had reached its end. The Romans, however, displayed their characteristic steadfastness and resolve. After these initial setbacks, the Romans continuously defeated both their enemies. In 308 the Etruscans sued for peace, which was granted on harsh terms. Four years later, in 304, the Samnites obtained peace on terms that were probably severe, but not crushing.

In 298 the Samnites renewed the war. The Etruscans, Gauls, and Umbrians, another northern–Italian tribe joined them. The Romans won a shattering victory over their combined forces at the Battle of Sentinum, in Umbria, in 295. The Samnites, nonetheless, fought on until a final defeat in 291 made further resistance hopeless. The following year peace was made on more favourable terms for the Samnites than Rome had granted to any of its other enemies.

Rome now completely controlled the wealthy and populous Campanian cities, both Italian and Greek. They were now allies of Rome, with varying degrees of independence. Roman military colonies were settled in Campania as well as on the eastern outskirts of the Samnite's territory. From 285 to 282 the Romans were again engaged in a campaign in the north against the Gauls and their sponsors the Etruscans. Victories in the battles near the Vadimonian Lake (283) and Populonia (282) brought this war to a successful conclusion. In 282 the Samnites again revolted, and were joined by the Etruscans, Lucanians, and Bruttians. The Roman victories in the north allowed them free rein to take the offensive in the south.

During their wars with the Italians the Romans had founded a number of colonies in Apulia and Lucania. The most important of these were Venusia and Lucera, both in Apulia. The Romans had settled Venusia with 20,000 colonists in 291. Luceria had been captured by the Romans in their wars against the Samnites in 315-4, and lay in a strategic position near to the territories of the Samnites and Lucanians. According to Diodorus, Luceria was an important base for the Romans in their campaigns against these peoples.[9] These two colonies in particular were seen by the Tarentines as a threat to their domination of southern Italy, and were a major factor in hardening their attitude towards Rome.

In 283 the Romans finally intervened in southern Italy, while the Lucanians were attacking the city of Thurii. As the Thuriians no longer trusted the Tarentines, they turned in desperation to the enemies of the Lucanians, the Romans, for help. The Romans placed a garrison in Thurii and won a victory over the Lucanians before the city. Other Greek cities – Locri, Croton and Rhegium – soon followed suit, and allied themselves with the Romans.

The more conservative politicians in Tarentum saw no reason to object to this spread of Roman power, but the democratic party was furious at Rome's intervention into what they considered to be their own sphere of dominance, guaranteed by the treaty of 302. At this moment, the Romans sent a small naval squadron into the Gulf of Tarentum, waters forbidden to it by the treaty. Although a war measure aimed at the Lucanians in defence of its Greek allies, it was a formal breach of the treaty, and certain to provoke the Tarentines. By chance, or ill-fortune, bad weather forced the fleet to seek shelter in the harbour of Tarentum.

As fate would have it, the city was celebrating the festival of the wine-god Dionysus, and many would have been extremely inebriated. The populace of Tarentum, reputedly, lost its head. Rather than negotiate with the Romans, they manned their ships and attacked the fleet while it lay at anchor. They captured and looted five ships, killed the commander and imprisoned the crews.

The Tarentines followed up this success with an attack on Thurii. They captured the city along with its Roman garrison. They held the Thuriians to be chiefly to blame for the Romans breaking the treaty. Even more to the point, they considered that the worst crime of the Thuriians was to prefer the Romans to their fellow Greeks. As a punishment for their behaviour, the Tarentines expelled the noblest citizens, considering them to be most likely pro-Roman, and pillaged the city. The Tarentines may also have now allied themselves with Rome's other enemies, the Etruscans, Gauls and Samnites. Although the attack on the Roman fleet is often described as the result of drunken spontaneity, its success and the subsequent successful attack on Thurii would suggest that the Tarentines had already begun preparations for war with Rome.

The Romans sent a delegation, led by an ex-consul Posthumius, to Tarentum to complain about the capture of their fleet and the attack on Thurii. The Romans' terms were to demand that the Tarentine's release the fleet, surrender Thurii, pay compensation, and hand over the Tarentine commanders to Rome for punishment. To refuse would mean war. Acceptance of the Roman demands would have meant an almost complete surrender on the part of the Tarentines. Negotiations in the form of an ultimatum do, however, seem to be the Roman's usual method of conducting such affairs.

The government of Tarentum was at this time a democracy. Important decisions, such as war and peace, would be debated in an assembly of all adult male citizens. When addressing this assembly, the Roman delegation was ignored and ridiculed by the crowd. On leaving the theatre Posthumius was, reputedly, accosted by a particularly-drunk Tarentine citizen, who soiled the envoy's sacred robe with faeces. This drove the assembly into even greater fits of laughter and derision. The exasperated Roman is reported to have replied, 'laugh while you may. For long will be the period of weeping when you wash this garment clean with your blood.'[10] The Roman ambassadors, having been publicly insulted in this fashion by the Tarentines, sailed away from the city and back to Rome.

This anecdote begins a theme that will remain constant in the sources throughout their narratives dealing with Pyrrhus' campaigns against the Romans. The Greeks, including Pyrrhus, will generally be portrayed as clever and wealthy, but fickle and always looking for an easy solution. The Romans by contrast are displayed as having the more basic virtues of incorruptibility, frugality and courage. Such portrayals are, of course, crude characterizations. They are the product of the historians' attempts to explain why the Romans were able to conquer the Greeks so easily. Their conclusions are best laid out by Dionysius, who claimed:

> That Rome from the very beginning, immediately after its founding,
> produced infinite examples of virtue in men whose superiors,

whether for piety or for justice or for life-long self-control or for warlike valor, no city, either Greek or barbarian, has ever produced.[11]

Anecdotes, such as the insulting of Posthumius, should be seen as a part of this comparison. When recording such incidents the ancient historians were more interested in whether they demonstrated their preconceived theme, and rarely checked their accuracy. The account of the assembly derives mainly from Dionysus of Halicarnassus who, like all ancient historians, was an aristocrat, and had the contempt of his class for democracies. Later in the same passage he condemns assemblies for being too easily influenced by demagogues. Democratic assemblies could, however, be extremely informal and ribald affairs, as can be seen in the writings of the more sober Athenian historian Thucydides and the playwrights. It is, therefore, extremely likely that the Tarentines did abuse and mock the Romans in fairly earthy terms. The Posthumius incident, and similar anecdotes, should, however, be treated with some scepticism, as they may represent the author's prejudices rather than recording actual events.

On the return of the embassy to Rome, the consuls called an immediate meeting of the Senate. Unlike the democracy of the Tarentines, the oligarchy of the Romans discussed foreign affairs in the Senate, the council of the upper classes. The session apparently went from dawn to dusk for many days. One faction argued that war with Tarentum should be postponed until the revolt of the Italians had been put down. Another group, appalled and insulted by the treatment of their ambassador, demanded immediate war. The war party won the vote. Once they had made such a decision it was then passed to the *Comitia Centuriata*, an assembly of all citizens who voted by order of wealth. In law, the *Centuriata* had the final say on matters of war and peace but rarely rejected the Senate's recommendations. On this occasion they voted for war.

According to Livy, the Romans were winning the war against the Italian alliance and were therefore able to open a new front against Tarentum. In 281 they began operations by ordering the consul Lucius Aemilius to break off his campaign against the Samnites and to invade the territory of the Tarentines. He offered peace on the same terms that the embassy had, but again they were rejected by the assembly of the Tarentines. Aemelius then proceeded to ravage 'the whole country of the enemy setting fire to the fields which had crops of grain already ripe and cutting down the fruit-trees'.[12] The Tarentines sent out sorties against him, but he easily defeated them. As a gesture of goodwill, designed to enhance the influence of the peace party in Tarentum he liberated some of the more wealthy prisoners. This succeeded, and one of the anti-war group, Agis, a noted friend of the Romans, was elected as general with full powers. The expression in Greek is *strategos autocratoras*,[13] commander with full powers, and usually means the individual would exercise political as well as military authority.

The Tarentine assembly met again to discuss the war with Rome. Reportedly the atmosphere was much more sober:

> This time they did not laugh for they saw the army. They were about equally divided in opinion until one of their number said to them as they doubted and disputed: 'To surrender citizens is the act of a people already enslaved, yet to fight without allies is hazardous. If we wish to defend our liberty stoutly and to fight on equal terms, let us call on Pyrrhus, king of Epirus, and designate him the leader of this war.' This was done.[14]

The vote had obviously been close, but the war party had prevailed. The Tarentines, with the war now on their own territory, did as they had done previously, and looked to the Greek mainland for allies. Sparta had its own problems and was no longer an option. The next most obvious choice was Pyrrhus, a noted commander with a relatively large army. They sent an embassy to Pyrrhus, probably in early 281, to ask for assistance.

Pyrrhus was now caught in a dilemma. The death of Lysimachus earlier in the year had briefly created the possibility of reconquering Macedonia. This was dashed, however, when Seleucus advanced into Europe with a huge force, consisting of both his own troops and many of the survivors of Lysimachus' army. The situation changed again in September, after Ptolemy Ceraunus' assassination of Seleucus.

Pyrrhus was carefully following these events while also negotiating with the Tarentines. This allowed him to drive a hard bargain and to make a number of demands on the Tarentines. They must pay the costs of the war, give him supreme command of the allied forces and, most importantly, allow him to place a garrison inside the city. In return the king promised to remain in Italy no longer than was necessary. Although Pyrrhus would, of course, decide how long this was to be.

The final decision to accept Pyrrhus' terms did not go unchallenged within Tarentum. There were those that foresaw that subordinating themselves to the king would impose severe limitations on their democracy and way of life. Both Dionysus and Plutarch tell the story of how one of the citizens of Tarentine, a certain Meton, entertained the assembly with a flute girl. When he spoke, however, he had a serious warning to give:

> Men of Tarentum, you do well not to frown upon those who wish to sport and revel, while they can. And if you are wise, you will also get some enjoyment still out of your freedom, assured that ye will have other business and a different life and diet when Pyrrhus has come into the city.[15]

He warned them against allowing the king and a garrison into their city. This was the same warning that Pyrrhus had earlier given the Athenians.

A Greek city, such as Tarentum, was an independent, sovereign state. The two things its people valued most were their freedom (*eleutheria*) and autonomy (*autonomia*). Autonomy simply meant being able to make and enforce their own laws, and not have them dictated from elsewhere. Such autonomy might be destroyed by foreign conquest and the imposition of a governor, puppet oligarchy or tyranny. The less powerful Greek states were always at risk of their autonomy being compromised by domination by more powerful states such as Sparta, Athens, the Persian Empire or, increasingly, the powerful Successor monarchies.

Somewhat perversely, the cities would often look to such powers to guarantee their freedom by entering into alliances with them. When entering these alliances the weaker states would usually seek assurances that the forced levying of its troops, and the imposition of tribute, would not compromise their autonomy. They would also expect to govern themselves according to their own constitution. Thucydides had defined the payment of tribute as the dividing line between autonomy and enslavement.[16] Under treaty obligations they could be required to provide men, ships and/or money. Such exactions of money were euphemistically called 'contributions' or 'expenses'. As such they were not considered 'tribute', and so did not compromise the cities' autonomy.

The biggest threat to a state's freedom, however, was the imposition of a foreign garrison within the city's walls. This, apart from being a powerful symbol, allowed the garrison to dominate the city and interfere in its internal politics at will. Antigonus, in his declaration at Tyre in 315, had promised to defend the freedom of the Greek cities. He guaranteed his promise by expressly committing himself to not introducing garrisons into the cities. Since this date the Greeks had sought similar assurances, whenever possible, from their more powerful allies. By allowing an Epirot garrison within their city walls, the Tarentines were putting their autonomy at immense risk. It is no wonder that the debates within the assembly were heated.

Despite these genuine fears, the war party was more scared of making peace than of an Epirot garrison. To do so would mean that they would be handed over to Romans and executed. They drove Meton from the assembly and voted for war. Apart from these personal considerations, accepting Rome's terms would have, in reality, meant surrender, subordination, and finally annexation by Rome. The other option may have meant subjection to Pyrrhus, but this would, hopefully, be only temporary. As the Tarentines had, however, already told the Thuriians, they believed it better to be subject to one's fellow Greeks than to barbarians. Plutarch clearly shows his prejudices when describing the Tarentine's final decision for war as 'owing to the rashness and villainy of their popular leaders'. Whereas, 'the sensible citizens, some who were directly opposed to this plan were overborne by the clamour and violence of the war party, and others, seeing this, absented themselves from the assembly.'[17]

A second delegation, representing Tarentum and a number of other Greek cities, was sent to Epirus accepting Pyrrhus' terms. The delegation promised that they, along with the Lucanians, Messapians and Samnites, could provide Pyrrhus with forces amounting to 20,000 horse and 350,000 foot. The claim was clearly exaggerated, modern estimates of the total manpower available to these states vary from 180-230,000.[18]

This latter figure would represent the total number of free, adult males of military age. In normal circumstances ancient states only called up adult males of certain property classes and ages, usually about half this total. As has been already discussed, even in major campaigns only about half of this reduced number would normally be raised. The poor, the young and the old were generally called up only in dire emergencies. Otherwise the poor, if they served at all, were usually only used in the navy, as labourers, or occasionally as poorly-equipped skirmishers.

The biggest limitation on the numbers raised would, however, be money. Ancient troops were paid, and the costs of raising an army of any size were enormous. A heavy-infantry man would expect to be paid roughly double the pay of a common workman, and cavalry even more.[19] Only the wealthiest states could afford to keep large numbers of troops in the field for long periods of time. Later in his campaigns Pyrrhus was reportedly so strapped for cash to pay his troops, that he committed the sacrilege of plundering one of the temples of Locris. So, although this lower estimate of troop numbers is theoretically possible, nothing like this number would have been enlisted at any one time.

While these negotiations had been dragging out, Pyrrhus' hopes of winning back Macedonia had suffered a considerable setback. Seleucus' army had gone over to Ptolemy Ceraunus and proclaimed him king. Pyrrhus may have made some attempt to confront Ptolemy in alliance with Seleucus' son Antiochus, perhaps hoping that the fickle Macedonian infantry would again change sides. His efforts were to no avail and the size of Ptolemy's army forced him to make peace. The only mention of this campaign is in Justin, where he states that 'Ceraunus negotiated an end to the wars with Antiochus and Pyrrhus, giving support to Pyrrhus, so that he could go to the defence of Tarentum against the Romans'.[20]

The problem with accepting the existence of this campaign is that there is no other record in the sources, and Justin is not the most reliable of historians. His work is an anthology, excerpted from the earlier work of the historian Pompeius Trogus. Unfortunately, Justin appears to have been extraordinarily careless in his method of composition and it is full of factual errors. He has been described as 'a thorough bungler who does not deserve to be called a historian'.[21] There is, however, an adage among some historians of the period that any ancient source is better than the best modern opinion - even Justin. On this occasion the surrounding details of the passage appear to be accurate and, therefore, there is no good reason to doubt that the campaign took place.

The Italian Greeks' acceptance of his terms, and his failure to overthrow Ptolemy, finally persuaded Pyrrhus to commit to the Italian expedition. After due consideration of the two opportunities fortune had presented to him, Pyrrhus opted for what he considered the more promising target, Italy. Even before he accepted the Tarentines' offer Pyrrhus was already looking around for further prospects of conquest. Sicily had been unsettled since the death of the self-proclaimed king, Agathocles of Syracuse, in 289. His alliance of the Greek cities had fallen apart. Pyrrhus had a potential claimant to Agathocles crown within his own family. His son Alexander was a grandson of the dead king. The prospect of following up his campaigns in Italy with a supposedly-easy conquest of a divided Sicily proved irresistible to Pyrrhus. He reasoned that, with the wealth and forces of the western Greeks behind him, he could then reconquer Macedonia and Greece.

Like all ancient rulers Pyrrhus consulted the oracles before making his final decision. The responses were, as usual, ambiguous. The Epirot oracle at Dodona stated that, 'you, if you cross into Italy, Romans shall conquer.' The temple of Apollo at Delphi responded circumspectly that Pyrrhus could defeat the Romans. Pyrrhus, naturally enough, chose to interpret the answers positively – 'for desire is very apt to deceive one'.[22]

To further sweeten the deal Ptolemy Ceraunus offered him the use of 5,000 Macedonian infantry, 4,000 cavalry and 50 elephants for a two-year period.[23] The last two figures are possibly an example of Justin's propensity to error, as Pyrrhus took only 3,000 cavalry and 20 elephants with him to Italy. No doubt Ptolemy saw this as a relatively cheap and easy method of removing the threat of the Epirot king. He could then turn his full force against his other rival, and Pyrrhus' former ally, Antigonus Gonatas, son of Demetrius.

To begin the campaign, and to prepare his allies, Pyrrhus sent his most trusted advisor Cineas, and his general Milon, ahead to Tarentum with 3,000 soldiers to act as a garrison. Their presence would also serve to weaken the influence of the peace party. Cineas was a Thessalian with a reputation for great wisdom. He had been a pupil of Demosthenes, the famous Athenian orator who had been a major opponent of Philip of Macedon. He was one of Pyrrhus' most trusted and effective ambassadors. The king claimed that he had won for him more cities by his eloquence than by his own arms. Pyrrhus also detained a number of the Tarentine delegates in Epirus, claiming he wished to discuss further matters with them. In reality they were hostages, held to further guarantee their city's loyalty.

Cineas' arrival gave the pro-war Tarentines the political ascendancy and they removed Agis from his office. While Cineas used persuasion, Milon used force to ensure the Tarentines' loyalty. He placed his garrison in the city's acropolis and took command of the manning of the walls. These measures ensured that the Tarentines kept to their agreement, sending supplies to the garrison and money to Pyrrhus.

The arrival of Pyrrhus' advance force had one immediate effect. The Roman commander, Lucius, decided to withdraw his invasion force. While marching along the coast he was ambushed in close terrain by both the Tarentine fleet and army. He suffered heavy losses to both the artillery on the warships and the missiles of the light infantry. He eventually made good his escape by the ruthless stratagem of using captured Tarentines as a human shield.

Once this initial force had been sent out, the Tarentines sent their fleet to Epirus to transport Pyrrhus' army. Antigonus may also have supplied ships; perhaps he too wished to speed the departure of the Epirot king. In early 280 Pyrrhus and his army crossed over to Italy. The force embarked consisted of 20 elephants, 3,000 horse, 20,000 heavy foot, 2,000 archers, and 500 slingers. Most of the heavy foot would have been the Macedonian and Epirot pikemen, although some may have been mercenaries.

For Pyrrhus' battles against the Romans, the pikemen and the elephants would prove to be the most effective parts of his army. The first Hellenistic general to face elephants was Alexander the Great. Although he gathered a considerable force of his own he did not use them in battle, most likely because he lacked the time to train his own troops to fight effectively alongside them. Alexander's Successors, however, consistently used their elephants in their battles.

One of the main advantages of the elephant in war was, apart from its size and strength, its ability to terrify the enemy. This was even more pronounced if they had not faced the animals before, but even troops who had previously met them could be reticent to face them. The later Roman historian and soldier, Ammanius, describes how 'past experience had taught us to dread them'.[24] Cavalry horses in particular were terrified of the beasts.

The historian Arrian gives a good description of the uses of elephants at Alexander's first encounter with them on the open field, at the Battle of the Hydaspes in 326. The Indian King Porus attempted to deploy his elephants so as 'to spread terror among the cavalry of Alexander' as it would 'make the horses uncontrollable.' Alexander took considerable care to ensure that his mounted troops avoided them. He had also enquired into the best way to fight the beasts. This was to attack them with infantry, 'giving ground when they charged', and 'shooting the drivers and pouring in a hail of missiles from every side upon the elephants themselves'. Despite this the elephants, unlike other troops, were able to force themselves into the phalanx by their sheer strength and did considerable damage to the Macedonian infantry. 'The monster elephants plunged this way and that among the lines of infantry, dealing destruction to the solid mass of the Macedonian phalanx'.[25]

The biggest weakness of elephants in battle was the danger they posed to their own side if wounded or panicked. At the Hydaspes the Macedonian infantry managed to box the elephants up and 'with no room to manoeuvre ... they trampled to death as many of their friends as the enemy'.[26]

The usual method of the Successor generals was to deploy the elephants along the front of their armies. They generally spaced them about fifteen to thirty metres apart, depending on numbers, and filled the gaps with light infantry. Pyrrhus would have learned all of this at the court of Antigonus and Demetrius. He would, however, deploy his elephants differently against the Romans, holding them in reserve. There are two likely reasons for this. The first being his experience at Ipsus, where he had learned from first-hand experience the value of an elephant reserve. The second was, most likely, sheer necessity, as Pyrrhus had only twenty elephants, nowhere near as many as even Antigonus' seventy plus. Spread out along the front of the army they would have had a negligible impact. Far better to hold them back until he could make the most of their impact at a crucial time in the battle, either to blunt an enemy assault or to spearhead one of his own.

There was one further military use of elephants. This was against fortifications, where using their size and strength, they could push over or tear up fortifications. Diodorus describes Perdiccas' elephants as 'tearing the palisades to pieces and throwing down the parapets'.[27] It is for this reason that commanders would often use their elephants in assaults on cities, despite the risks involved being even greater in the confined spaces of such attacks. As shall be seen, this use would later prove to be disastrous to Pyrrhus.

The biggest challenge for Pyrrhus in his crossing to Italy was the transportation of his elephants across the sixty-five, or more, kilometres of open sea. This was certainly the first time such an attempt had been made. In 319 Antipater had taken elephants back to Macedonian from Asia, but he had only crossed the relatively narrow and protected Hellespont. But even such a relatively simple crossing could be difficult. Polybius describes the problems faced by Hannibal when he attempted to take his elephants across the River Rhone. He was forced to build a number of rafts and disguise them as solid land by piling 'up a quantity of earth on all the line of rafts, until the whole was on the same level and of the same appearance as the path on shore leading to the crossing... and they now drove them along over the earth with two females in front, whom they obediently followed.'[28] There is no record of how Pyrrhus managed to get his elephants aboard ship but a similar ruse was probably used.

Getting the animals on board ship was, however, only the start of his problems. Even during Hannibal's crossing of the Rhone, some of the elephants 'becoming very alarmed, at first turned round and ran about in all directions,' and 'some were so frightened that they threw themselves into the river'.[29] During Pyrrhus crossing to Italy the fleet was rocked by storms. If the elephants were prone to panic crossing a river then the situation on board a ship during a storm must have been terrifying. How their handlers managed to calm a panicking five tonne animal while on board a twenty-metre long ship is not recorded, but manage it they did, as despite the storm all the elephants were eventually landed safely in Italy. Somehow, Pyrrhus and his officers had solved a novel problem, and completed a potentially dangerous operation.

The storm that had terrified the elephants had also scattered Pyrrhus' fleet and wrecked a part of it. Pyrrhus landed in Apulia, accompanied by less than 2,000 infantry and two elephants. He then marched with this small force into Tarentum, where he joined Cineas and the vanguard. At first, commanding such a small force, Pyrrhus did nothing to upset the Tarentines. Once the remainder of the fleet arrived the situation rapidly changed. The warnings of Meton were realized as Pyrrhus forced the population to billet his soldiers, and closed the gymnasia and other public areas. He also put a stop to the drinking parties, revels, and festivals. He enrolled the men for military service, and forced them to drill regularly. The Tarentines were separated, and groups assigned to Epirot regiments, both to enforce their training and prevent them from uniting against the king. Many Tarentines, not used to such strict discipline, deserted the city despite Pyrrhus posting guards to prevent them. The Tarentines were beginning to see the consequences of allowing a king and foreign garrison within their walls and supposedly 'repented, since they found in Pyrrhus a master instead of an ally.'[30]

Now in complete military control of Tarentum, Pyrrhus set about removing any political opposition to his presence. He began to remove those politicians who might favour the Roman cause, most he sent to Epirus on various pretexts to join the other hostages; while a few of the most dangerous he quietly assassinated. One of the most influential of the Tarentine aristocrats was a certain Aristarchus. At first Pyrrhus tried to win him over, but when this proved impossible, 'invited' him to travel to Epirus. Instead, Aristarchus fled to Rome, where he became the leader and main propagandist of the Greek opposition to Pyrrhus.

The Romans also set about ensuring the loyalty of their allies, which they were able to do without any pretence. Once the war with Pyrrhus looked inevitable they placed garrisons in many of their allied cities. In those where they suspected sympathy for the Tarentine cause, they arrested and executed the leaders of the anti-Roman factions. These expedients would ensure that most of the Italian cities remained loyal, or at least neutral, during the coming period of Epirot victories.

With Pyrrhus now in control of Tarentum, the Roman Senate made preparations for the coming war. They kept a strong garrison in Rome itself, raised a legion to garrison Campania and reinforced their garrison in Locri. In addition, they sent a garrison to the Greek city of Rhegium, at the invitation of its government. The garrisons in Locri and Rhegium would threaten the Bruttians from the south. An army under the previous year's consul, Aemellius, was sent to ravage the territory of the Samnites. Another force, under the new consul, Tiberius Coruncanius, was sent north to attack the Etruscans. These last two forces were designed to keep potential allies of Pyrrhus occupied and unable to unite with him.

The other new consul, Publius Valerius Laevinus, was given command of the largest force, four legions plus allies. He was ordered to march directly against Tarentum, ravaging the territory of the Lucanians along the way. In their usual manner the Romans had taken the offensive in an attempt to wrest the initiative away from Pyrrhus. This also ensured that the territories of their enemies, rather than their own, would be ravaged. The Roman plan was clearly to force Pyrrhus to fight a battle as quickly as possible, while preventing his allies from reinforcing him. The usual method for an ancient army to force another to do battle was to plunder their enemy's countryside.

The Roman plan succeeded. Pyrrhus, learning that the Roman army had advanced south and was threatening the Greek city of Heraclea, advanced out to save the city before he could be joined by his Italian allies, as he thought it 'an intolerable thing to hold back and suffer his enemies to advance any nearer'.[31] According to Polyaenus:

> Before Pyrrhus engaged in a war, he always tried to bring the enemy
> to terms; by making clear to them that otherwise there would be
> terrible consequences, by trying to convince them where their own
> interests lay, by demonstrating to them the miseries that must come
> with the war, and by urging every just and reasonable argument
> against it.[32]

In keeping with this, he then sent a letter to the consul. The message began with Pyrrhus telling the Romans that he had come to Italy in response to the call of the Greek cities, and the Italians, in order to defend their freedoms. Pyrrhus went on to brag about his abilities as a general and the courage of the Epirots in battle. He offered to arbitrate between the parties 'with complete justice', then threatened that this would involve the Romans paying compensation for any damages they had done to the allies, and handing over hostages. Then he promised that he would ensure the peace and aid the Romans if they were attacked. Finally, he ended with another threat that if the Romans did not keep the peace, he would:

> Not permit you to make desolate the country of men who are my allies, to plunder Greek cities and sell freemen at auction, but I shall prevent you by force of arms, in order that you may at last stop pillaging all Italy and treating all men arrogantly as if they were slaves. I shall wait ten days for your answer; longer I cannot wait.[33]

Pyrrhus' offer to the Romans followed a long tradition of such ultimatums by powerful rulers or states. It began with the so-called King's Peace of 387, where the Persian King Artaxerxes asserted that 'the other Hellenic cities both small and large should be autonomous ... and whoever does not observe this peace, against them I shall make war, both by land and sea, with ships and money.'[34] The peace did not last long, and Persia was not strong enough to enforce its threats, but the tradition had been begun. In the next half-century there are at least six more known examples of a 'common peace'.

Rather than a guarantee of peace and autonomy, such arrangements were in fact the method by which the great powers dominated the weaker ones. Beginning with Philip II, the Hellenistic kings followed this historical precedent by enacting other 'common peaces'. In his treaty, following the Battle of Charoenea, Philip guaranteed the territorial integrity and the existing constitutions of the members would be defended, with all agreeing to wage war on any transgressors. Philip was also elected commander-in-chief (*hegemon*) of the armed forces of the alliance and for his proposed war against Persia. His control was ensued by the dominance of Macedonian arms and the presence of his garrisons at strategic points, justified on the grounds of general security. In effect, Philip had ensured his supremacy and the survival of those regimes favourable to him, while presenting himself as the protector of the 'freedom' and 'autonomy' of the Greeks. The terms outlined in Pyrrhus' letter are almost identical. Rather than a genuine offer to arbitrate, it was, in reality, a demand for surrender.

The Roman reply was not surprising. As already noted, Rome's idea of peace was imposing terms on the enemy after a victorious war. Laevinus wrote that such intimidation should only be directed at one's subjects, whereas a prudent man would not threaten those whose valour he had not tested. He went on, somewhat insultingly, to add that this showed a certain foolishness and lack of discrimination. The Romans, on the other hand, 'are wont to punish our enemies, not by words, but by deeds'. He also rejected Pyrrhus' offer of arbitration, but warned him to make himself ready as 'our opponent, not as our judge'. Laevinus further told Pyrrhus, 'to put aside your threats and drop your regal boastfulness, then go to the Senate and inform and persuade its members, confident that you will not fail of anything that is either just or reasonable'.[35]

With the peace offer rejected, the two sides were now determined to decide the fate of Italy by force of arms. The coming battle would occur just outside of the ancient city of Heraclea, modern Policoro.

Chapter V

Heraclea

'Pyrrhus became famous for his victory and acquired a great reputation from it.' - Cassius Dio, 9.39

'it was clear that he was pleased and proud because with his own troops and the Tarentines alone he had conquered the great force of the Romans.'
- Plutarch, *Pyrrhus*, 17.

The coming battle between Pyrrhus and the Romans would be the first clash of arms between a Hellenistic king and the newly-emerging Italian power. It would also be the first battle between two different military systems, the Macedonian, as created by Philip and Alexander the Great, and the Roman.

During its wars with its Italian neighbours Rome's military tactics and equipment had undergone considerable change. Initially, its infantry had been armed with the traditional hoplite equipment, a spear, some body armour, a helmet and a large shield. The Roman infantry would have fought in a close-packed phalanx, with each man able to support his neighbour with his shield. Rome's Etruscan overlords and enemies may have taught them this method of fighting. It was also the method of fighting of many of its other foes, namely the Latins, Campanians and Greeks. Battles were fought on open plains and decided by a clash of the opposing phalanxes, in a similar fashion to such battles between the Greek cities.

From the writings of the Greek historians and poets we have some idea of the course of such battles. Most often the two sides would line up and march towards one another. The battle would inevitably be decided by a clash of the two infantry lines. If both sides' morale held up there would be a terrible collision as the two lines smashed into one another. Sometimes, if one side's nerve failed, this initial impact would decide the battle. If, however, this first clash failed to break one side, the fighting could degenerate into a pushing match. Eventually, one side would prevail, either by superior numbers, courage or formation. The other side would break and flee the battlefield. This moment of collapse was the most dangerous: the beaten side would expose its unprotected rear to the enemy, and it was here that the heaviest casualties often occurred. Pursuit was usually short, due to the exhaustion of the victors.

This method of fighting was effective so long as both sides adhered to the same tactical system. Many of Rome's enemies, however, did not adhere to these rules of engagement. The Italian hill tribes, given the broken nature of their terrain, tended to fight in looser formations and smaller units. They preferred to shower their enemies with javelins from afar and give ground when pressed. Ambushes and skirmishing were their normal method of fighting, rather than a straightforward battle of close-order spearmen. If such troops could be forced into open battle they would usually be beaten by the phalanx, but this could be difficult to achieve.

The other enemy the Romans faced, from 390 onwards, was the Gauls, a Celtic people. The Celtic method of fighting was again different. According to the ancient writers, it consisted of a mad rush, preceded by a shower of javelins, to bring the Gauls into hand-to-hand combat. They then fought as individuals, slashing at their enemies with long swords. Their size and ferocity intimidated their smaller, southern neigbours. Such a charge could sweep away the inflexible hoplite phalanx. In the Galatian invasion of Greece in 279 the Greek hoplite phalanx could not withstand the fierce charge of the Celtic Galatians. The successes of the Gauls against the Etruscans and Romans in the early-fourth century suggest that they had similar problems.

The Romans, after their experiences fighting against both the Gauls and hill tribes, adapted their tactics and equipment. They broke their infantry up into smaller units of about 120 men, called *maniples* (handfuls). These were more flexible and could manoeuver to support one another. They also deployed in three lines, rather than the traditional one. The first line was now used to break up the enemy attack. It could then fall back through the gaps in the maniples of the second line, or be reinforced by them. The reserve lines could then renew the assault on the enemy.

They also re-armed the troops of the first line with throwing spears and a new shield, the *scutum*. This was a longer and narrower shield, giving more protection to the wielder, but, unlike the hoplite shield, none to his neighbour. At some stage, certainly before 290, the throwing spear had become the much heavier *pilum*. Although of shorter range, it had the advantage that if it struck an enemy shield its weight would render the shield useless. Troops so armed now fought more individually, with sword and shield, rather than as a phalanx. They also fought in more open and shallower formations. The attack would begin with a shower of thrown spears, followed up by a charge into contact using sword and shield. The second line, the *principes*, was also re-armed with the *pilum* at some stage, although not by the time of Pyrrhus' invasion.[1] The third line, the *triarii*, although maintaining the thrusting spear, also adopted the *scutum*.

Livy describes how the new formations worked:

When the battle formation of the army was completed, the *hastati* were the first to engage. If they failed to repulse the enemy, they slowly retired through the intervals between the companies of the *principes* who then took up the fight, the *hastati* following in their rear. The *triarii*, meantime, were resting on one knee under their standards, their shields over their shoulders and their spears planted on the ground with the points upwards, giving them the appearance of a bristling palisade. If the *principes* were also unsuccessful, they slowly retired to the *triarii*, which has given rise to the proverbial saying, when people are in great difficulty 'matters have come down to the *triarii*.' When the *triarii* had admitted the *hastati* and *principes* through the intervals separating their companies they rose from their kneeling posture and instantly closing their companies up they blocked all passage through them and in one compact mass fell on the enemy as the last hope of the army. The enemy who had followed up the others as though they had defeated them, saw with dread a new and larger army rising apparently out of the earth.[2]

That the Romans actually fought in this three-line, chequerboard formation has sometimes been disputed by later scholars. It has been argued that such a broken formation would have been swept away by a more compact enemy line, as they would push through and outflank the isolated Roman *maniples*. Therefore, the argument goes, the Romans must have formed a single front line before contact with the enemy. This argument is not supported by any of the ancient sources. As Goldsworthy has pointed out, the enemy advancing through the gaps in the Roman first line would be confronted by the *princeps* of the second line. If they turned to take the *hastati*'s flanks their own flanks would then be in danger.

Hand-to-hand fighting carrying protective armour was extremely fatiguing, emotionally stressful and much more tentative than is often thought. The usual way to get the enemy line to collapse was to force a gap in it and then to attack the exposed flanks of the enemy. To do this, soldiers would have to press forward into any gaps in the enemy line caused by casualties, before they could be filled by the rear ranks. To do so, however, required considerable courage, as those pressing forward would be surrounded by the enemy. If the initial clash did not decide the battle then the two sides would separate and rest. It was then up to their officers to get them to renew the struggle. The longer the battle went the more difficult this would become. This is when the Roman method of holding troops in reserve gave them the advantage, as fresh troops would be more willing to renew the struggle.[3]

The Roman method of raising armies was also changed. Troops were now organized into legions. As well as the heavy infantry, each legion also included light infantry, *leves* and *roraii*, and another class, the *accensi*. The exact nature of the *accensi* is not known; they were most likely either poorly-armed camp servants or a camp guard equipped with spear and shield. Livy describes them as those 'who were least to be depended upon, and were therefore placed in the rearmost line'.[4] The total numbers in each legion were usually about 5,000 infantry and 300 cavalry. The usual size of a Roman consular army was two legions of Romans and an equal, or more often greater, number of Latins or other allies. The size of this army would often be increased in order to meet more serious threats.

These changes in armament and tactics made the Roman infantry line more flexible and better able to deal with the tactics of their opponents. The exact dates of all these changes are unknown, but most were certainly in place by the time of Pyrrhus' invasion.

This new manner of fighting would, however, place the Romans at a disadvantage when facing the pike-armed Epirot infantry. When formed up, the pikes of the first rank of the phalanx would extend four metres beyond the line. In addition, the spearheads of the next four ranks would reach past the first rank. The following eleven ranks would angle their pikes overhead to provide a shelter from enemy missiles. Although they would not prevent such missiles from landing, the velocity and damage caused would be considerably reduced. On no recorded occasion did the Roman initial missile barrage halt the charge of a pike-armed phalanx. The only time a phalanx was disordered by missiles was at Magnesia in 190, when the Seleucids foolishly remained stationary in the face of a prolonged Roman missile attack, as well as interspersing their line with elephants. The frontline Roman infantryman, being in a looser order than his Greek opponent, would be faced by as many as ten spear points. The only way through these was to try to hack away the pikes or seize them by hand. Neither method was particularly successful.

As Polybius concludes, 'nothing can withstand the frontal assault of the phalanx as long as it retains its characteristic formation and strength.[5] The only way for the Romans to defeat a pike phalanx was to break up its formation, either by luring it onto broken ground, or taking it in the flank or rear. The unstoppable nature of the phalanx often worked to its disadvantage. As it pressed forward the reserve lines of the Romans could be used against its susceptible flanks, if its own supporting troops failed to keep pace with it. This is what happened at the Battle of Cynoscephalae in 197, when a Roman commander:

> Wheeling his force ... and thus getting behind the Macedonians, he fell upon them in the rear. As it is impossible for the phalanx to turn right about face or to fight man to man, he now pressed his attack home, killing those he found in his way, who were incapable of

protecting themselves, until the whole Macedonian force were compelled to throw away their shields and take to flight.[6]

At the Battle of Pydna in 168, the phalanx advanced onto broken ground and lost formation. Once its front was broken up the Roman infantryman, usually heavier armoured, having a larger shield, and better trained and equipped for such close combat than the pikeman, was at a huge advantage:

> The strength and general efficiency of the phalanx was lost when it was thus broken up; and now that the Macedonians engaged man to man or in small detachments, they could only hack with their small daggers against the firm and long shields of the Romans, and oppose light wicker targets to their swords, which, such was their weight and momentum, penetrated through all their armour to their bodies. They therefore made a poor resistance and at last were routed.[7]

The slaughter of the Macedonian pikeman at these two battles is testimony to their vulnerability to such attacks.

At Heraclea, the Romans were at a disadvantage as they had never before faced a pike-armed phalanx. The above tactics would only be worked out through hard-earned experience over the next century. Nor had the Romans previously faced Pyrrhus' other major weapon, his elephants, in battle.

Numbers for both sides in the forthcoming battle are not recorded in the sources but a reasonable estimation can be attempted. Laevinus' army most likely consisted of four Roman legions plus allies. A fourth legion is certainly recorded as being present.[8] The army would have been, if at full strength, at least 40,000 infantry and 2,400 cavalry. Pyrrhus had embarked 25,500 infantry, 3,000 cavalry and 20 elephants for Italy. Some of these had been lost in the storm and some would be used to garrison his allies. In addition, he would have the Tarentine levies, which had numbered 20,000 infantry and 2,000 cavalry in 302.[9] The Tarentine numbers may have been reduced somewhat by the reported desertions. These departures may have impacted most heavily on the cavalry, as the wealthy classes who made up their number were those most opposed to the war. Making allowances for losses, garrisons and desertions, a reasonable estimate of Pyrrhus' army would be about 35,000 troops, of which about 4,000 may have been cavalry, and 20 elephants.[10] The sources are consistent in claiming that the Romans had a numerical advantage over Pyrrhus. This would have increased their desire to bring on a battle as soon as possible, before Pyrrhus' Italian reinforcements arrived.

Exactly how the Tarentines were armed is a matter of some speculation. Prior to Pyrrhus' coming they were most likely to have been the traditional Greek hoplite. Pyrrhus had, however, following his arrival, imposed a rigorous training regime upon them and attached them to Epirot units. This makes it likely, although not certain, that he may also have re-armed them as pikemen. If they were fighting in the same units as the Epirots they must have been re-equipped. At the Battle of Asculum in 279, conversely, Frontinus records them as forming up separately, in the centre, where Homer advised that the weakest troops should be stationed. The comments of both Strabo and Frontinus, added to Dionysius' description of their earlier rout by Aemelius, infer that the Tarentines were of limited military value.

There is a widespread belief that during the Hellenistic period the Greek cities abandoned the use of citizen soldiers and replaced them with mercenaries. Such a view is a gross distortion of the situation. Throughout the Hellenistic period, it was generally considered both an obligation and an honour for citizens to serve their state in war. As Chaniotis argues, 'nevertheless, a study of the documentary evidence shows that in many, if not most, Hellenistic cities, citizen armies survived and were an important element of local pride. Military service was regarded as an honor, and only priests were temporarily exempted from it.'[11]

These forces might be augmented by mercenaries, especially for specialist roles such as artillerymen, skirmishers or engineers. However, the overwhelming majority of the Greek cities' armies consisted of their own population. Only the wealthiest of the Successor kings and those tyrants who could not trust their own citizens relied heavily on mercenary forces. The few states that did rely on mercenaries for their defence, such as Messina, often lost their freedom as a consequence. The army that Pyrrhus took to Heraclea was built primarily around the citizen levies of both Epirus and Tarentum.

This view may, however, simply reflect the contempt that the later historians had for the democratic Greek cities. It should be remembered that the Tarentines had captured the city of Thurii from a Roman garrison prior to Pyrrhus' invasion, no mean feat of arms. They had also launched a successful ambush of Aemelius' army while it was withdrawing. Clearly the Tarentines did possess some skill at arms and a will to fight. In the coming battle they would have made up nearly half of the infantry line, and there is no reference to their lack of fight, even though the Romans gained the advantage in the fighting on at least three occasions. They also provided Pyrrhus with a fleet that appears to have won naval superiority, as there is no record of the Roman navy playing any role in the coming campaigns. It should also be noted that when Pyrrhus dedicated part of his spoils from the battle to the temple at Dodona, he attributed the victory to both the Epirots and the Tarentines. How dedicated they were to Pyrrhus' cause after he had imposed a garrison upon them is, perhaps, more debatable.

Pyrrhus, unlike the Romans, wished to delay any battle until all his Italian allies had arrived. The Roman army had, however, now entered Tarentine territory and was threatening her colony of Heraclea. They were engaging in the usual method used by ancient armies to bring an enemy to battle, that of plundering the countryside. In order to prevent these ravages Pyrrhus was forced to advance to confront the Roman army. His plan was, most likely, to follow the Roman army, harass it, inhibit its capacity to send out foraging parties, but avoid an immediate battle. The Romans on the contrary wished to bring on a battle as soon as possible. Pyrrhus advanced to the plain west of Heraclea. Here he made his camp on the opposite side of the River Siris to the Romans, no doubt still hoping to keep the river between the two sides and prevent a general engagement.

The most likely site of the battle is a river plain about six kilometres to the west of the site of ancient Heraclea. The local population certainly believe this to be the location of the battle, as they have named an incredibly ugly, modern shopping-centre in its honour. Although it is sometimes considered that the battle may have been fought slightly further to the north, that appears most unlikely. Further north of this site the hills either side of the plain rapidly become quite precipitous, and the movement of large numbers of troops would be extremely difficult. There is a low hill just to the east, that gives a commanding view of the plain and the hills to the west of the river, an ideal place for Pyrrhus' first view of the Roman army and camp.

Pyrrhus, learning that the Romans were encamped just the other side of the river, went forward in person to observe them. He was reputedly amazed to see the disciplined way they organized their watches, and the arrangement of their camp. Here the sources are somewhat contradictory. Frontinus describes that at this time Roman camps were disorganized and unfortified like 'Punic huts'. He claims that it was only after they captured Pyrrhus' camp in 275 that they began the practice of concentrating the army within one entrenchment.[12] The numerous references to the good order of Roman camps in Livy prior to this battle would favour Plutarch's testimony over that of Frontinus.

Apart from his personal reconnaissance, Pyrrhus also sent a spy into the Roman camp. Laevinus, having caught the spy, drew up the whole army in line of battle and displayed it for him. He then released the spy to relate to Pyrrhus the strength and discipline of the Roman army. Impressed by what he had learned, Pyrrhus was now even less confident of victory, and more determined to wait for his allies. He stationed patrols on the bank of the river to check the Romans in case they should decide to attempt to force battle. This story mirrors Herodotus' tale, where Xerxes released captured Greek spies for much the same reason.[13] In both cases, the anecdote appears to be a warning against hubris, as both would later suffer defeat at the hands of their Greek enemies.

The Romans were still eager to bring Pyrrhus to battle before his allies arrived and while they held superiority in numbers. They attacked with their infantry across the river at a ford. At the same time, their cavalry swam across at a number of different places. Threatened with being outflanked by the Roman cavalry, the Epirot pickets withdrew. Observing the Roman attack, Pyrrhus ordered his infantry to stand to arms and form a line of battle. None of the surviving accounts of the battle record the exact dispositions of the two armies. From the course of the battle it would appear most likely that Pyrrhus deployed his elephants, and some of his cavalry, in reserve. This was a tactic that he would use successfully the following year at Asculum.

Meanwhile, Pyrrhus led an attack with 3,000 horsemen, hoping to catch the Romans scattered and in disorder while they were crossing the river. The Roman vanguard had, however, already crossed and was advancing in good order. Pyrrhus formed up his cavalry and led them to the attack. In the ensuing melee Pyrrhus showed his experience of battle, and the role of a commander in this sort of situation. Despite fighting vigorously himself, he did not become confused by the noise, dust, and confusion of the battle, but constantly moved to wherever his troops looked to be in difficulty. His richly-ornamented, distinctive armour ensured that his men were both aware of, and inspired by, his presence.

It is during this encounter that the following incident occurred. One of the Roman cavalry sought to make a name for himself by engaging Pyrrhus in individual combat. Single combat was one of the methods by which an ambitious Italian noble could win *gloria*. Despite his companions noticing the threat, Pyrrhus chose to ignore it, trusting in both his own skill and his bodyguards' prowess. Seizing his chance, the Roman attacked. In spite of his own horse being struck down by one of Pyrrhus' bodyguards, he managed to force his way through a gap and run the king's horse through with his spear. Pyrrhus was lifted up and rescued by his friends. His assailant, fighting to the last, was killed, but some of his companions recovered his body after a sharp struggle. According to Dionysius, the king, alarmed by his near escape, then ordered that his own cloak, purple-dyed and shot with gold, and his distinctive armour, should be worn by the most faithful of his companions, and the bravest in battle, Megacles. Pyrrhus himself then wore the other's dun cloak, breastplate and his felt head-gear, in order to make himself less conspicuous in battle.[14]

Despite Pyrrhus' intervention, the cavalry fight began to swing the Romans' way. Possibly the Roman infantry had completed their crossing of the river and were supporting their mounted troops. The Epirot horse fell back to rally on their own infantry, probably forming up on one or, more likely, both flanks, with some placed in reserve. The Roman cavalry would have deployed on both flanks. At this point, Pyrrhus could still have avoided battle and retreated back to his fortified camp. Such a course was not, however, in Pyrrhus' nature. Instead, he ordered his infantry forward and again personally joined the fighting, leading his phalanx against the enemy. Perhaps he was hoping to destroy the Roman army by trapping it with its back to the river.

The infantry combat probably began with the light infantry skirmishing with one another. Such fighting was generally ineffectual and eventually both sides would have fallen back, either behind the heavier infantry, or to their flanks. The main lines of heavy infantry would have now approached each other. When close enough, both sides would have let out their war cries, crashed their weapons against their shields, and then charged. The Romans would have thrown their *pila* and drawn their swords, while the front ranks of the Epirots would have levelled their pikes and advanced in their close-packed formation. Although the Roman missiles would have caused some casualties, the overhead pikes would have deflected many, and any holes in the line caused by casualties would have been replaced by the rear ranks. The combat would have proceeded as already described, with the Roman infantry trying to find a way through the forest of Epirot spearheads. The Roman infantry appear to have found some way of fighting back. For Plutarch relates that for a long time the battle remained in the balance as the fighting swung backward and forward seven times, as each side either retreated or pursued.[15]

The ability of the Romans at Heraclea to stand against the pike phalanx of the Epirots does call into the question the reality of the ancient historians' claim that the phalanx was unstoppable. Possibly they have overstated its effectiveness for rhetorical reasons, creating the stereotype that it was invincible in order to magnify the Romans later victories over the Macedonia kings. The ancients believed that the greater the challenge, the greater the glory in victory. It is possible, however, that the writers' views were correct. It may have been that the Roman's tactical system of multiple reserve lines allowed them to temporarily gain the upper hand, as the fresh troops charged into the tiring pikemen.

At one stage Pyrrhus' trick of dressing Megacles in his armour almost caused a disaster when Megacles was killed in combat. The perceived death of their king caused consternation in the ranks of the Epirots and improved the morale of the Romans. Pyrrhus was forced to ride along his battle line, with his face bare, to prove that he was still alive.

The battle was decided when Laevinus

> who had horsemen in hiding somewhere outside the battle, ordered them to attack the enemy in the rear. As a counter-move to this, Pyrrhus raised the signal for the elephants. Then, indeed, at the sight

of the animals, which was out of all common experience, at their frightful trumpeting, and also at the clatter of arms which their riders made, seated in the towers, both the Romans themselves were panic-stricken and their horses became frenzied and bolted, either shaking off their riders or bearing them away.[16]

The Roman cavalry fled in disorder. Pyrrhus seized his opportunity, he ordered forward his Thessalian cavalry, probably from reserve, attacked the Romans while they were in disarray and completed the rout.

With one wing of the Roman cavalry driven off the field, the flank of the infantry centre would now have been exposed. Pyrrhus now turned his elephants against the isolated Roman infantry. Zonaras describes the final stage of the battle:

Disheartened at this, the Roman army was turned to flight, and in their rout some soldiers were slain by the men in the towers on the elephants' backs, and others by the beasts themselves, which destroyed many with their trunks and tusks (or teeth) and crushed and trampled under foot as many more. The cavalry, following after, killed many.[17]

During the pursuit one of the retreating Romans managed to wound one of the elephants. Its cries of pain panicked the others and threw them into disarray. This confusion caused Pyrrhus to call off the pursuit and the Romans thereby were able to cross the river and make their escape off the field. Frontinus claims, however, that Pyrrhus in his treatise on war recommended:

Never to press relentlessly on the heels of an enemy in flight, not merely in order to prevent the enemy from resisting too furiously in consequence of necessity, but also to make him more inclined to withdraw another time, knowing the victor would not strive to destroy him when in flight.[18]

When an ancient battle line broke the most natural response for those in it was to simply throw away their weapons, particularly the heavy shield, and make a run for it. The throwing away of the shield did incur the odium of society, hence the Spartan mother's entreaty to her son to 'come back with your shield or on it', meaning to fight or die bravely. A more realistic view is that of the poet and soldier Archilochus, who unashamedly claimed that, 'some barbarian is waving my shield, since I was obliged to leave that perfectly good piece of equipment behind under a bush. But I got away, so what does it matter? Life seemed somehow more precious. Let the shield go; I can buy another one equally good.'[19]

Despite this bravado, the throwing away of one's arms and leaving oneself defenceless was extremely hazardous, and could lead to the massacre of the fleeing army.

Some braver souls did, however, maintain their arms. Rather than turn and flee, they would group together in bodies and withdraw slowly. When threatened by the pursuing enemy they would turn and threaten to sell their lives dearly. This is the manner in which the Athenian general Alcibiades describes how the philosopher Socrates escaped from the defeat at Delium in 424. 'The result was that both he and his comrade got away unscathed: for, as a rule, people will not lay a finger on those who show this disposition in war; it is men flying in headlong rout that they pursue.'[20] These are the types of men that Pyrrhus no doubt had in mind when he recommended a cautious pursuit, and those who wounded one of his elephants.

Whatever the real reason for Pyrrhus' lack of a vigorous pursuit, a large part of the Roman army was able to withdraw back across the River Siris and escape to safety. That night they retreated north, heading for their base at Venusia, in Apulia. Pyrrhus followed up his victory by taking the abandoned Roman camp and securing much booty. Casualties for both sides in battle differ in the sources. Dionysius states that Roman losses were nearly 15,000 and Pyrrhus' 13,000, whereas Plutarch gives the casualties as 7,000 and 4,000 respectively.[21] As Plutarch is claiming to be citing the contemporary historian Hieronymus, his figures are more likely to be accurate. In addition, Pyrrhus captured 1,800 Roman prisoners. Pyrrhus' losses were also reported to have been particularly heavy among the Epirot commanders. It was a great albeit costly victory. Pyrrhus is reputed to have commented after the battle that 'if we ever conquer again in like fashion, it will be our ruin.'[22]

Livy claims that Pyrrhus later inspected the bodies of the Romans that had fallen during the fight and noticed that they were all facing towards their enemy.[23] This appears to be the usual patriotic propaganda of the writer, as it ignores the reality of the Roman rout described in the other sources. All the sources agree, nonetheless, that the hard fight put up by the Romans came as an unwelcome surprise to Pyrrhus, giving him a greater respect for their courage and fighting ability. He buried the Roman dead with great honours.

Pyrrhus also celebrated his victory by dedicating some of his spoils to the temple at Dodona with the following inscription, 'King Pyrrhus and the Epirots and the Tarentines over the Romans and their allies to Zeus Naius.'[24]

According to Plutarch, the Romans blamed the defeat on Laevinus, claiming that 'it was not the Epirots who had conquered the Romans, but Pyrrhus who had conquered Laevinus, being of the opinion that the Roman defeat was not due to their army, but to its general.'[25] This would appear to be unfair to Laevinus, who, in the opening stages of the battle, had clearly outmanoeuvred Pyrrhus and forced him to fight a battle while outnumbered.

His defeat was more a result of being faced by a new and, at least on level-ground, superior tactical system. Livy, perhaps more correctly, claimed that the defeat was 'because the soldiers were not used to the elephants and were terrified.'[26]

Cassius Dio asserts that it was by this victory that Pyrrhus obtained his reputation as a great general. From our limited knowledge of the battle this appears to be overstated. Pyrrhus' generalship seems to have consisted of forming up his army skillfully and inspiring it by leading from the front. This, however, was what was expected of any competent ancient general. His only inspired action was to attack with his elephants at the correct moment, although if Zonaras is to be believed this was in response to Laevinus' ambush. Pyrrhus did, however, show the ability to fully exploit this success, supporting the attack with his cavalry, and turning an advantage into a rout. The later historians of Pyrrhus' campaign were, however, writing after all the other Successor kingdoms had been easily defeated in all their battles against the Romans. With the benefit of this hindsight, Pyrrhus' victories over the Romans must have appeared as shining lights in an otherwise dark tale of failure.

Despite blaming him the Romans did not depose Laevinus, but showed their usual stoicism by rallying around him. They would, seventy years later, show similar support to Varro, the loser of a much more catastrophic defeat at Cannae.

Following the battle, Pyrrhus' rebuked his Italian allies for their delay in bringing up their forces. He did, nonetheless, give them a share of the booty from the Roman camp. This, plus the great prestige won by the victory, convinced many of the Italian cities who had been watching the turn of events, to commit fully to the cause. As a result Pyrrhus won over many new allies, both former allies of the Romans, and those who had remained neutral up to that point. These included the Greek city of Locri, which, with the help of the Tarentine fleet, revolted from Rome and captured its garrison. Croton came over to Pyrrhus, as did the Bruttians.

In the aftermath of the battle, the Campanian allies of the Roman garrison in Rhegium revolted. They massacred the adult-male population, sold the children into slavery, and seized the woman and property of the city. They justified their actions by claiming that the citizens were about to hand the city over to the Tarentine fleet. In reality, they were emulating their kinsmen who had similarly seized the Sicilian-Greek city of Messina and set up their own independent state in 288.

After his defeat of the Romans in battle, most of Italy south of Campania had come over to Pyrrhus. It is at this point that Pyrrhus, while in a position of strength, decided to send an embassy, led by Cineas, to offer peace to the Romans. Cineas was well provisioned with both money and gifts of women's clothing, in case the wives of the Senators proved more amenable than their husbands. After entering the city Cineas continued to delay meeting the Senate on various excuses, while he visited individual Senators, offering them gifts. How successful this campaign was depends upon which source is read. Plutarch claims that no one, men and women alike, would accept the gifts. Zonaras, on the other hand, states that 'he was visiting the houses of leading men, and by his conversation and gifts was gradually extending his influence over them,' and not until 'he had won over a large number, he entered the Senate chamber.'[27]

Cineas began with a defence of Pyrrhus' actions, stating that he had entered Italy not to make war on the Romans but only to ensure the independence of Tarentum. He further pointed out the king's goodwill, in that he had so far refrained from pillaging the countryside, nor had he marched on the city. He furthermore offered to ally himself with Rome. If Plutarch is to be believed, he even promised to assist the Romans in subjugating the rest of Italy provided they guaranteed immunity for the Tarentines. This, if true, would have been a terrible betrayal of his other Italian allies, and would appear to be highly unlikely given his position of apparent strength. Far more likely are the much harsher terms recorded by Appian:

> He offered them peace, friendship, and an alliance with Pyrrhus, provided the Tarentines should be included in the same treaty, and provided the other Greeks dwelling in Italy should remain free under their own laws, and provided the Romans would restore to the Lucanians, Samnites, Daunii, and Bruttians whatever they had taken from them in war. If they would do this, he said that Pyrrhus would restore all his prisoners without ransom.[28]

Acceptance of these terms would be a huge capitulation by Rome, abandoning all its gains south and east of Campania. Despite this, after some deliberation the senate was considering the acceptance of these terms, although the reasons again vary according to the sources. Plutarch states that they were demoralized due to the loss at Heraclea and the large numbers of allies that had defected to Pyrrhus. Zonaras infers that it was because of the bribes of Cineas. The true reason could, possibly, be a combination of the two.[29]

At this point, fate, in the person of a retired and blind senator named Appius Claudius, intervened. He had himself carried into the Senate chamber by his sons and son-in-law. He was supposedly outraged that the senate was supporting peace and rose to address them:

> He stated that to even consider peace with the Epirots was a disgrace as they: were ever the prey of the Macedonians, and yet you tremble

before Pyrrhus, who has ever been a minister and servant to one at least of Alexander's bodyguards, and now comes wandering over Italy, not so much to help the Greeks who dwell here, as to escape his enemies at home, promising to win for us the supremacy here with that army which could not avail to preserve for him a small portion of Macedonia. Do not suppose that you will rid yourself of this fellow by making him your friend; no, you will bring against you others, and they will despise you as men whom anybody can easily subdue, if Pyrrhus goes away without having been punished for his insults, but actually rewarded for them in having enabled Tarentines and Samnites to mock at Romans.[30]

He urged them to dismiss Cineas from the city with the message that Rome would never make peace until Pyrrhus had withdrawn from Italy. The senate was won over by Appius' rhetoric and voted unanimously to continue the war.

Although thwarted in his attempts to make a treaty with the Romans, Cineas had also used his mission as an intelligence-gathering trip. He was suitably impressed by the Roman's resolve and their capacity to absorb losses and raise new troops, describing them as a 'hydra for them to fight against, since the consul already had twice as many soldiers collected as those who faced their enemies before, and there were many times as many Romans still who were capable of bearing arms.'[31]

Pyrrhus was to be continually surprised at the Roman refusals to make peace after a defeat in battle, as Hannibal would later be. It is here that the Roman view of war is often compared to that of the Hellenistic kingdoms. Rome went to war to destroy its enemies' capacity to be a future threat. Rome's wars ended only with the enemy being totally defeated and accepting their position as a subordinate ally of Rome. The only other alternative was Rome's total defeat. This attitude varied only slightly in the case of Pyrrhus, a foreign invader. Here the Romans refused to consider peace unless Pyrrhus completely withdrew his troops from Italian soil. In contrast, it is often argued that the Hellenistic kingdoms expected a war to be completed with a negotiated peace that reflected the balance of power. The victor would be satisfied with winning concessions from the defeated. Total destruction of the enemy was not contemplated.

In reality, the attitude of the Greeks and Macedonians to war was slightly more complicated than this. Early wars between city states certainly fit this characterization. They were usually small, seasonal conflicts for limited goals, most likely for the control of agricultural land. The later wars of the Hellenistic kingdoms, once they had solidified after the wars of Successors, also fit this pattern. During the period between these two eras, however, wars were often fought to the total defeat of the enemy. The almost thirty-year-long Peloponnesian war did not end until Athens was starved into surrender. The Thebans, part of the victorious alliance, argued forcefully for the complete destruction of the losing city. The early wars of the Successors were, whenever possible, fought until one of the dynasts had been completely defeated, and usually killed. Only once power had been firmly established in three distinct kingdoms did the later pattern emerge.

Where this characterization is perhaps more accurate is in the dealings between the Macedonian kings and the Greek cities. Usually, a single defeat would force the Greeks to surrender on terms. Philip II's victory at Chaeronea, and Antipater's at Crannon, are examples of such instances. The Greeks were incredibly fickle in these alliances and would constantly re-align themselves with whoever was most powerful at the time. The rival political factions in the Greek cities aided in this outcome, as the kings could play them off against one another. Philip II claimed that he had won more cities with money than with soldiers:

> For he had learned by experience that what could not be subdued by force of arms could easily be vanquished by gold. So, organizing bands of traitors in several cities by means of bribes and calling those who accepted his gold 'guests' and 'friends' ... he corrupted the morals of the people.[32]

Pyrrhus most likely believed that the Romans would behave in a similar manner. In expecting the Romans to negotiate peace on his terms, Pyrrhus clearly expected them to behave like a Greek city, rather than as a major power. His attempts to use Cineas to bribe parts of the Senate confirm this attitude. As such, he was severely underestimating the power of Rome. Pyrrhus' surprise at the wealth and the military power of the Romans is continually emphasized in the sources.

One of the main strengths of the Romans when dealing with the Hellenistic kings was their overwhelming manpower. At this time Rome, along with its Latin and Campanian allies, had possibly 275,000 men available for military service.[33] With numbers like these the Romans could afford to suffer a defeat like that at Heraclea and simply, as they did, raise new troops like a 'hydra'. For a Hellenistic king such as Pyrrhus, with a military manpower of less than 40,000 men, such a defeat could be a catastrophe, requiring an entire generation to recover from. This explains Pyrrhus' pessimistic utterances regarding his losses after Heraclea. It was this relentless arithmetic of attrition that allowed the Romans to maintain their intractable attitude towards their enemies.

Foiled in his attempt to win the Romans over, Pyrrhus decided to break the Roman hold over Campania. Outside of the Latin homelands, this region was the most important to the rise of Roman power. It was both wealthy and a large source of manpower. The control of Campania and its resources had been the major cause of Rome's Samnite wars. Sixty years later, Hannibal would employ a similar strategy. Pyrrhus marched from Heraclea against Capua, the major city of Campania.

Meanwhile, the Romans, as was their usual practice, had rallied behind Laevinus, refusing to dismiss him. They raised two new legions, possibly by temporarily abolishing the property qualification required for enlistment, and sent them as reinforcements to him. Once he had rebuilt his army, Laevinus pursued and harassed Pyrrhus. He also managed to enter Capua before the Epirots could arrive and prevent him from capturing it. Robbed of the chief prize, Pyrrhus then turned south and attempted to take the important port of Neapolis (Naples), but the precautions the Romans had taken prior to the campaign showed their value. The Roman garrison deterred Pyrrhus from attempting to capture the city.

Foiled in his attempts to capture Campania, Pyrrhus decided to advance directly against Rome. He followed the route of the Via Latina rather than the more strongly garrisoned and mountainous Appian Way. First, he took Fregellae and then Anagnia. Finally, he advanced on the Etruscan city of Praeneste (Palestrina), which had fallen to the Romans in 338. The citizens of Praeneste were strongly anti-Roman. A number of their senators had been taken to Rome and executed earlier that year in order to ensure the town's loyalty. This measure had failed, and the citizens surrendered the city to Pyrrhus.

This was a great coup for Pyrrhus as Praeneste, with three massive lines of walls, was supposedly impregnable. The fortifications, which can still be viewed today, are truly immense. Praeneste lay on the edge of the Apennine hills, and from here Pyrrhus could see the acropolis and the smoke of Rome, less than thirty-five kilometres away. Unfortunately, even on a clear winter's day, this view is no longer possible due to modern pollution. Praeneste would continue to make poor choices in picking sides during wartime. Sulla would execute the entire adult-male population, 12,000 in all, for siding with Marius during a later civil war.[34]

Along the march, Pyrrhus, much to the chagrin of his troops and allies, had refused to ravage the rich countryside as he went. He was hoping that such moderate conduct would win the Romans over without further recourse to arms. The king was reputed to have been favourably impressed by the territory of the Romans, which 'had all kind of trees, vineyards, and tilled fields, and expensive farm fixtures; whereas the districts of his own friends had been pillaged to such an extent that it was impossible to tell whether they had ever been settled.'[35] Years of Roman victories had clearly devastated the lands of Rome's enemies. He was now forced to confront the obvious strength and wealth of Rome, and to compare it to the weakness of his own allies.

Alarmed at Pyrrhus' approach, and his presence so close to Rome, the Senate made peace with the Etruscans. They then ordered their other consul Coruncanius, who had been campaigning in Etruria, to march south to Rome with his entire force, most likely the usual consular army of 20,000 men. In attempting to win Rome's allies away from them, Pyrrhus was using a strategy that Hannibal would also follow. Both expected that a victory on the battlefield would compel Rome's allies to abandon her and force her to make a negotiated peace. Both would enjoy some success with this strategy, but ultimately would be disappointed.

Pyrrhus advanced to within six kilometres of Rome but baulked at an assault on the city. The walls had been strengthened in 387 after the Gallic assault, and the city was reputed to be impregnable. A strong garrison also held the city. Pyrrhus now found himself in a difficult military position. He faced three different Roman forces: Coruncius was advancing on him from the north; Laevinus' army was still dogging his footsteps to the south; and the garrison of Rome to his west. Pyrrhus began to fear being surrounded on all sides while he was in unfamiliar and enemy territory. Any attempt to besiege such a strong city over winter, in hostile territory, while threatened by two consular armies would prove impossible. Despite the entreaties of his new allies, who would be left to the vengeance of the Romans, Pyrrhus decided to retreat south.

Laevinus rushed south in order to again protect Campania. Coruncius, reinforced by part of the Roman garrison, cautiously tailed Pyrrhus' army. Quite possibly, Pyrrhus hoped that by retreating from Rome he might be able to isolate and defeat one of the Roman consuls. During this retreat, Pyrrhus appears to have lost control of his army, which resented being deprived of their earlier opportunity to pillage Roman territory. Both his Epirot troops and his Italian allies are accused of ravaging indiscriminately the territory of their own allies and those of Rome's. This was a further stroke of fortune for the Romans, as many of the Italians, who were still considering whether to ally themselves with Pyrrhus, now held back.

Pyrrhus once again confronted Laevinus' army in Campania. Both sides drew up for battle. In an attempt to intimidate the Romans, he ordered his soldiers to strike their spears against their shields and call out their battle cry, while he had his trumpeters and elephants join in the display. Rather than be overawed the Romans responded with their own war cry, supposedly terrifying Pyrrhus' troops. More likely is that Pyrrhus, seeing the heavily-reinforced army of Laevinus, realized that it either matched or exceeded his own in size. Pyrrhus declared, perhaps artfully, that the omens were bad and refused to give battle. Laevinus, still wary of fighting an enemy who had already defeated him, allowed him to retreat unmolested. His major task, the

rhus, son of Aeacides and descendant of the hero Achilles. King of the Epirots (306–302, .72 BC), the Macedonians (288–284, 273–272) and the Sicilians (278?–276). He was given the ame 'the Eagle' by his troops after his victory over the Macedonian general Pantauchus. The s held in the Museo Archeologico Nazionale, Naples. (Author's photograph)

2 (*left*). Seleucus I Nicator, son of Antiochus and commander of Alexander the Great's foot guards, the 'Shield-bearers'. He was one of the joint victors over Antigonus the One-eyed at Ipsus. This defeat was most likely Pyrrhus' first experience of a major battle. Seleucus was murdered by Ptolemy Ceraunus on his return to Macedonia, leading to the chaos that allowed Pyrrhus to make his second attempt at the Macedonian crown. The bust is held in the Museo Archeologico Nazionale, Naples. (Author's photograph)

3 (*right*). Demetrius Poliorcetes, son of Antigonus the One-eyed, brother-in-law of Pyrrhus and his protector during his second period of exile. The two would later fall out and fight a series of wars for the control of Macedonia and Epirus. The bust is held in the Museo Archeologico Nazionale, Naples.

4. A bridge at Cosenza, ancient Consentia, at the base of three distinct hills. This is a possible site for the death in battle of Alexander of Epirus, Pyrrhus' second cousin. He accepted an invitation from the Tarentines to intervene in Italy in 334 and was killed in 332. His expedition created the precedent for the later request to Pyrrhus to come to Italy and take command of the forces of Tarentum in their war against the Romans. (Author's photograph)

5. The old port at Taranto (Tarentum), now a fishing boat harbour. It is from here that the Tarentines would have launched a fateful attack on the Roman fleet and given the Romans a cause to go to war. (Author's photograph)

6. 'In the city of Tarentum ... the majority of the inhabitants are always ready for sexual intercourse as well as drinking' – Theopompus. A third century vase held in the Museo Archeologico Nazionale, Taranto (Author's photograph)

7. The remains of the acropolis of Heraclea in Italy. The city, a colony of Tarentum, was captured back from the Italians by Alexander of Epirus. It was later used as a base by Pyrrhus for his first battle against the Romans. (Author's photograph)

8. The likely site of the Battle of Heraclea, as seen from a hill behind the Greek lines. It is likely it was from this position Pyrrhus obtained his first view of a Roman army. (Author's photograph)

9. The island of Ortygia in Syracuse, the wealthiest and most powerful of the Greek cities of Sicily. It is from this stronghold that the tyrants, and Pyrrhus, dominated the city. (Author's photograph)

The beach at Taormina (Tauromenium), site of Pyrrhus' first landing in Sicily. (Author's photograph)

11. The straits of Messina, looking out from the harbour of Messina across to Reggio (Rhegium), site of Pyrrhus' naval defeat by the Carthaginians. (Author's photograph)

12. The cliffs of the eastern side of Erice (Eryx). Such features protect two of the three sides of the city.
(Author's photograph)

13. The 'Punic Walls' of Erice. It was against these walls that Pyrrhus woul have launched his assau
(Author's photograph)

14. Remains of a tower, part of the 'Punic Walls' of Erice.
(Author's photograph)

15. Cape Boeo and the harbour at Marsala (Lilybaeum), the closest point on Sicily to Africa, and the Carthaginians' main base on the island. In ancient times the harbour was much bigger and enclosed by two breakwaters. (Author's photograph)

16. The remains of the Carthaginian ditch at Marsala. It was dug as an a line of defence against yrrhus' assault and was ted to have been twenty netres deep. It was later restored and used in ending the city during a siege mounted by the ans. (Author's photograph)

17. The third level of walls of the town of Palestrina (Praeneste). The city, built by the Etruscans on the slope of a steep hill, was defended by three lines of massive walls. It was considered impregnable, but was surrendered without a fight to Pyrrhus by its anti-Roman population. It was from the acropolis above that Pyrrhus obtained his first view of Rome. (Author's photograph)

18. A frieze from a third-century Greek temple showing a cavalryman in action. It may represent an idealised heroic scene of Alexander fighting the Persians, but the equipment would be typical of the cavalry in Pyrrhus army. In battle, this equipment would also include a helmet and a spear or javelins. The remains of the temple are on display in the Museo Archeologico Nazionale, Taranto. (Author's photograph)

19. A war elephant with tower, from a stamp, probably Coptic Egyptian, now in the Allard Pier Museum, Amsterdam. Towers on elephants were used around the time of Pyrrhus' campaigns and has been proposed that he may have invented the At this time the tower would probably have been occupied by two men armed with javelins. It is th extra height of the tower that probably allowed t elephants to win their missile duel with the Rom. wagons at Asculum. (Image courtesy of Jona Lenderin;

20. An early third-century Greek infantryman being bid farewell by his wife or mother as he leaves for war, a common image over centuries of vase painting. In battle he would usually have also worn a helmet. Such troops would have made up the allied, subject and mercenary Greek infantry in Pyrrhus' armies. Pyrrhus' Epirot pikemen would have dressed much the same but have been armed with a pike and smaller shield. From a vase held in the Museo Archeologico in Agrigento. (Author's photograph)

defence of Campania, had been successfully accomplished. Once he was clear of Laevinus' army, Pyrrhus dismissed his allies and withdrew with his own forces back to his base at Tarentum.

The majority of the Roman forces went into winter quarters in the Latin colony of Firmum, in northern Apulia. The Romans, never tolerant of defeat, decided to punish the survivors of Heraclea. The cavalry were demoted to infantry, and the infantry to the less prestigious role of skirmishers. They were also forced to winter outside the main camp and refused supplies, forcing them to forage for food.

After he had entered into winter quarters in Tarentum, Pyrrhus was approached by a Roman embassy, sometime during the winter of 280/279. In order to get them safely into the city, past the Tarentines, Pyrrhus was forced to send a detachment of his own troops. Clearly, anti-Roman sentiment was still strong among the Tarentines. The delegation consisted of no fewer than three ex-consuls and was lead by one Gaius Fabricius, who had been consul two years previously. As consul he is recorded as winning victories over the Samnites, Lucanians and Bruttians. Pyrrhus had hoped that such an impressive delegation had come with full powers to discuss peace. Fabricius quickly disillusioned him. The embassy had come only to discuss the ransoming, or exchange, of prisoners.

Following his initial discussions with the Roman embassy, Pyrrhus consulted with his advisors. His general, Milon, claimed that he should not release the prisoners but continue the war. Cineas, on the other hand, advised that releasing the prisoners without ransom would produce goodwill and make the Romans more inclined to make peace in the future. At first Pyrrhus was inclined to accept Cineas' advice, but eventually the intransigence of the Roman delegation forced him to follow the counsel of Milon.

At first, Pyrrhus tried to bring round the delegation by entertaining them lavishly. He was reputedly greatly impressed by the bluff, no-nonsense Fabricius and his reputation as a soldier. Pyrrhus attempted to win over Fabricius and convince him to use his political influence to get the Senate to reconsider his peace proposals. After learning that he was inordinately poor for a senator, he offered him a large gift of gold. Fabricius replied by giving Pyrrhus a long lecture, claiming that he had no desire for wealth, was content with his small farm and had deliberately refused to take his share of the plunder after successful campaigns. He also extolled the supposed virtues of the Republic stating that despite his poverty he was able to:

Hold the highest magistracies, am sent on the most distinguished embassies, am entrusted with the most sacred rites in connection with sacrifices, am thought worthy to express my opinion upon the most urgent matters ... am second to none of the most powerful, and am regarded as a model of uprightness for the rest, though spending nothing of my substance for these honours, ... with the result that the poorest man enjoys no less esteem than the richest when it is a question of awarding honours, but all the Romans who are worthy of these honours by virtue of their uprightness are on an equal footing with one another.[36]

Fabricius went on to state that if he accepted Pyrrhus' offer his reputation would be ruined and his name would be struck from the Senate roll by the censors. He would thereby bring disgrace on both his ancestors and his descendants. Fabricius continued, claiming that it is better to be a poor man with honour in a free state than the slave of king or tyrant. He also claimed that Pyrrhus would never be content while he had no limit to his greed, but would be as unhappy as the poorest of beggars.

Next, Pyrrhus tried to frighten Fabricius by surprising him with an elephant while the two dined together. To which Fabricius is reputed to have replied calmly that, 'your gold made no impression on me yesterday, neither does your beast today.'[37]

Later, Fabricius indulged in a discussion with Cineas regarding philosophy. Cineas was a follower of Epicurus, a philosopher who taught that the way to happiness was through seeking a tranquil life. This was done by limiting one's desires, avoiding politics if possible and always seeking a peaceful resolution to problems. This was the philosophical underpinning of the earlier debate he had with Pyrrhus before leaving for Italy. Such philosophies were, of course, anathema to a patrician Roman. Fabricius lived in a world where glory and reputation were attained by political advancement and military conquest. Both were essential for one's own reputation and one's ancestors' position in society. Naturally enough, Fabricius scoffed at Cineas' beliefs: 'O Hercules, may Pyrrhus and the Samnites cherish these doctrines, as long as they are at war with us.'[38]

The endless moralizing of Fabricius' reply to Pyrrhus must be seen in the context of the sources. All wrote under the later Republic or the Empire, when the supposed virtues of the early Republic, courage and incorruptibility, were idealized and compared unfavourably with the supposed greed and decadence of the Roman nobility of their own times. Thus Pyrrhus is cast into the role of the greedy tyrant and compared unfavourably to the upright senator.

The longest version of Fabricius' reply comes from Dionysius of Halicarnassus. This author wrote during the reign of Augustus. His primary motive was to reconcile the Greeks to the rule of Rome. He claimed that the Greeks should not:

Rail at Fortune for having wantonly bestowed upon an undeserving city a supremacy so great and already of so long continuance, particularly when they shall have learned from my history that Rome from the very beginning, immediately after its founding, produced infinite examples of virtue in men whose superiors, whether for piety or for justice or for life-long self-control or for warlike valour, no city, either Greek or barbarian, has ever produced.[39]

Fabricius is, therefore, one of Dionysius' examples of Roman virtue.

As discussed earlier, such anecdotes should not be taken literally, as the ancient historians used them to make pre-determined moral points. This is particularly true of speeches and conversations. Even Thucydides, one of the most reliable of ancient historians, admits to concocting such speeches. 'So my habit has been to make the speakers say what was in my opinion demanded of them by the various occasions.'[40]

Having failed to win over the Roman embassy, Pyrrhus eventually reiterated his terms; he would only release the prisoners if the Romans accepted the peace terms that Cineas had already proposed to the Senate. If they accepted, he would release the prisoners without ransom. If not, he would not hand over such a large number of brave men to fight against him. Pyrrhus then instigated another plan for obtaining peace. He released the prisoners into the custody of Fabricius so that they could go home to attend the festival of Saturn, on the condition that if the Senate accepted the peace terms offered by him they should remain free, but if not that they should return to him at the end of the festival. This dates the embassy to December of 280 at the latest. Pyrrhus also attempted to obtain their goodwill by showering them with clothes and money for the trip.

Cineas was again sent to Rome to try and win the senators over. Despite the pleas of the prisoners, and the persuasiveness of Cineas, the Senate again rejected Pyrrhus' terms. They also passed a decree that at the conclusion of the festival, the prisoners must return to Pyrrhus on the day specified, otherwise they would be executed. All returned, and in this way Pyrrhus learned that the only way open to him to overcome the Romans was by force of arms. The war would continue into 279.

Chapter VI

Asculum

"'if I win a victory in one more battle with the Romans, I shall not have left a single soldier of those who crossed over with me"' ... In very truth, all of his victories were, as the proverb has it, Cadmean; for the enemy, though defeated, were in no way humbled, since their dominion was so great, whereas the victor had suffered the damage and disaster that goes with defeat.' - Diodorus, 22.5

With the Romans refusing to make peace Pyrrhus was forced to resume the offensive against the Romans in the following year, 279. Since his victory at Heraclea the Italian tribes had flocked to his banner. Contingents of Samnites, Lucanians, Bruttians, and the Sallentines of southeastern Italy are all recorded as joining Pyrrhus' army. Pyrrhus had clearly re-thought his strategy after the previous year's campaign had almost ended in disaster, with his army nearly being trapped by separate Roman forces, with hostile territory to its rear. To avoid such a situation recurring, Pyrrhus decided on a more cautious approach. Instead of the more direct advance into the Roman stronghold of Campania, he decided on a more careful advance, north into the Roman allied territory of Apulia. By capturing the Apulian cities as he went he would ensue that his rear, and his communications back to Tarentum, would be secure.

The territories of the allied Lucanians and Samnites would protect Pyrrhus' western flank. This axis of attack promised several benefits to Pyrrhus. A successful campaign along the Adriatic coast would help secure his sea communications back to Epirus. The capture of Apulian cities might induce more of Rome's allies to change sides. Once Apulia was made safe he would have the choice of advancing west into Campania, or against Rome itself.

In the spring of 279, Pyrrhus began his advance. Unopposed by any Roman forces, he managed to capture, or win over, a number of Apulian cities and to threaten the important Roman colonies of Venusia and Luceria. Up to this point, the Romans had been reluctant to confront Pyrrhus after their defeat at Heraclea the year before. However, the threatened loss of two of their more important cities, as well as the possible loss of all of Apulia, forced them to advance in order to confront the army of Pyrrhus. The Roman army had wintered in northern Apulia, and was now commanded by the new consuls Publius Sulpicius Saverius and Publius Decius Mus. With

Pyrrhus threatening to capture Venusia, they advanced south and met Pyrrhus south of the Apulian city of Asculum (Ascoli Satriani). The scene was now set for a second battle between the two enemies.

The Roman army is recorded as numbering more than 70,000. This figure included 20,000 from Rome itself. The cavalry contingent numbered about 8,000. Pyrrhus' army totalled 70,000 infantry, more than 8,000 cavalry and nineteen elephants. Dionysius states that the Greeks who had accompanied Pyrrhus amounted to 16,000. He does not say whether this number also includes Pyrrhus' Macedonians, but probably does not, as he later mentions the Macedonians separately.[1] The total of Macedonian and Epirot pikemen was perhaps around 20,000. Dionysius' numbers are often rejected in favour of the lower figure of 40,000 as recorded by Frontinus.[2] There would, however, appear to be no good reason to reject Dionysius' numbers, especially as he claims to have had access to Pyrrhus' memoirs. Both sides had made considerable efforts to recruit their allies. Pyrrhus had been joined by the Samnites, a people who previously had fielded armies of 40,000 men on their own. A century later, the Lucanians and Bruttians had a total military manpower of at least 48,000.[3] With both these allies having joined Pyrrhus' force, there is little doubt he could gather an army of 80,000 men, provided that sufficient money could be found to pay for it. Frontinus' work is generally considered to be unreliable, as it is full of later additions and errors.

The Romans encamped on the opposite side of a fast flowing river, almost certainly the River Aufidus, (Ofanto). The river at this point was swift-flowing, its banks heavily wooded, and difficult to cross. Zonaras claims that both sides were unwilling to risk crossing the river and bring on an engagement from dread of the other. The Romans feared to face an enemy that had already defeated them, whereas the Epirots worried that the Romans would be driven by the courage of despair.[4] For a number of days both sides avoided combat and remained on their own side of the river.

During the wait, one of the Romans, a certain Decius, was rumoured to be preparing himself for a *devotio*. This was a sacred form of suicide. The devotee would throw himself into the thick of the fighting, seeking death, as a form of sacrifice to the gods for victory. There was a history of such sacrificial actions in Decius' family. His grandfather, also named Decius, had been one of the consuls commanding in a battle against the Latins and Campanians, in about 340. The priest sacrificing before the battle had declared that the omens were favourable for victory but had also foretold Decius' death.

During the battle, as the Latins were gaining the upper hand, Decius took an oath to Jupiter that he would devote his own life if the gods would grant the Romans victory. He then leapt upon his horse and charged into the middle of the enemy. According to Livy:

To those who watched him in both armies, he appeared something awful and superhuman, as though sent from heaven to expiate and appease all the anger of the gods, and to avert destruction from his people and bring it on their enemies. All the dread and terror, which he carried with him, threw the front ranks of the Latins into confusion, which soon spread throughout the entire army. This was most evident, for wherever his horse carried him they were paralysed as though struck by some death-dealing star; but when he fell, overwhelmed with darts, the Latin cohorts, in a state of perfect consternation, fled from the spot and left a large space clear.[5]

The Romans then charged into the gap with renewed vigour, as if the battle had just begun. After hard fighting, the Romans gained the upper hand and won the battle. The honour for the victory was shared equally between the consuls, one for his generalship and one for his sacrifice. Livy goes on to add that such a sacrifice need not be the general himself, but he can select anyone he chooses. If the man is killed then the offering is duly performed, if he survives then a seven foot image must be built and a prisoner sacrificed instead. Supposedly Decius' father had also sacrificed himself in the same manner.

Learning of this legend, and Decius' intention of repeating it, Pyrrhus called an assembly of his army to discuss the rumour and find a method to overcome it. He reportedly advised them:

Not to be disheartened or terrified by such talk. One human being, he said, could not by dying prevail over many, nor could any incantation or magic prove superior to arms and men. By talking to this effect and confirming his words by arguments Pyrrhus encouraged his army. He also inquired into the details of the costume which the Decii had used in devoting themselves, and gave orders to his men, if they should see anybody so arrayed, not to kill him, but to seize him alive.[6]

Once Pyrrhus had given these orders he sent a messenger to the Roman consul telling him of the preparations he had made and 'that if he were taken alive, he should perish miserably'. The Roman consuls retorted ' that they were in no need of resorting to such a deed, since they were sure to conquer him in other ways.' [7]

Despite their fear of defeat, both sides desired to decide the issue in battle. Pyrrhus needed a decisive victory, both to ensure the loyalty of his allies, and to force the recalcitrant Romans to come to terms. The Romans, most likely, wished to protect their colonies and to remove the Greek threat from Italy once and for all. The Romans eventually approached Pyrrhus and:

Inquired whether he chose to cross unmolested himself, while they retired, or whether he would allow them to cross, in order that the forces might encounter each other intact, and so from a battle with conditions equal the test of valour might be made an accurate one. The Romans delivered this speech to overawe him, but Pyrrhus granted them permission to cross the river, since he placed great reliance upon his elephants.[8]

Pyrrhus' elephants had proved a nasty surprise for the Romans at Heraclea and had been decisive in his victory in the battle. In the meantime, the Romans had developed a novel mechanism in order to defeat them. They had taken common Italian, four-wheeled wagons and turned them into mobile strongholds drawn by oxen. The carts had been fortified with wicker screens in order to protect the crews. The wagons were further equipped with offensive weapons. Dionysius describes these as consisting of:

Upright beams on which were mounted movable traverse poles that could be swung round as quick as thought in any direction one might wish, and on the ends of the poles there were either tridents or sword-like spikes or scythes all of iron; or again they had cranes that hurled down heavy grappling-irons. Many of the poles had attached to them and projecting in front of the wagons fire bearing grapnels wrapped in tow that had been liberally daubed with pitch, which men standing on the wagons were to set afire as soon as they came near the elephants and then rain blows with them upon the trunks and faces of the beasts.[9]

Each cart also had a crew of bowmen and slingers. A number of other troops were also attached to each wagon to guard it from attack. In the coming battle the limited mobility of these carts would prove them to be more vulnerable to missile fire, and light infantry attack, than the more mobile elephants they were designed to combat. They were, however, an ingenious response by the Romans to a new and serious tactical threat.

The major problem for any attempt to recreate the Battle of Asculum is the difference in the sources regarding the length of the battle. The only detailed account, by Dionysius of Halicarnassus, describes a one-day battle. Zonaras' brief account also mentions only one day of fighting. Plutarch, however, describes a two-day battle, while admitting that he knows of Dionysius' account.[10] There are a number of different ways of explaining these discrepancies. One possibility is that Dionysius simply omitted the break of day in his account of the battle. This is unlikely as there is no obvious place in his account to place such an interruption.

The simplest explanation is that Plutarch has it wrong, but as he acknowledges Dionysius' version and went out of his way to discount it, this would appear unlikely. It is more probable that Plutarch had an alternative source or, more likely, sources. Plutarch had certainly read widely when preparing his lives of the various Successors. He, on various occasions, cites by name no less than five of the contemporary historians of Pyrrhus' times, whose works are now lost: Hieronymus of Cardia, Duris, Diyllos, Philochoros and Demochares. He also claims that he had access to various forms of primary evidence such as the memoirs of Pyrrhus. Although Plutarch is not always the most reliable of historians, on this occasion it would appear preferable to accept his explicit statement of the battle lasting two days.

The problem then becomes whether to accept Dionysius' detailed account as a description of either the first or the second day's fighting. As both he and Zonaras end their accounts with the completion of the battle, and the withdrawal of Pyrrhus' army due to the capture of his camp, the more likely course is to date their accounts to the second day of the battle. This is supported by Plutarch's brief account, as he describes the initial day's fighting as taking place in difficult terrain where Pyrrhus could not deploy his whole army effectively. He also states that the decisive charge of Pyrrhus' elephants took place on the second day. As this attack is also described in Zonaras' account, on balance it would appear to be most likely that Dionysius' narrative describes the second day's fighting.

Plutarch describes the first day as an indecisive but bloody fight amongst dense terrain. The Romans, despite their previous boasting, had obviously occupied a defensive position protected by wooded areas, where Pyrrhus' 'cavalry could not operate and his elephants could not charge and engage the enemy's phalanx. Therefore, after many had been wounded and slain, for the time being the struggle was ended by the coming of night.' [11] This was most likely a deliberate ploy on the Romans' part as Frontinus, in his *Stratagems*, describes, 'Manius Curius, as observing that the phalanx of King Pyrrhus could not be resisted when in extended order, took pains to fight in confined quarters, where the phalanx, being massed together, would embarrass itself.' [12] Although this describes an incident four years later, it is possible that Curius first learned the value of this tactic at Asculum.

In order to prevent a repetition of these tactics, Pyrrhus sent overnight detachments of troops to occupy the unfavourable parts of the field and to ensure that the Romans ' having no opportunity for sidelong shifts and counter-movements, as on the previous day, were obliged to engage on level ground and front to front.' [13] Here Pyrrhus' pike phalanx, and most importantly his elephants, would have the tactical advantage.

Dionysius gives a detailed account of the dispositions of both armies. On his far left Pyrrhus positioned the cavalry of the Lucanians, Tarentines and Greek mercenaries. His infantry, posted from left to right was: the Samnites,

Greek subjects and mercenaries, in the centre the Epirots, next the Bruttians and Lucanians, the phalanx of Tarentines, the Ambracians, and in the position of honour on the right, the Macedonians. His right wing cavalry consisted of the Samnites, Thessalians, Bruttians and the mercenaries hired by the Tarentines. The light infantry and the elephants he divided into two groups and placed them behind both wings, at a reasonable distance, in a position slightly elevated above the plain. He joined the royal bodyguard of 2,000 picked horsemen, which was held in reserve, so that he might intervene anywhere that his line was hard pressed.[14]

Frontinus gives a different version of Pyrrhus' dispositions. He states that Pyrrhus, following the Homeric verse (*Iliad* 4.299), placed his weakest troops, the Tarentines, in the centre, with the Samnites and Epirots on the right, and the other Italians on the left. The cavalry and elephants were held in reserve.[15] Given the already noted limitations to Frontinus' work, it would again appear to be more realistic to accept Dionysius' more detailed description. Both agree, however, that Pyrrhus kept his elephants and a strong force of cavalry in reserve.

There were sound tactical reasons for this. Much of Pyrrhus' infantry, certainly more than half, was made up of his Italian allies. Artistic representations of these troops show them to be more lightly armoured than their Roman opponents. Body armour, if it was worn at all, generally consisted of a triangular or square breastplate about 24cm wide. Their offensive weapons and tactics also differed. The infantry of southern Italy, equipped mostly with a shield and javelins, preferred to skirmish from afar, showering their opponents with javelins and then withdrawing to safety. The Samnites were regarded by the Romans as the bravest and most determined of their Italian opponents. Livy describes that it was the usual practice ' of both the Gauls and the Samnites to make a furious attack to begin with, and if that were successfully resisted, it was enough; the courage of the Samnites gradually sank as the battle went on.' [16]

The Romans' heavier equipment and system of reserve lines gave them considerable advantage in a protracted fight. As a result, in their long series of wars against the Samnites, the Romans had little problem defeating them in open battle The only victories won by the Samnites seem to have been when they were able to ambush the Romans, or force them to fight in difficult terrain. On one occasion Livy records an incident where:

> The Samnites, finding all chance of a surprise hopeless, since matters
> would have to be decided by an action in the open, thought it better
> to meet their foes in a pitched battle. Accordingly, they came down to
> the lower ground, and placed themselves in the hands of Fortune with
> more of courage than of hope.[17]

*

As usual the Romans won this battle after a hard fight. In an open battle, such as Pyrrhus was about fight, they were generally swept away by the more heavily equipped Romans.

The evidence suggests that the Lucanians and Bruttians fought in a similar way to the Samnites, but possibly without the same courage. Livy describes the Lucanians as 'fickle and reckless' . Justin, in contrast, claims that the Bruttians 'seem to have been the bravest and most powerful people of the country' and that 'the Lucanians were accustomed to breed up their children with the same kind of education as the Spartans Öthus were they prepared for the toils of war.' [18] The performance of the two contingents at Asculum would tend to favour Livy' s view. Pyrrhus was most likely hoping that his Italian allies could hold the Romans long enough to allow his Macedonian and Epirot pikeman to defeat their opponents. He wisely kept his elite cavalry and elephants in reserve in order to plug any holes in his line that their defeat may open, or to deliver the decisive blow if the infantry fight went his way.

Polybius states that Pyrrhus had made his phalanx more flexible by placing units of the more lightly-armed Italian infantry between the units of his pikemen.[19] He does not, however, state when this was first done. Dionysius' description of Pyrrhus' battle line mentions only distinct ethnic divisions. Supporting Polybius' claim is the amount of the front occupied by the small numbers of Pyrrhus' Macedonians and Epirots. These 16,000 to 20,000 men are recorded by Dionysius as facing off against two of the four Roman legions - implying that they occupied about half of Pyrrhus' line. In order for these units to have such a long frontage they, most likely, did include Italian contingents. The smallest known unit of the pike-phalanx was about 250 men, whereas the Italian infantry may have fought in units as small as 120 men, as the Romans did. If each unit of the phalanx was interspersed with a *maniple* of Italians, there would still be plenty of Italian infantry remaining to form up in their separate, ethnic contingents. Unfortunately for this theory, Polybius claims that they were interspersed cohort by cohort. That this formation was used at Asculum can, however, only be conjecture, given the lack of detail in the sources.

The Romans arrayed on their left wing the first legion, facing the Macedonians, Ambracians and the Tarentine mercenaries. Next, they positioned the third legion, opposed to the Tarentine phalanx and the Bruttian and Lucanian allied contingents. To the right of the third legion they placed the fourth, facing the Epirot phalanx. The second legion was placed on the right wing, opposite the mercenaries from Greece and the Samnites. The Romans divided their allies, the Latins, Campanians, Umbrians, Volscians, Marrucini, Peligni, Ferentani, and their other subjects, into four divisions, and interspersed them between the Roman legions. Whether whole divisions of allies were placed between entire Roman legions, or the troops were intermingled cohort by cohort is not made clear. Dionysius claims that this was done to ensure that no part of the line was weak, implying that they were intermingled.[20] The normal practice of the Romans, however, was to field their legions as an entity with their allies alongside them. Given the unusually large number of allies present, it is possible that the Romans may have altered their standard deployment. As with the case of Pyrrhus' army, it is impossible to determine exactly how the Romans deployed their infantry.

The Romans divided their cavalry, both their own and that of their allies, and placed them equally on both wings. Behind the main battle line they stationed their own reserve of light-armed troops and the three hundred wagons, held back specifically to fight Pyrrhus' elephants.

The coming battle would be one of the largest of the battles of Alexander's Successors. Pyrrhus' Epirot, Macedonian and Tarentine pikemen most likely formed up in their usual sixteen-deep formation. His Italians would have fought in shallower formations, probably in the more usual eight ranks. This would have meant that the Epirot infantry would have had a frontage of about 6-7,000 men. Even without gaps between formations, the infantry front line would have covered around six kilometres. With cavalry formed up on both wings the total frontage must have been at least seven kilometers long. The Romans formed up in shallower formations than the Epirots, but their use of three supporting lines would have meant that their frontage was similar to that of Pyrrhus' army. None of the sources for the battle mention either side as outflanking the other, so it is likely that their frontages were equally matched. In an age where communications depended on visual or sound signals, or horse-mounted messengers, control of both armies would have been made even more difficult by the unusual size of the battle.

As they advanced towards one another, the opposing armies first chanted their war songs, and when the signals were given to advance raised their various war-cries. The cavalry, stationed upon both wings, fought with their usual tactics. The Romans, armed with heavier thrusting spears, attempted to bring the opposition horse into hand-to-hand combat. The Greek and Italian cavalry of Pyrrhus, generally being more lightly armed with javelins, preferred to fight at a distance, employing flanking and evasive manoeuvres. The Romans, when they were hard pressed by the Greeks, would close up their ranks and fight shoulder-to-shoulder as if an infantry phalanx. The Greeks, when confronted by these tactics would swerve to the right and attempt to charge the enemy's flanks.[21]

The fighting was at first hard and indecisive, with neither side breaking.

Instead, those that were hard pressed maintained good order, remaining with their standards and protecting themselves with their shields while gradually falling back. Both sides had placed their best infantry on their right flank. On the king's side, the Macedonians drove back the first Roman legion and the Latins arrayed with it. On the Roman right, the second legion was gradually winning their struggle with the Samnites. Pyrrhus, seeing his left wing under pressure, ordered the elephants to be led up to the part of the line that was in difficulties. The Romans responded by driving forward their wagons that had been specially designed to counter such a move. An epic struggle developed between the two weapon types. At first the wagons got the better of the elephants, the crews striking at them with their spiked poles and targeting their fire-bearing claws at the elephants' eyes. The elephants' crews responded by withdrawing their beasts slightly and engaging the wagons by hurling their javelins down from above. The light-armed troops, who accompanied the elephants, cut through the wattled screens surrounding the wagons and hamstrung the oxen. The crews of the carts abandoned them and fled to seek refuge with their nearest infantry. Their panicked flight caused great confusion among the nearby Roman infantry.

The disarray caused by this flight appears to have halted the Roman advance on their right. It is likely that both sides were disorganized by the unusual nature of the fighting and neither side was in any position to immediately renew the offensive. There is no further description of any fighting in this portion of the battlefield and Pyrrhus was later able to withdraw troops from his left.

The Romans, however, won a crucial breakthrough when their third legion (Dionysius states the fourth, but this must be an error as they were arrayed against the Epirots) broke the Lucanians and Bruttians, stationed on the centre-right of Pyrrhus' battle-line. They fled after only the briefest of fights. Their rout exposed the vulnerable flank of the Tarentine phalanx, stationed to their left. With their flanks threatened, the brittle morale of the Tarentines collapsed. Demoralized, they also turned and fled.

The Roman infantry had torn a huge hole in the Epirot line. The third legion and its accompanying allies poured into the gap. A breach of over a kilometre had been torn through the Epirot front, and nearly 20,000 Roman infantry advanced into it. Here was a great opportunity for the Roman commanders, if they could retain control of their troops they could swing them either left, right, or both, into the exposed flanks of the Macedonian and Epirot phalanxes. The rigid formations and unwieldy pikes of these infantry would make them easy prey to the more mobile Romans. Such an attack on the flanks of a phalanx could end in carnage.

On this occasion, however, the Roman consuls were either unable, or unwilling, to control and reform their troops. The Romans appear to have simply charged straight ahead into the gap, pursuing their fleeing opponents. The Roman generals were, most likely, fighting at the front of their troops. If so, the noise and confusion of battle may have prevented them from even learning of the breakthrough. A century later, at the Battle of Cynoscephalae a junior Roman officer, a tribune, would take the initiative and lead his troops into the flank of the Macedonian phalanx. That was, however, a veteran army and far more professional than those of the early third century.

Breaking the enemy line could also be confusing for the troops taking part, especially for armies made up of numerous, allied contingents. Once the lines had been broken, the soldiers could change alignment and intermingle, making it difficult to tell friend from foe. At the Battle of Delium in 424 the Athenians, having broken the Thebans front and swung onto their flanks 'fell into confusion in surrounding the enemy and mistook and so killed each other.' [22] In the turmoil of battle, the victorious Romans appear to have behaved as leaderless mobs often do, and charged straight ahead, bunching together as they did.

Pyrrhus, however, displayed a much greater level of generalship. As was described at Heraclea, he limited his involvement in the fighting and thereby was able to maintain control of the battle. Upon learning of the breakthrough, he gathered together a force of cavalry, from both his own bodyguard and from his right wing. He sent this force under one of his officers with orders to attack the pursuing and, probably, disordered Roman infantry. Before Pyrrhus could put this plan into effect, however, a second crisis was reported to him.

A contingent of Rome' s Apulian allies, from the city of Argyrippa, consisting of 4,000 foot and 400 horse, had been marching to the assistance of the Romans.[23] They arrived on a hill overlooking the Epirot camp. Given their likely line of march, they probably arrived behind Pyrrhus' right flank. This was a fortuitous result for the Romans as the Apulians had been marching by pure chance along the road that led to the Epirot rear. The arriving Apulians witnessed the battle in full fight and delayed for a brief period in order to decide on their next action. Eventually, they resolved not to descend from the heights and take part in the battle, since the confusion and dust of the battlefield made it difficult to determine friend from foe. Instead, they decided on an easier and much more profitable action, to attack and sack Pyrrhus' camp. They justified this decision with the excuse that the sight of the blazing camp, which was about three-and-a-half kilometres from the battle, would demoralize Pyrrhus' army. The Apulians captured some Epirot foragers and learned that the camp was only lightly guarded. They then surrounded the camp and attacked it from all sides.

Made aware of the attack on his camp by an escaping cavalryman,

Pyrrhus rode back to conduct a personal reconnaissance. Pyrrhus did not panic but instead 'decided to keep the rest of his forces in the plain and not to recall or disturb the phalanx, but sent the elephants and the boldest of the horse, carefully selected, as reinforcements for the camp.' [24] He reinforced the cavalry force he had just collected with a force of elephants. These were most likely drawn from his now-dormant left as his right wing elephants would soon be in action elsewhere. This force was now ordered to attack the Apulians but they arrived too late to prevent the sack and firing of the camp. The victorious Apulians, observing Pyrrhus' troops coming down from the heights against them, and content to secure their booty, withdrew to the summit of a steep hill, which could not easily be ascended by the mounted troops of the relief force.

Pyrrhus' soldiers arrived too late to save the camp. Instead, they turned against the Romans of the third legion. These troops had advanced far ahead of their supports after routing the Bruttians, Lucanians and Tarentines who had faced them. The victorious Roman infantry would have lost formation as they pursued their beaten enemies. Suddenly faced by a new enemy, they became terrified at the thought of facing Pyrrhus' cavalry and elephants while out of formation and on level terrain. They quickly retreated to a thickly-wooded hill and reformed their ranks. The elephants and cavalry could not successfully attack such a position. Instead, they surrounded it, and isolated the Romans. The Epirots then brought up bowmen and slingers, who had either been accompanying the elephants, or had been withdrawn from their position in reserve behind the main Epirot battle line. The Epirot light infantry were able to fire their missiles from all sides, killing and wounding many of the isolated Roman force. The Romans were trapped, as they could not leave the hill in order to drive off their tormentors for fear of the Epirot elephants and cavalry.

When the Roman commanders became aware of the situation they sent a force of cavalry to support the isolated infantry. Again, this most likely came from their right wing. Pyrrhus responded by withdrawing a detachment of infantry, made up of the Athamanians, Acarnanians and some of the Samnites from his main line and dispatching them to support the attack. A battle within a battle now broke out between all these forces, with both sides, reportedly, inflicting heavy casualties on the other.

According to Dionysius, the battle was brought to a halt by the fall of night and the Roman consuls recalled their troops, withdrew back across the river, and led them back to their camp. Plutarch has a different version of the end of the battle. He claims that after a long struggle the Romans were being driven back at the point where Pyrrhus himself was leading the assault and that the:

Greatest havoc was wrought by the furious strength of the elephants, since the valour of the Romans was of no avail in fighting them, but they felt that they must yield before them as before an onrushing billow or a crashing earthquake, and not stand their ground only to die in vain, or suffer all that is most grievous without doing any good at all.[25]

The Romans broke and fled back to their camp in confusion.

Zonaras' account, although claiming that the battle was a Roman victory, lends some support to Plutarch. He states that the Romans were forcing the Epirot army back, 'slowly but surely, until Pyrrhus, bringing his elephants to bear, not opposite their wagons, but at the other end of the line, routed their cavalry through fear of the beasts even before they had come close.' [26]

As Zonaras' states that Pyrrhus led the decisive attack against the wing opposite to the wagons it is safe to infer that Pyrrhus' decisive assault was launched against the Roman left wing. This also fits in with Plutarch' s account which links this attack to the earlier success of the Macedonian phalanx. The most likely reconstruction is that after he had dispatched his relief forces to contain, or destroy, the Roman breakthrough, he then moved to the right. Here he organized and personally lead the final assault by his already-successful Macedonian phalanx. He supported this attack by bringing forward the unengaged elephant reserve from behind his right wing. These quickly routed the Roman cavalry opposed to them. Meanwhile, the elite Macedonian pikemen continued their assault on the Romans, who 'fought fiercely with their swords against the Macedonian spears, reckless of their lives and thinking only of wounding and slaying, while caring naught for what they suffered.'[27]

Despite their courage, the Roman infantry had no answer to the veteran Macedonian pikemen. The combined assault by the Macedonians and elephants finally broke the Roman left. These then fled to the safety of the Roman camp. The separate struggle between the Roman third and fourth legions and Pyrrhus' relief force was probably that which Dionysius refers to as being brought to an end by nightfall. Both contingents were, perhaps, content to slip away under the cover of night.

The battle won, Pyrrhus' forces now withdrew to the supposed safety of their own camp. Instead they found it destroyed. Having lost their tents, pack-animals, and all their baggage, they were forced to encamp in the open, upon a hill. Here they spent the night without cover or supplies. These privations and the loss of their equipment caused many of the wounded to die, whereas they might have survived if they had received the necessary treatment.

Plutarch, alone among the sources, claims that the battle was a clear victory for Pyrrhus. He records that the Romans lost 6,000 dead and the Epirots 3,505, citing Pyrrhus' own memoirs. Again, Plutarch goes out of his way to contradict Dionysius' account. According to Dionysius, there was no Roman rout and the fighting lasted until ended by nightfall. Plutarch also claims that Dionysius stated that Pyrrhus lost 15,000 men.[28] This figure, however, does not appear in the text that has come down to us, so either Plutarch is in error, or, more likely, this part of Dionysius' account has been lost. According to Frontinus and other Roman historians, the battle was a Roman victory, with them losing 5,000 dead and the Epirots 20,000.[29] The Epirot losses had, as at Heraclea, fallen heavily on Pyrrhus' friends, commanders and the troops Pyrrhus had brought across from Greece. Pyrrhus himself had been badly wounded in the arm by a javelin.

It was the usual practice for Greek armies to set up a trophy on the field after a victorious battle. This usually consisted of a tree trunk decorated with arms of a defeated enemy soldier. The Romans do not appear to have set up battlefield trophies. Instead, they commemorated their victories by setting up monuments in Rome itself. If the victory was substantial enough the general would be awarded a triumph, a parade through Rome. Unfortunately, the sources do not record who set up a trophy to claim victory at Asculum. Tellingly for Roman claims of victory, however, is the fact that there is no triumph recorded for the consuls of this year.

Although Plutarch's figures for the numbers of dead appear low for a battle of this size, it is clear from the aftermath of the battle that both sides had considerable numbers of wounded. This is probably because both sides had routed only a portion of the enemy battle line. Under these circumstances, the injured of both armies would have had a good chance of escaping the battlefield, rather than being hunted down and killed by any pursuing enemy.

Here again, it is best to accept Plutarch's verdict and casualties, as he cites contemporary sources. The battle appears to have been a narrow tactical victory to Pyrrhus. It was, however, clearly a hard-fought and costly one. Pyrrhus is reported to have rued the cost of victory as he had after the Battle of Heraclea. He could not afford to continue to sustain such losses among his limited number of Epirot and Macedonian troops.

The generals of both Rome and the Greek cities were also elected politicians. They often owed their position to factional politics rather than military competence. These men would often have had considerable military experience and some were fine commanders, but generally their experience would be intermittent. Pyrrhus, by contrast, had been born to command in battle and his life and education was largely directed to these ends. He himself had claimed that the only true art for a king to study was warfare.

Large-scale hoplite battles had often seen portions of both battle lines breaking. In general, the victorious troops would merely pursue their immediate beaten enemies. Victory often went to the side that had broken more of the enemy. The notable exception to this was the Spartans at the Battle of Nemea in 394. The Spartans had beaten their opponents but the rest of their allies had fled. Rather than pursue their foes, the Spartan commanders retained control of their troops and swung them into the flanks of the pursuing enemy. They were therefore able to turn defeat into an overwhelming victory. The Spartans did, however, pride themselves on their military professionalism as compared to the amateurism of the other Greek states.[30] When the Romans had breached Pyrrhus' line they acted as armies had for centuries before: they simply pursued the broken troops in front of them.

It was not until the reigns of Philip, Alexander, and his Successors that generals, other than the Spartans, would demonstrate greater control over the course of the battle. The first occasion that a general consciously used a reserve line was Alexander the Great's victory at Gaugamela. According to Curtius, Alexander deliberately formed up a second line in order to prevent being encircled by the numerically-superior Persians. He placed infantry reserves to his rear and light infantry behind his wings. Curtius claims that these formations were already facing to the rear and sides. Arrian merely records the presence of the infantry reserve to prevent attack from the rear. He, more credibly, has them facing forward.[31] As Alexander's victorious right wing advanced, a gap opened between them and his centre. A group of Persian and Indian cavalry broke through the line at this point and penetrated to the rear of his position, where they raided the baggage animals. Alexander's reserve formation proved its worth as it about-faced and drove off the Persian cavalry.

At Gaugamela, Alexander had initially retained control of the battle, feeding units into the fighting in order to neutralize any Persian threats. Only once a hole had opened in the Persian line did he commit himself into combat, leading the decisive charge of the Companion cavalry against the exposed flank of the Persian centre.

After Alexander's death his Successors also demonstrated greater control over the course of the battle than had the earlier Greek generals. At the Battle of Paraetacine, both Antigonus and his opponent, Eumenes, placed themselves on the far right of their lines. They both protected themselves with advance and rear guards of cavalry, enabling them to avoid the initial fighting and remain aware of the tactical situation as it unfolded. At the crucial point of the battle, Eumenes was able to withdraw a unit from his left wing and then lead it personally in an outflanking attack around Antigonus' left. Eumenes' attacks on his right and centre were successful and soon their opponents were in rout.

Antigonus, however, refused to be panicked, and demonstrated how much battlefield control had improved under the tutelage of Alexander. Eumenes' advance had opened up a breach between his left and centre. Antigonus seized the opportunity and advanced with his own, uncommitted, bodyguard through the gap. He then turned right and attacked the exposed flank of Eumenes' left wing. This was quickly rolled up and put to flight. Antigonus then sent the swiftest of his cavalry to relieve his defeated centre and left. By these means Antigonus stabilized his battleline and turned a certain defeat into a drawn battle.

Pyrrhus had spent much time at Antigonus' court and no doubt heard of Antigonus' tactics from both him and others present at the battle. Perhaps of even more influence on Pyrrhus was his experience at the Battle of Ipsus. Here he learned the value of holding one's elephants in reserve. Pyrrhus clearly displays the value of these lessons at Asculum, where he too was able to turn an apparently-certain defeat into a hard-fought victory.

During the battle he was able to respond effectively to no less than three crises. First, he had sent a reserve of elephants and light infantry to check the Roman success on his left. Next, he gathered a relief force to deal with the threat to his camp, although this proved to be unsuccessful. Most importantly, in a similar way to his mentor Antigonus, he refused to panic when a large part of his line broke and fled. Instead, he sent a reserve force to neutralize the breakthrough. Not until all these threats had been neutralized did he emulate Alexander, place himself at the head of his bodyguard, and lead the decisive assault. By the standards of his time this demonstrated remarkable, possibly unparalleled, battlefield leadership.

Although the battle was a tactical victory to the Epirots, the final result was clearly a strategic loss. Pyrrhus' casualties, the loss of his camp and equipment, and possibly his own wounding, forced him to retreat to Tarentum immediately, before the Romans learnt of his distressed position. Zonaras claims that despite their losses the Romans later crossed the river to offer further battle. They then discovered that Pyrrhus' army had retreated. They too then withdrew, being unable to pursue the enemy on account of their large numbers of wounded.[32] The Romans went into winter quarters in Apulia. Pyrrhus' retreat undid the gains that he had won in Apulia earlier in the year. Twice in two years Pyrrhus had won a tactical victory over the Romans. On both occasions, however, he had been unable to convert these victories into long-lasting strategic successes. Pyrrhus had been unable to break Rome's control of either Latium or Campania.

After arriving in Tarentum, Pyrrhus released his allies and went into winter quarters. Here he sent messages to Epirus asking for reinforcements and money, but none were forthcoming. The heavy casualties among his

Epirots and commanders had clearly disheartened him. He also observed that his allies in Italy were becoming exhausted by the struggle. Meanwhile, the Romans were easily able to obtain replacements from their massive reserve of manpower. Nor had their defeat in two battles caused them to lose courage or the determination to continue the war. As Plutarch records, ' the army of the Romans, as if from a fountain gushing forth indoors, was easily and speedily filled up again, and they did not lose courage in defeat, nay, their wrath gave them all the more vigour and determination for the war.' [33]

Following the battle, both sides appear to have remained inactive for the rest of the year. They were probably recovering from the fighting. A certain amount of war weariness also seems to have affected both sides. Even the usually-belligerent Romans appear to have been unsettled, as Polybius records that 'the commons, however, worn out as they were by the recent wars, had need of any and every kind of restorative.'[34] It is also possible that Pyrrhus was observing events that were unfolding back in Greece. The Galatian invaders of Greece had killed Ptolemy Ceraunus in battle in early 279. His death again threw the prize of the Macedonian kingship back into the ring.

Early the next year, while both sides were still recovering, the Romans sent another delegation to Pyrrhus, led by the newly-elected consul, the ever-present Fabricius. He too was reported to have fought and been wounded at Asculum. The exact content of their discussions is not known, but the Romans had already learned that Pyrrhus was considering leaving Italy for either Sicily or Macedonia. They most likely considered that this was an ideal time to pressure him into making an agreement more conciliatory than his previous offers.

During the negotiations a traitor within Pyrrhus' ranks approached Fabricius and offered to assassinate Pyrrhus for money. Fabricius was horrified by such treachery and sent a letter to Pyrrhus warning him of the plot. As usual Fabricius used the opportunity to compare the virtue of the Romans to the supposed perfidy of the Greeks:

> It would appear that you are a good judge neither of friends nor of enemies. You will see that the men with whom you are at war are honourable and just, but that those whom you trust are unjust and base. And indeed we do not give you this information out of regard for you, but in order that your ruin may not bring infamy upon us, and that men may not say of us that we brought the war to an end by treachery because we were unable to do so by valour.[35]

After Pyrrhus had read the letter he executed the traitor and used his skin to make a bridle, which he gave to Milon as a gift. Grateful to Fabricius for his warning, Pyrrhus released his prisoners without ransom. The Romans, naturally enough, punished them by disgracing them in the same way they had the survivors of Heraclea. Not wishing to be indebted to Pyrrhus in any way they also released, without ransom, an equal number of Tarentine and Samnite prisoners.

After the discussions with Fabricius, Cineas was once again sent off to Rome to continue negotiations for a truce with the Romans. The most likely terms are an acceptance of the *status quo*, with both sides retaining what they currently held. In the meantime, however, the Senate' s attitude had hardened again, helped by an offer of assistance from their allies the Carthaginians. They reiterated their position that they would make no terms with Pyrrhus until he had quit Italy completely. Pyrrhus was now forced to embark on his next adventure, a campaign in Sicily, without having achieved any assurances for the security of his Italian allies.

Chapter VII

Sicily

'Pyrrhus, the only man whom all the Sicilians had accepted as their leader and king deliberately out of affection.' - Polybius, 9.23

'and after he had brought under his power all Sicily with the exception of the city of Lilybaeum, the one city which the Carthaginians still held, he assumed the arrogance of a tyrant.' - Dionysius, 20.8.

While Pyrrhus was wintering in Tarentum two new opportunities for conquest arose. First was the news that Ptolemy Ceraunus had died in battle against the forces of the invading Galatians. His death created the possibility that Pyrrhus could return and reclaim the kingship of Macedonia. There also came to Tarentum ambassadors from the Sicilian Greek cities of Agrigentum, Syracuse and Leontini. This delegation offered to place their cities under the command of Pyrrhus, provided that he drove the Carthaginians from the island. Plutarch claims that, 'Pyrrhus rated Fortune soundly because occasions for two great undertakings had come to him at one time and thinking that the presence of both meant the loss of one, he wavered in his calculations for a long time.'[1]

In 279 the Galatians, a group of Celtic tribes, had invaded Macedonia. The ancient historians claim that the Celtic invasion was a result of overpopulation. One group, following the omen of a flight of birds, had invaded Illyria. They won numerous victories before settling in Pannonia. Flushed with their success, they then moved south into Greece and Macedonia, laying waste to all before them. Ptolemy Ceraunus, the new king of Macedonia, learning of the approach of the Gauls, hurried to meet them with a small force. An embassy from the Dardanians, an Illyrian people, had offered to ally with him and provide 20,000 men. Ptolemy spurned their offer and insulted the embassy. Justin claims he said that:

> The Macedonians were in a sad condition if, after having subdued the whole east without assistance, they now required aid from the Dardanians to defend their country; and that he had for soldiers the

sons of those who had served under Alexander the Great, and had been victorious throughout the world.[2]

The Dardanian king is supposed to have observed that as a consequence 'the famous kingdom of Macedonia would soon fall as a sacrifice to the rashness of a raw youth.'

The Galatian commander, Belgius, sent ambassadors to Ptolemy to offer him peace if he would pay a ransom. Ptolemy retorted that the Galatians only desired peace because they feared war. He replied that 'he would grant peace only on condition that they would give their chiefs as hostages, and deliver up their arms; for he would put no trust in them until they were disarmed.'[3] The Galatians attacked a few days later, and the Macedonians were heavily defeated. Ptolemy, after receiving several wounds, was captured. The victorious Gauls, as was their custom, cut off his head and stuck it on a lance.

When the news of the defeat spread through Macedonia, panic spread and the gates of the cities were slammed shut. Macedonia fell into confusion as a number of claimants to the throne came forward. First was Meleager, an uncle of Ptolemy Ceraunus. Antipater, a nephew of Cassander, drove him out after only a few days rule. He, in turn, ruled for only forty-five days. While the Macedonian nobles bickered, the Galatians ravaged the Macedonian countryside unopposed. Eventually, Sosthenes, a former general of Lysimachus, assembled what troops he could, drove back the Galatians and saved Macedonia from devastation. In gratitude, the army saluted him as king, above the claims of many of the nobles that aspired to the throne. Sosthenes, supposedly of humble birth, refused to take the title of king. Instead, he made the soldiers swear an oath to him as general.

Pyrrhus eventually decided that the prospect of gaining the great wealth of the Sicilian Greeks was the more attractive offer. This decision is not surprising given the unsettled nature of Macedonian politics, and the unknown threat posed by the formidable Galatians. Pyrrhus possibly hoped, at least initially, that he could create a Sicilian kingdom using the claims of his son Alexander. Alexander was the grandson of the dead Syracusan tyrant and self-proclaimed king, Agathocles. In addition, Pyrrhus had long planned that he could use Sicily as a springboard for an invasion of Africa, while leaving Sicily securely under Alexander's rule.

As was his usual practice, Pyrrhus sent his chief ambassador Cineas to Sicily to prepare for his arrival. The Tarentines, learning of Pyrrhus' plans, were extremely displeased. They demanded that he either continue the war against the Romans, the task for which he had been invited, or else withdraw completely from their territory. Pyrrhus had no intentions of giving up Tarentum, or any of the other Greek cities now that he had control of them. He imposed strong garrisons, placing more than half of his Epirot troops in the cities, and ordered the Tarentines to continue to obey him until he returned. Such were the risks for the Greek *poleis* when they invited foreign kings into their cities and allowed them to install a garrison. No Hellenistic king would willingly give up control over such a rich prize as Tarentum.

The Sicily to which Pyrrhus was heading had long been a battlefield between the Greeks and Carthaginians. Carthage was a Phoenician city on the northern coast of what is now Tunisia. It was settled by Phoenician colonists, according to the literary evidence, in either 814 or 751. The archaeological evidence favours the earlier date. The Phoenicians were great merchants and miners, and over the next two centuries they established trading posts and opened mines in Sicily, Spain and Sardinia. In Sicily, they appear to have limited themselves mostly to small trading stations on headlands or offshore islands. They also seem to have established friendly relations with the three already-existing peoples of Sicily, the Elymians, Sicanians and Sicels.

The Greeks, to the contrary, had arrived as settlers. They established their first colony at Naxos, on the eastern coast, around the year 733. This was rapidly followed by others. Syracuse, which would later become the dominant Greek city on Sicily, was founded soon after. Over the next century, they continued their colonization westwards, mostly along the eastern, northern and southern coasts. This expansion was conducted chiefly at the expense of the native Sicels, who they drove into the more inaccessible, central, mountainous areas. Rather than confront the Greeks, the Carthaginians had initially withdrawn their existing far-flung trading posts and concentrated around the settlements of Motya, Soluntum and Panormus (Palermo) on the western end of Sicily.

With the foundation of Himera, around 648, on the north coast, and Selinus, in either 651 or 628, on the southern coast, the Greeks had advanced as far westward as they could without coming into direct conflict with both the Carthaginians and Elymians. War between Phoenicians and Greeks first broke out, however, not in Sicily but in southern France, against the Greek city of Massilia, modern Marseille. The cause of the conflict was probably a perceived threat to Carthage's trade routes from the Atlantic. In 600, a Massilian fleet defeated the Carthaginians in a sea-battle. This victory allowed colonists from Massilia to encroach into Spain and threaten Carthage's mining interests.

In 580 the Greeks attacked the Carthaginians and Elymians. An expedition of settlers from Cnidos and Rhodes, lead by a certain Pentathos, seized Lilybaeum, a headland dominating the Bay of Motya. At the same time, an expedition from Selinus attacked the Elymian city of Segesta. Confronted by the aggression of the Greeks, the Elymians and Phoenicians allied. Their combined army scored a decisive victory over the Greeks.

Pentathos' expedition was driven out of Lilybaeum and settled instead in the Lipari Islands, off northeastern Sicily. Selinus, cowed by its defeat, ceased to be aggressive to its neighbours.

Greek threats to Phoenician interests in the western Mediterranean were not long abated by this defeat. In about 581 the Greek city of Agrigentum was founded on the southern coast of Sicily, to the east of Selinus. Under the rule of the tyrant Phalaris, who reigned from 571-555, it launched a war of expansion against the native Sicels. He soon came to dominate central Sicily, and was given command of the forces of Himera. In 565 the Greeks also set up a colony on the island of Corsica. In Africa, the Cyrenian Greeks pressed westward, and reputedly defeated the Carthaginians at sea. The Phoenician's interests were being threatened by the Greeks throughout the western Mediterranean.

The challenge of confronting the Greeks fell to the city of Carthage. Over the previous century Carthage had made itself the dominant Phoenician city in Africa, and had brought much of the nearby African hinterland under its control. Sometime during the reign of the Persian king Cyrus, 559-529, the Carthaginians sent an army to Sicily for the first time. Its commander, Malchus, campaigned successfully, imposing hegemony over all the Phoenician towns in Sicily and the Elymians. He also appears to have forced Selinus into an alliance with Carthage.

After consolidating Carthaginian power in western Sicily, Malchus led an expedition to Sardinia. The western Greeks had been heavily reinforced by refugees from the Persian conquest of Ionia. The Etruscans of Italy also felt threatened by the expansion of Greek colonisation, and the inevitable piracy that accompanied it. They allied themselves with the Carthaginians. In about 540 the allies sent a fleet of 120 ships to attack the Greek colony of Alalia on Corsica. Despite being outnumbered two-to-one, the Greeks won the ensuing naval battle, but suffered heavy losses. Herodotus described this as 'a Cadmean sort of victory with more loss than gain', the first known use of the term.[4] The battered Greeks abandoned Alalia and retreated to the city of Rhegium, on the toe of Italy.

Successful generals were, however, generally mistrusted by the civilian government in Carthage. The Carthaginians recalled Malchus, accused him of plotting a coup, and executed him. Despite this, Carthage continued its path of expansion, taking Sardinia and bringing the Phoenician cities of Spain under its control. The Greek colonies in eastern Spain were destroyed. Only the Massalians held out, defeating the Carthaginians in two sea battles. In 490 a treaty was signed between Carthage and Massalia, fixing the boundary between the two in Spain at Artemision (Denia). In Africa, the Carthaginians also drove back the Greeks, and again a frontier was agreed upon, at the altar of the Philainoi, near modern El Agheila in western Libya.

These frontiers would remain fixed for the next two centuries. Only in Sicily would the two peoples continue to wage war on one another.

A new wave of Greek expansionism began in Sicily in the early fifth century. In 505, a certain Cleander had seized power in the city of Gela. Gela lay on the southern coast, to the east of Agrigentum. Cleander was murdered seven years later and his brother, Hippocrates, seized power. Hippocrates, with the army of Gela strengthened by many mercenaries, conducted a campaign of conquest against both the Sicels and his fellow Greeks. By 494 he dominated most of the eastern part of the island. Only the city of Syracuse succeeded in fighting him off. In 491 Hippocrates was ambushed and killed by the Sicels. He was succeeded as tyrant by his cavalry commander Gelon. In 485 taking advantage of the perennial class warfare between rich and poor in Syracuse, Gelon was able to seize control of the city. Gelon then turned Syracuse into his capital. It had two good harbours, unlike most other Greek cities in Sicily that had none. Under Gelon, Syracuse flourished and soon became the dominant city among the Greeks in Sicily. Gelon was now the most powerful ruler in the Greek world. In 481 a delegation from Greece arrived in Sicily, seeking help in the coming war against Persia. A sign of Gelon's strength was his reported offer of 28,000 troops and 200 warships.[5] Gelon's offer was refused as it came with the condition that he was to be made commander of all the Greek forces.

Gelon's expansion caused fear and apprehension among those Greek cities that still remained independent. In the manner of Greek cities, they were often more afraid of the ambitions of their fellow Greeks than those of non-Greeks. Selinus and Himera sought alliances with the Carthaginians. It was the annexation of Himera by another tyrant, Theron of Agrigentum, that again provoked the Carthaginians into action in Sicily. In 480, the same year that the Persians invaded Greece, the Carthaginians sent a massive expedition to Sicily. Most likely the Carthaginians of Sicily, like their nearest Greek neighbours, feared to leave unchecked the expansionism of Gelon. The army is reputed to have been 300,000 strong,[6] most likely an exaggeration; possibly half this number is credible. It consisted of the usual mix of troops the Carthaginians recruited from their empire and enlisted mercenaries: Africans, Spaniards, Ligurians from northern Italy, Corsicans and Sardinians. Part of the fleet, including all of the cavalry horses, was lost in a storm, but most landed safely in the bay of Panormus. After landing they advanced on Himera.

Once the location of the invasion force was known, Gelon, aided by his ally Theron, advanced rapidly to meet them. The combined Greek army was reputed to have been 50,000 infantry and 5,000 cavalry.[7] The Greek's total superiority in cavalry proved decisive. They were able to dominate the plain, killing the Carthaginian foragers and confining them within their camp. The

Greeks then launched a surprise assault, from both land and sea, on the Carthaginian camp. The attack was overwhelmingly successful and the enemy army was destroyed. In victory Gelon's terms were mild, demanding only an indemnity of 2,000 talents, enough to pay the cost of the war, from Carthage. The Punic settlements were allowed to remain. In the Machiavellian world of Greek politics, Gelon likely saw them as a useful threat to his rival tyrant, and erstwhile ally, Theron.

Following their defeat at Himera, the Carthaginians followed a defensive policy in Sicily for the next seventy years. The Greeks, meanwhile, continued their usual practice of expansion at the expense of the Sicels and of intercinal warfare, both between the cities and among the rich and poor classes within the cities. This situation lasted until 410. Carthage had become alarmed at the increasing strength of Syracuse, especially after its defeat of the Athenian invasion of 413. The peace finally broke down when Selinus once again attacked Elymian Segesta. The Carthaginians sent an army of 50,000 in 409, led by a general called Hannibal. This Hannibal was supposed to hate all things Greek, just as his later namesake reputedly hated all things Roman. Selinus fell within nine days and the population was massacred. Himera fell soon after.

Hannibal returned to Carthage, and in his absence the Syracusans recovered Selinus and Himera. The Carthaginians responded by sending Hannibal back to Sicily in 407 with an even larger force. He quickly recaptured Selinus and Himera. Pushing further east, he took Agrigentum. The Syracusans responded by appointing a supreme commander, or tyrant, Dionysius.[8] This would become the usual Greek response to any threat from the Carthaginians, and Syracuse from that point forward would intermittently be under the control of tyrants. Dionysius was unable to stop the Carthaginians, who went on to capture Gela and Camarina. Syracuse was saved from attack only by the outbreak of a plague that decimated the Carthaginian army and killed the commander, Hannibal. The two sides concluded a treaty, leaving Carthage in control of the greater part of the island, including the lands of the Sicels, Elymians and those Greek cities they had taken, which were forced to pay tribute.

The Syracusans could not allow the Carthaginians to control cities so far east and so close to Syracuse itself. In 398 Dionysius marched westward with an army of 80,000 men.[9] He attacked and took the main Carthaginian base at Motya. This was a remarkable piece of siege craft for the time. Motya lay on an offshore island. Dionysius repaired the mole leading out to the island and:

> Advanced war engines of every kind against the walls and kept hammering the towers with his battering-rams, while with the catapults he kept down the fighters on the battlements; and he also

advanced against the walls his wheeled towers, six stories high, which he had built to equal the height of the houses.[10]

This capture showed how much the Syracusans were in advance of the other Greeks in siege technology, at least until the time of Philip of Macedon. This expertise would be of great assistance to Pyrrhus during his Sicilian campaign.

A new Carthaginian force landed at Panormus and in a complete reversal of fortune drove the Greeks all the way back to Syracuse, destroying Messina on the way. Again Syracuse was saved by an epidemic among the Carthaginian army. This was supposedly caused by divine retribution for the Carthaginian desecration of a number of Greek temples and shrines. In 396 the Carthaginian commanders deserted their army and fled back to Africa. The war dragged on to 392, but both sides were now exhausted. A treaty was signed, which guaranteed the autonomy of the Greek cities and freed them from tribute. Dionysius could claim, with some justification, that he had liberated them.

In 385 Dionysius also intervened in Epirus on behalf of the exiled King Alcetas. Dionysus sent 2,000 Greek troops and recruited the Illyrian king Bardyllis to attack Epirus. They ravaged the region, killed 15,000 Molossians in battle and succeeded in returning Alcetas to his throne.[11]

During the following years he campaigned in southern Italy, capturing Rhegium, which gave him full control of the Strait of Messina. In 383–378 he attacked the Carthaginians again, but was unsuccessful. The Carthaginians and Greeks finally decided that the border between their territories was to be at the River Halycus, lying between Selinus and Agrigentum.

Dionysius died in 367, and over the following twenty years Syracuse was racked by internal political struggles. In 347 a previously ousted tyrant, Dionysius II, son of the earlier Dionysius, even invited a Carthaginian fleet into the harbour of Syracuse. This internal strife led to a collapse of Greek power, as Greek cities broke away from Syracusan control and the native tribes regained their strength.

The Sicilian Greeks were, however, saved by outside help. Syracuse's mother city, Corinth, sent an expeditionary force, commanded by one of their generals, Timoleon, to Syracuse in 343. Timoleon arrived in Syracuse at a time when there were two rival claimants for the tyranny, one being Dionysius II. He defeated one and drove the other into exile. Timoleon then defeated the Carthaginians at the Battle of Crimisus. The border between the two peoples was again set at the River Halycus in a treaty signed in 339. He then tried to revive the Greeks' fortunes in Sicily by bringing 60,000 Greek settlers to the island. Rather than seize the tyranny for himself, Timoleon reorganized the constitution, mixing elements of democracy, oligarchy, and monarchy. He then retired from public life. His intervention laid a solid foundation for stability, peace, and prosperity for a generation.

Such stability was, nonetheless, usually short-lived in the Sicilian cities, and the new Syracusan constitution eventually broke down into the usual conflict between the rich and the poor. In 316 a general named Agathocles defeated the oligarchs and seized power as yet another tyrant. By 311 his popularity was in decline, so he played the age-old political ruse of diverting public opinion by provoking a foreign war. He attacked the Carthaginians but was defeated at the Battle of Himera.

The Carthaginians again besieged Syracuse. Agathocles decided upon a remarkable gamble. In August 310 he sailed away from Sicily, and invaded the Carthaginian homeland, in modern Tunisia. As well as catching the Carthaginians off-guard, this also removed the sons of the middle-classes, the hoplites, from Syracuse, making them effectively hostages. Agathocles defeated the Carthaginians in battle and advanced on Carthage itself. Both sides' capitals were now blockaded. The deadlock was broken when in 306 Agathocles concluded a peace treaty with Carthage that left him in control of eastern Sicily. The border was again set at the River Halycus.

This peace lasted until Agathocles' death in 289. In the following years no single leader emerged to unite the Greeks of Sicily. Rival tyrants seized control of the cities and chaos ruled. Again a Carthaginian fleet sailed into Syracuse's harbour. Syracuse itself was divided by rival claimants for the role of tyrant. Sosistratus of Agrigentum, reputedly the ruler of thirty cities, held the town, whereas the fortified island of Ortygia, the stronghold by which Syracuse's tyrants dominated the city, held by a certain Thoenon. Italian mercenaries, the Mamertines, had seized the city of Messina in northeastern Sicily. Some of the Greek cities allowed Carthaginian garrisons within their walls rather than accept rule by a local tyrant. The Carthaginians, taking advantage of the disunity of the Greeks, marched into eastern Sicily and once again laid siege to Syracuse.

This was the backdrop to the Sicilian approach to Pyrrhus. The Sicilian Greeks were plagued with two constant problems: the military threat from the Carthaginians and the class struggle within their cities. Their traditional solution was to appoint a strong leader, usually a tyrant, who they believed could solve their troubles.

Embassies came to Pyrrhus from the cities of Agrigentum, Syracuse, and Leontini, and 'begged him to help them to drive out the Carthaginians and rid the island of its tyrants'.[12] This last claim appears to have been a rhetorical flourish by Plutarch, as it was the tyrants of Sicily who approached Pyrrhus, and who would later flock to his banner. Most likely they hoped that he would be another Timoleon, waging war for them and then conveniently retiring.

While the Sicilians were approaching Pyrrhus, Mago, a general of the Carthaginians, approached their long-time allies the Romans, offering to send 120 ships to their aid. He went to the Senate, saying that 'the Carthaginians were much concerned that they should be distressed by war in Italy from a foreign prince; and that for this reason he had been despatched to assist them; that, as they were attacked by a foreign enemy, they might be supported by foreign aid.'[13] It is probably at this point that the Romans renewed their alliance with the Carthaginians for the third and final time. The terms of the treaty were:

> If they make an alliance against Pyrrhus, both shall make it an express condition that they may go to the help of each other in whichever country is attacked. No matter which require help, the Carthaginians are to provide the ships for transport and hostilities, but each country shall provide the pay for its own men. The Carthaginians, if necessary, shall come to the help of the Romans by sea too, but no one shall compel the crews to land against their will.[14]

The treaty allowed for both sides to land forces in the others sphere of interest if they were there to assist the other in making war against Pyrrhus. This was contrary to the terms of the earlier treaties, which forbade either from sending forces into each other's domains.

Having made the alliance with the Romans, Mago then sailed to Pyrrhus in Tarentum. He claimed to be seeking peace between Pyrrhus and Carthage, but supposedly his real intention was to discover the king's views with regard to Sicily. The Carthaginian aim was, most believably, according to Justin, to prevent Pyrrhus from landing in Sicily and to keep him in Italy fighting the Romans.[15]

The Carthaginians also succeeded in forming an alliance with the Mamertines. They sent a fleet, including 500 Roman marines, to Messina to prevent Pyrrhus landing in Sicily. The Carthaginians, in accordance with their new treaty, landed with their Roman allies and assaulted the rebel garrison of Rhegium but were unable to take it. They took their fleet at Messina to guard the straits against the expected crossing of Pyrrhus.

Pyrrhus departed Tarentum two years and four months after he had arrived in Italy, probably in the late summer of 278. Prior to departing Italy, he installed garrisons in all of the Greek cities. This ensured their loyalty, but of course violated their autonomy and was greatly resented. He first sailed to Locris, where he left his son Alexander in charge of an Epirot garrison. Pyrrhus had been invited to Sicily by a group of aristocratic tyrants, sworn enemies of Agathocles and his legacy. For now the appearance of Alexander in Sicily would have been a political liability instead of an asset.

Pyrrhus' fleet consisted of sixty warships from Tarentum plus numerous transports. His invasion force was recorded as consisting of his elephants and 8,000 cavalry.[16] The latter figure is clearly wrong and is usually interpreted as either 8,000 men in total or 8,000 men plus the cavalry.

Pyrrhus managed to avoid the Carthaginian blockade and landed on the west coast of Sicily at the city of Tauromenium (Taormina), where the local tyrant had already declared his allegiance to him. Next he sailed to Catana (Catania), where the citizens are supposed to have welcomed him with great enthusiasm and presented him with golden crowns, believing he had come to liberate them from the hated Carthaginians. At Catana he disembarked his army and received reinforcements from the two cities, perhaps about 3,000 men.[17] Pyrrhus then advanced on Syracuse, both with his fleet and with his army marching by land.

The Carthaginians were reputed to have had an army of 50,000 men and a fleet of 100 ships besieging the city and pillaging the countryside. Pyrrhus' rapid advance had caught the Carthaginians unprepared, and a part of their fleet, thirty ships, had been sent away. At the unexpected sight of Pyrrhus' fleet in full battle array advancing on them, they refused to engage and allowed Pyrrhus' ships to occupy the port unopposed. Pyrrhus sailed triumphantly into the harbour and accepted control of the island of Ortygia. He then effected reconciliation between the two rival tyrants and took total control of the city. Pyrrhus was now able to take possession of the Syracusan fleet of 141 warships.[18] Although the fleet was over a decade old and under-crewed (hence its inability to break the Carthaginian blockade) it did increase Pyrrhus' potential fleet to over 200 vessels and gave him numerical supremacy over the Carthaginian navy.

Despite heavily outnumbering the Epirot army, the Carthaginians withdrew without a fight. Given the disparity in numbers, it appears to be a surprising decision, but without naval supremacy the continuation of the siege would have been fruitless. The Carthaginian generals possibly also feared to face a renowned general and his elephants in open battle. It is also very possible that the Greek historians may have exaggerated the size of the Carthaginian army. Whatever the reasons for the Carthaginian withdrawal, Pyrrhus now was in full control of the most powerful city in Sicily. In addition to the fleet, Pyrrhus also gained control of the Syracusan siege-train. Pyrrhus' possession of their equipment and expertise would be invaluable during the coming campaign.

The Carthaginian forces that Pyrrhus faced in Sicily were different in a number of ways from those of the Greeks, Macedonians and Romans. According to Polybius, 'the Carthaginians wholly neglect their infantry, though they do take some slight interest in their cavalry. The reason is that they employ foreign mercenaries – rather than citizen levies'[19] This statement is perhaps exaggerated, as the Carthaginian citizens did in fact serve in defence of their own city, and in the fleet. It is, however, generally correct when applied to Carthaginian overseas armies. These were made up of a number of different nationalities commanded by Carthaginian officers drawn from the aristocracy. The bulk of the army at this time generally appears to have consisted of African spearmen drawn from Carthage's Libyan conquests, and to a lesser extent troops from Spain. To label such troops mercenaries is perhaps misleading. They were recruited from Carthaginian-ruled areas, and 'auxiliaries' may be a more accurate, or less pejorative, term. These troops were usually supplemented with genuine mercenaries recruited from outside Carthage's empire. Gauls, Italians, Numidians and Greeks are all recorded. In Sicily, the latter were probably most numerous.

Tactically, however, the Carthaginians fought in a similar manner to the Greeks. They formed up for battle in the traditional Hellenistic manner, a single line of deep-formed infantry units in the centre, with cavalry on the flanks, rather than the multiple-line Roman method. In their early wars against the Greeks in Sicily, the Carthaginians relied predominately on their infantry centre. The Carthaginian army during this campaign appears to have been either incapable of defeating Pyrrhus' army in the field, or possibly unwilling to even face it. Their battle line, consisting mostly of close-order, spear-armed troops, would have had no answer to Pyrrhus' pike-armed infantry and elephants.

After settling affairs in Syracuse, Pyrrhus took control of the city of Leotini. He then marched on the city of Agrigentum where he took control from the already-allied Sosistratus. Pyrrhus also took over the thirty other cities that Sosistratus had controlled. These cities provided him with 8,000 infantry and 800 cavalry, supposedly excellent troops equal in ability to the Epirots. Good news also came from the city of Enna, which had expelled its Carthaginian garrison and allied itself with Pyrrhus. These reinforcements brought Pyrrhus' army up to a total of 30,000 infantry, 2,500 cavalry, and his elephants.[20]

So far Pyrrhus' campaign had been a triumphant procession through southeastern Sicily, winning over the Greek cities without a fight. From Agrigentum he would then have to cross the River Halycus and invade the hostile territory of the Carthaginians. Unfortunately, we have no detailed source for Pyrrhus' Sicilian campaign. Diodorus' account, which would have been based predominantly on the historian Hieronymous of Cardia, and therefore probably detailed and reliable, has been lost. All that remains is an epitome compiled by a later Byzantine librarian. Its account is brief and mostly lacking in detail. It describes a number of successful sieges but no battles against the Carthaginians.

Justin claims, however, that Pyrrhus 'fought many successful battles with the Carthaginians'[21] He uses the Latin word *proliea*, which is generally applied to land or naval battles rather than sieges. From this, it could be inferred that as well as besieging a number of cities Pyrrhus also defeated the Carthaginians in a number of battles. Unfortunately, Justin is an incredibly careless historian and cannot be relied on in isolation. It is possible that he has simply used the wrong word, *proleia*, rather than the more exact *obsidio*, meaning siege. Elsewhere in his work, however, Justin does use *obsidio* when mentioning sieges. On this occasion it is possible that he has accurately recorded events that have been lost in the other sources.

Goldsworthy points out, however, that the mountainous geography of Sicily does not favour the movement of large armies and creates many good defensive positions. This makes it difficult for a commander to force battle on an unwilling enemy. The key to controlling Sicily was to control its cities.[22] This would make sieges far more important than battles to any would-be conqueror of the island. Justin may therefore be referring to the two battles that took place in the last year of the campaign, against the Mamertines and Carthaginians. Diodorus' account may then be an accurate portrayal of the first two years of the war.

The exact dating of the incidents in Pyrrhus' Sicilian campaign is not recorded. Most likely events up to the gathering of his forces at Agrigentum occupied the remainder of 278. Pyrrhus began the next year by continuing his march west to the city of Heraclea. Here, the Carthaginians stood to defend their own border. Pyrrhus stormed the city, capturing it from its Carthaginian garrison. He then captured Azones. From there, he marched on Selinus, which came over to him without a fight.

Up to this point, Pyrrhus had been operating against cities occupied by the Carthaginians but inhabited by Greek populations. From this moment on Pyrrhus would be advancing into territory inhabited by the Elymians and the Carthaginians themselves, and could expect greater resistance. Despite this, the Elymian cities of Halicyae and Segesta also came over to him without resistance. Pyrrhus then moved against the Elymian city of Eryx, modern Erice. This city was held by a large Carthaginian garrison and occupied a naturally strong position, situated on a mountain 750 metres high. On the summit stood a magnificent temple of Venus. The city extended along the hill under the actual summit, the ascent to it being very long and steep on all sides. Here the Carthaginians again chose to stand their ground.

The city is roughly triangular in shape, with two sides protected by precipitous slopes. It is against the third side, which faces southwest, that Pyrrhus, and later the Arabs and Normans, must have launched their assaults. The remains of the walls on this side have been dated back to about 700, and are known as the 'Punic walls', although they were probably built by the Elymians. Eryx was also famous for being the site of one of the hero Hercules' 'labours'. Hercules had, according to legend, killed the king of the Elymians in a wrestling match.

Pyrrhus was forced to besiege the city as the garrison offered strong resistance. After a brief siege, he determined on an assault. Diodorus claims that Pyrrhus himself led the assault, 'desiring to win high renown and vying to rank with Hercules. Plutarch has a slightly different version, claiming that Pyrrhus merely 'made a vow to Hercules that he would institute games and a sacrifice in his honour, if the god would render him in the sight of the Sicilian Greeks an antagonist worthy of his lineage and resources.'[23]

Pyrrhus first cleared the walls with the missiles from his siege engines and then brought up his scaling-ladders. He was the first to mount the walls, and being easily recognizable in his ornate armour became the target of the Carthaginian defenders. Pyrrhus was reported to have fought heroically, pushing defenders from the walls:

> But most he laid dead in heaps about him with the strokes of his sword. He himself suffered no harm, but was a terrible sight for his enemies to look upon, and proved that Homer was right and fully justified in saying that valour, alone of the virtues, often displays transports due to divine possession and frenzy.[24]

After the capture of the city, he made good his promise, sacrificing to Hercules in a magnificent fashion and putting on spectacles and athletic games. Pyrrhus secured the city with a garrison.

In personally leading the assault on Eryx, and being the first man upon the walls, it is possible that Pyrrhus was not only attempting to emulate Hercules, but also that god's alleged descendant Alexander the Great. Alexander had supposedly being trying to outdo Hercules when he had besieged the fortress of the Rock of Aornos. Alexander had been the first to set foot upon it, but after he and his companions had engaged 'the enemy in hand-to-hand fighting – received more wounds than they inflicted – and signalled the retreat.'[25] Alexander only managed to capture Aornos after it had been deserted by its defenders. In taking Eryx by storm, Pyrrhus could claim not only to have equalled Hercules but possibly to have outshone Alexander.

Pyrrhus next advanced on the city of Iaetia, which he planned to use as a base for an assault on one of the main Carthaginian ports, Panormus. This city was reputed to have the finest harbour in all Sicily. The name in Greek means 'all harbour', and is used in the context of always being fit for mooring in all weathers. Iaetia surrendered immediately. Pyrrhus successfully took Panormus by storm.

He followed up his success by taking the fortress of Herctae. This lay near the sea between Eryx and Panormus on the plateau of a high hill rising up from a plain. Polybius describes the strength of the position:

> On the side looking to the sea and on that which faces the interior of the island, this plateau is surrounded by inaccessible cliffs, while the parts between require only a little slight strengthening. There is also a knoll on it which serves for an acropolis as well as for an excellent post of observation over the country at the foot of the hill. Besides this, Herctae commands a harbour very well situated for ships making the voyage from Drepana and Lilybaeum to Italy to put in at, and with an abundant supply of water. The hill has only three approaches, all difficult, two on the land side and one from the sea.[26]

Now all of Carthaginian Sicily had fallen to Pyrrhus except for the Carthaginian's main base at the city of Lilybaeum, which occupied the closest point of Sicily to Africa. The Carthaginians had founded it after Dionysius had destroyed Motya. In what was probably less than one campaigning season, Pyrrhus had succeeded in taking by storm three cities and a fortress held by the Carthaginians, two of which had occupied extremely-strong natural positions. The skills that he had learned at the court of Antigonus, along with the siege train of the Syracusans, had served Pyrrhus brilliantly up to this point.

Justin records that Pyrrhus' success up to this time had made him so popular that he 'received the title of king of Sicily as well as of Epirus.'[27] Such a title was not unprecedented as Agothocles had earlier emulated the other Successor monarchs and called himself king. Exactly how the title was bestowed and what it entailed is unknown.

Pyrrhus now made ready to besiege Lilybaeum. Its capture would give him complete control of Sicily. The Carthaginians now took extreme measures to prevent its capture. Diodorus states that they were able to move in reinforcements, as they had gained control of the sea. Unfortunately, our sketchy sources do not tell us the fate of Pyrrhus' fleet. Over a year later, after attempting to raise a new fleet, his forces departed Sicily aboard only 110 warships. Presumably at some stage either the Carthaginians had defeated the Greek fleet in battle, or it had been destroyed by a storm. This latter event was a common fate of fleets in the later wars in Sicily between the Carthaginians and Romans. Carthaginian naval supremacy would make the siege especially difficult.

Diodorus records that the Carthaginian control of the sea allowed them to bring over from Africa large amounts of grain, armaments and a considerable army. They also recruited mercenaries from Italy. So many men and arms were sent that they, reputedly, could not all be contained within the walls of the city. In preparation for the siege the garrison strengthened the city's defences by walling off the land approaches, building towers and digging a great ditch nearly twenty metres deep.[28] The ditch was about twenty-five metres from the walls, and so could easily be protected by missile fire from the city. This same ditch was cleared and re-used for a later siege against the Romans. Parts of it are still visible today.

Lilybaeum also occupied a naturally strong position, being on a promontory, and surrounded by the sea on two sides. The city was square in shape, with two walls running up from the sea on either side of the cape. They joined at a high point, now occupied by a medieval bastion, which would have dominated both the city and the attackers. The harbour, much bigger then than now, was protected by two breakwaters.

Prior to the siege beginning, the Carthaginians sent an embassy to Pyrrhus to discuss peace. They offered him a large amount of money and to loan him ships if an alliance was made. At first Pyrrhus was inclined to accept the terms, leaving the Carthaginians in control of Lilybaeum. His advisors and Greek allies, however, convinced him to reject the terms and drive the Carthaginians out of Sicily forever. They pointed out that allowing them to hold Lilybaeum would give them a future base for any subsequent recovery and expansion. Given the history of the preceding two centuries the advice was most likely correct. Pyrrhus was convinced and replied to the ambassadors that, 'there could be no settlement or friendship between himself and them unless they abandoned all Sicily and made the Libyan Sea a boundary between themselves and the Greeks.'[29]

Pyrrhus encamped near the walls and tested the defences by making constant attacks with relays of troops. The Carthaginian defences were, however, too strong and the defenders easily beat off the assaults. Pyrrhus settled in for a siege and began building even larger siege engines than those he had brought from Syracuse. He also began mining operations under the walls. For two months the siege continued, but the Carthaginians' preparations had paid off and Pyrrhus' forces made no headway.

With winter about to close in, Pyrrhus decided to lift the siege. The Carthaginian defences and their control of the seas had proven to be too strong. Pyrrhus now decided to embark on a new venture. He would attempt to emulate Agathocles and invade Africa while still engaged with the Carthaginians in Sicily. Before he could invade Africa it would, however, be necessary to build a new fleet. Pyrrhus ordered the Greek cities to provide the resources and the crews for the new fleet.

Pyrrhus' siege of Lilybaeum would be the high-water mark of his Sicilian campaign, from this point on his position would rapidly disintegrate. His order to build the new fleet was greatly resented by the Sicilian Greeks, as was his lifting of the siege. Like the Greeks of Tarentum they strongly opposed his decision to launch a new campaign before finishing what he had promised. They quite correctly saw him as abandoning their needs for his own selfish interests. The abandonment of the siege was a crucial error on Pyrrhus' part. The history of the two previous centuries had shown that the Carthaginians could quickly recover and use Lilybaeum as a base for re-conquest of the island. It would have been far better for Pyrrhus to have continued the siege until it was successful.

Garoufalias, a strong admirer of Pyrrhus, justifies his decision by claiming that Pyrrhus 'could not mount an efficient siege or capture the city without simultaneously blockading it from the sea as well.'[30] This is perhaps correct, but does not excuse Pyrrhus' decision to lift the siege while the fleet was being constructed. Some locations during the Hellenistic period were of great strategic importance and well worth whatever effort was necessary to capture them. Lilybaeum was one of these, as were, for example, Athens, Corinth, Byzantium and Tyre. Pyrrhus' former protector, Antigonus the One-eyed, had shown what could be achieved through perseverance. He had begun his siege of Tyre in 315 while suffering from inferiority in naval forces. He too planned to build a fleet to overcome this shortcoming. Unlike Pyrrhus, however, Antigonus resolutely continued his siege for over eighteen months, despite his enemies using their naval strength to both assist the garrison and ravage his territory. In the end, Tyre fell to Antigonus and remained a cornerstone of his family's empire for decades to come. Plutarch is no doubt correct in his judgement that 'what he won by his exploits he lost by indulging in vain hopes, since through passionate desire for what he had not he always failed to establish securely what he had.'[31]

Pyrrhus' orders to the Greeks to construct a new fleet were the catalyst for his sudden decline in popularity. It is possible that this would not have been the case if Pyrrhus had clearly demonstrated that he intended to use the fleet to capture Lilybaeum, as the Greeks had insisted that he do prior to beginning the siege.

Plutarch states that when he had first arrived in Sicily he had treated the Greek cities as allies, winning hearts and minds 'by gracious intercourse with them, by trusting everybody, and by doing nobody any harm.' Now Pyrrhus showed the true nature of his kingship:

> Not dealing with the cities in an acceptable or gentle manner, but in a lordly way, angrily putting compulsion and penalties upon them – he ceased to be a popular leader and became a tyrant, and added to his name for severity a name for ingratitude and faithlessness.[32]

Dionysius supports Plutarch's accusations and adds some of his own. According to him, Pyrrhus stole the estates of Agathocles' relatives and friends and gave them to his own friends, he replaced the chief magistrates in the cities with his own officers and he arbitrarily interfered in the law courts and civil administration, deciding some cases himself and in others would refer them to his rapacious courtiers.[33]

Pyrrhus, aware that many of the Greeks were now hostile to him, introduced garrisons into the cities, using the excuse of the threat of the now-recovered Carthaginians. Pyrrhus had violated the Greek cities' freedoms in almost every possible manner, not even leaving them the facade of autonomy. Finally, he had committed the ultimate transgression of imposing garrisons upon them. Rather than rid themselves of their tyrants, the Greek cities had merely replaced them with another, even more demanding autocrat.

It is possible that Pyrrhus' harshness in dealing with the Greek cities was exacerbated by the death of his chief diplomat, Cineas. He is generally portrayed as the voice of moderation as opposed to the harsher counsel given by military men such as Milon. Cineas vanishes from the sources after going to Syracuse prior to Pyrrhus' arrival. The most likely explanation is that he died sometime during the campaign.

After abandoning the siege of Lilybaeum, Pyrrhus marched back to the eastern end of the island. Here the Mamertines of Messina had been extorting tribute from the neighbouring Greek cities. Pyrrhus seized the Mamertines' tax-collectors and put them to death. He then defeated the Mamertines in battle, despite their reputation for being 'numerous and warlike' and destroyed many of their strongholds.[34] By this victory Pyrrhus briefly restored some of his lost reputation.

For a while, the Greeks put up with Pyrrhus' demands, no doubt intimidated by his garrisons and his military prowess. Eventually, however, the Greek rulers that had originally called for Pyrrhus' aid, Thoenon and Sosistratus, fell out with him. Pyrrhus began to suspect that they were plotting against him, despite the fact that they had loyally provided him with aid and assisted him in his campaigns. Sosistratus wisely took fright and deserted but Thoeon was arrested and executed.

His death was only the beginning. Pyrrhus now embarked on a purge of all those Sicilian Greeks who he suspected of opposing him:

> He banished and put to death many who held office and many who had called him in to help in their disputes, partly because he was displeased with them, on account of remarks to the effect that he had become master of the state through their influence, and partly because he was suspicious of them and believed that just as they had come over to his side so they might go over to someone else.[35]

This appears to have been the final straw. The simmering unrest of the Greek cities exploded and they rose in open rebellion against him. Many allied with the Carthaginians. Some even sought protection from their former oppressors the Mamertines, such was their 'terrible hatred' towards the king. To the Sicilian Greeks, Pyrrhus' title as king of Sicily must now have seemed like a bitter imposition rather than an appellation of honour.

The Greek revolt against Pyrrhus appears to have revived the fortunes of the Carthaginians. They were reinforced from Africa and, according to Zonaras, they 'took up the war vigorously'. They harboured the Syracusans who were exiled and harassed him so severely that he abandoned not only Syracuse but Sicily as well.'[36] Pyrrhus fought and won a battle against the advancing Carthaginians, but it appears to have been yet another 'Cadmean victory' as 'though he had the advantage, yet, as he quitted Sicily, he seemed to flee as one defeated; and his allies, in consequence, revolted from him, and he lost his dominion in Sicily as speedily and easily as he had obtained it.'[37]

At this point, with the island in revolt against him and the Carthaginians on the offensive, Pyrrhus received letters from the Samnites and Tarentines. Since his departure from Italy they had been steadily losing territory to the ever-advancing Romans. They were struggling to maintain the war and begged for his assistance. This gave him a face-saving pretext for deserting Sicily. As Plutarch says, 'without its being called a flight or despair – but in truth it was because he could not master Sicily.'[38]

Pyrrhus had failed in Sicily for many of the same reasons that the earlier tyrants had. The individual Greek cities clung ferociously to their concepts of 'freedom' and 'autonomy'. In dire emergencies they might ally together, and even surrender some of their autonomy to a war leader. But once the immediate threat had passed they would revert to type, chafing under the demands and restrictions imposed upon them. Pyrrhus' autocratic manner and insatiable desire for conquest and glory would not have helped. The Greek cities, most likely, saw themselves being forced to fund and participate in an unending series of wars of conquest, beginning with an invasion of Africa. Pyrrhus' initial campaign had removed the immediate Carthaginian threat. His failure at Lilybaeum had, however, shown him incapable, or unwilling, to meet their demands to drive the Carthaginians completely from their island. The Greek cities now reverted to type. They turned on their failed liberator, and settled for making the best deal they could for themselves in the new political reality.

Pyrrhus' campaign in Sicily had lasted from 278 until 276, but had in the end achieved nothing. His hopes of a Sicilian and African empire were dashed. His Italian allies were resentful and had lost ground to the Romans. Plutarch claims that as he sailed away from Sicily he supposedly said, 'my friends, what a wrestling ground for Carthaginians and Romans we are leaving behind us!'[39] This quote is almost certainly apocryphal, as the next year would show Pyrrhus had not yet abandoned his hopes of defeating the Romans and creating an Italian empire.

Chapter VIII

Beneventum

'This gave the victory to the Romans, and at the same time the advantage also in the struggle for supremacy. For having acquired high courage and power and a reputation for invincibility from their valour in these struggles, they at once got control of Italy, and soon afterwards of Sicily.' - Plutarch, *Pyrrhus*, 25.

After Pyrrhus' departure to Sicily, his Italian allies had come under constant pressure from the Romans. The Roman offensive began as soon as Pyrrhus had departed for Sicily. The new consul, Fabricius, is recorded as campaigning successfully against the Lucanians, Bruttians, Tarentines and Samnites. His victories were of such an extent as to have earned him a triumph.

A triumph was a solemn procession in which the victorious general in a chariot, his troops and the captives and spoils of war paraded through Rome. At its finale the white bulls were sacrificed at the temple of Jupiter. Such awards were not lightly given and had to be voted on by the Senate. A number of prerequisites had to be met. These included that at least 5,000 of the enemy should have been slain in a single battle and that the Roman losses should have been small compared with that of their adversaries, and that war should have been brought to a victorious conclusion, with the enemy reduced to a state of peace that would allow the troops to be withdrawn in order to march in the triumph.

During the later Republic ambitious politicians would deliberately provoke wars, usually with weak enemies in order to gain a triumph and enhance their *gloria*. They hoped that their friends in the Senate would vote them a triumph, overlooking the prerequisites. Such an example was Cicero, who tried to claim a triumph after defeating some bandits in his province of Cilicia. He was, quite rightly, albeit generously, granted a lesser award, a *supplicatio*. During the more austere days of the earlier Republic the system does not appear to have been abused as it was later. The granting of a triumph to Fabricius would indicate that his campaigns had been successful.

The following year, 277, the consul Junius was also voted a triumph for a victory over the Lucanians and Bruttians. Zonaras gives us a narrative of events in Italy during this year. He claims that:

> The Romans on learning of his absence recovered courage and turned their attention to punishing those who had summoned him. Postponing till another time the case of the Tarentines, they invaded Samnium with their consuls, Rufinus and Junius, devastated the country as they went along.[1]

With both consuls present this must have been a large force, at least 40,000 men. The Samnites withdrew before the Roman advance, taking their families and valuables into the mountains for safe keeping. The overconfident Romans pursued them into the mountains. The territory they advanced into was difficult country – hilly and overgrown, perfect for the tactics of the Samnites. They ambushed the Roman army, inflicting heavy casualties and taking many prisoners.

The two consuls blamed each other for the defeat and split their forces. Junius continued to ravage the territory of the Samnites – so casualties may not have been as heavy as Zonaras claims – or more likely only a portion of the army had been defeated. Rufinus attacked the territories of the Lucanians and Bruttians. He then advanced on the city of Croton, which had revolted from Rome. The rebels had invited in a garrison from Milon, Pyrrhus' governor in Tarentum. Ignorant of the Epirot force, Rufinus approached the city without proper precautions. The Epirots made a sortie and drove the Romans back.

Rufinus now devised a stratagem by which to capture the city. He sent two agents into the town who pretended to be deserters and claimed that the Romans were marching against Locris, as the city had been betrayed to them. Given the fickle nature of the Locrians this would have been easily believed. Rufinus broke his camp and pretended to march towards Locris. The Epirot commander, Nicomachus, fell for the ruse and attempted to reach Locris before the Romans. Rufinus, meanwhile, turned back on Croton. He attacked the unprepared city from out of the mist and succeeded in capturing it. Nicomachus, when he learned of the attack on Croton, returned to the city but was unable to recapture it. He then had to fight his way back to Tarentum, harassed by the Romans along the way.

The Locrians were always ready to change with circumstances. Confronted by the army of a Roman consul, they rose up against their Epirot garrison, killed them and surrendered the city to the Romans. The Romans went on to capture the nearby city of Caulonia, which was pillaged by their Campanian allies.

Again, in 276, one of the consuls was granted a triumph for a victory over the Samnites, Lucanians and Bruttians. Livy's lost book 13 is supposed to have contained an account of successful wars against the Lucanians, Bruttians, Samnites, and Etruscans during these years. It would appear that, following Pyrrhus' withdrawal from Italy, the Romans had enjoyed three years of successful campaigning against their Italian and Greek enemies. With these successes the Romans had come to dominate most of Italy. Only a few of the Greek cities, those that were still garrisoned by Pyrrhus' troops, continued to hold out against them.

The exact route of Pyrrhus' return to Italy is unknown. Appian says he sailed straight to Rhegium but Diodorus claims that he landed at Locris. It is unlikely that he landed at either, as both were held by hostile garrisons. Zonaras records that Pyrrhus captured Locris before returning to besiege Rhegium.[2] The most likely explanation is that Pyrrhus landed somewhere along the coast between Locris and Rhegium. Here he disembarked his army and marched on Locris, in order to recapture the city and punish those who had put to death his garrison and their commanding officer. The Locrians, showing their usual flexibility, rose up, killed their Roman garrison and surrendered the city to Pyrrhus.

With Locris now secured as a base, Pyrrhus then marched on Rhegium. He had returned to Italy in a fleet of 110 warships and an even greater number of merchant vessels. This may have been the fleet Pyrrhus had ordered the Sicilians to build and crew, but was more likely the remnants of his earlier fleet. Supposedly the fleet was weighed down by the wealth he had exacted as tribute from the Sicilians. A Carthaginian fleet of either 120 or 130 vessels was waiting for him in the straits between Messina and Rhegium. The Carthaginians attacked and decisively defeated Pyrrhus' fleet, sinking seventy ships, and disabling all the rest except twelve.[3] With most of his fleet lost, Pyrrhus was forced to give up any attempt to capture Rhegium.

During his retreat to Locris he came under further attack. Prior to his landing in Italy, the Mamertines had sent a force of more than 10,000 men across into Italy,[4] probably to assist their fellow Italian occupiers of Rhegium. This force was not sufficient to match him in open battle. Instead, they ambushed him on the march as he passed through difficult terrain. They inflicted heavy losses on his rearguard and killed two elephants. Pyrrhus was forced to intervene in person, after riding back from his position at the head of the army. Leading the attack, he was compelled to fight at the head of his troops in order to inspire his men against the triumphant Mamertines. One of the enemy wounded him on the head with a sword stroke and he was forced to withdraw from the combat.

The Mamertines were now even more inspired. One of them, reputed to be a giant of a man and well armoured, advanced out from his lines and in a bold voice challenged Pyrrhus to come out and meet him, if he were still alive. Pyrrhus was enraged by the audacity of the challenge and, despite the opposition of his bodyguards, pushed his way through them to confront his challenger. According to Plutarch he was a terrifying figure, 'full of wrath, smeared with blood, and with a countenance terrible to look upon.' Before the Mamertine champion could even strike a blow, Pyrrhus dealt him an enormous sword cut to the top his head. So strong was the blow and so excellent the steel of his blade that it reputedly 'cleaved its way down through, so that at one instant the parts of the sundered body fell to either side.'[5] An impossible stroke, but one that has often been attributed to heroes throughout history. The defeat of their champion supposedly overawed the Mamertines and caused them to believe that Pyrrhus was some sort of divine being.

Pyrrhus was now able to march back to Locris unmolested. He had not, however, forgotten the Locrians' previous betrayal. His defeat at the hands of the Carthaginians and his harassment by the Mamertines had put him in an unforgiving mood. He executed the leaders of the pro-Roman faction and fined many more. Nor, as it shall be seen, had he finished with Locrians.

After dealing with Locris, Pyrrhus was able to march unmolested to Tarentum. At this point his forces numbered 20,000 foot and 3,000 horse.[6] This was a force considerably more than the 8,000 or so that he had taken to Sicily. The additional troops were, most likely, Sicilian Greek mercenaries. Pyrrhus then reinforced his army with the pick of the Tarentine troops. More of a problem for Pyrrhus was money. His Italian allies had been drained by five years of almost constant warfare and were unwilling to provide enough contributions to maintain his forces. The loss of his fleet had, moreover, left him short of cash. Much of his Sicilian plunder must have been lost in his defeat by the Carthaginians. Pyrrhus, therefore, sought about for ways to raise further money and troops.

Back in Macedonia, Antigonus Gonatas, the son of Demetrius, had taken advantage of the confusion after the death of Ptolemy Ceraunus. He had marched into Macedonia, defeated the Galatians and seized the throne. His hold on the kingship, however, could not yet have been secure. Pyrrhus decided to take advantage of this and attempt to blackmail him into sending support. He sent ambassadors to Antigonus threatening that, 'unless he sent him some, he should be obliged to return to his kingdom, and to seek that enlargement of his dominions from him, which he had wished to gain from the Romans.'[7] This was a long-shot that did not succeed. Antigonus, with Pyrrhus far away, simply ignored the threat.

A group of Pyrrhus' advisors came up with an easier scheme. With their king short of funds:

> The worst and most depraved of his friends, Euegorus, the son of Theodorus, Balacrus, the son of Nicander, and Deinarchus, the son of Nicias, followers of godless and accursed doctrines, suggested an impious source for the raising of funds, namely, to open up the sacred treasures of Persephone.[8]

This temple was located in Locris. It reputedly held great wealth, including large amounts of gold buried for safekeeping. It could not have taken much persuading for Pyrrhus to agree to the idea, as 'his necessity was stronger than any scruples.'[9] Such exactions were not unique among the Greeks. The temple had already been plundered previously by the tyrant Dionysius. Such sacrilege was, nonetheless, generally abhorred. When the Phocians had plundered the treasures of Delphi seventy years earlier, their enemies had used it as pretext for war and a justification to mete out terrible vengeance. The walls of their cities were torn down, a tribute was imposed, their leaders were condemned *in absentia* and a curse placed upon them. All those placed under the curse soon died horribly: by fire, murder, death in battle, falling over a cliff and of a lingering disease.

Bad luck dogged the sacrilegious expedition. After the ships carrying the treasure had left Locris, the wind changed direction. Some were sunk and others driven back onto the Locrian shore. The crews perished and the money was cast upon the shore. This was naturally seen by the Greeks as justified retribution by the goddess. Pyrrhus was terrified that he too might become the victim of divine justice. He returned all the recoverable wealth to the temple and executed those who had given the advice and had been delegated to carry it out. The ancient historians attributed Pyrrhus' final defeat in Italy to this sacrilege, claiming that it, 'ruined the cause of Pyrrhus, but rather the wrath of the goddess whose sanctity had been violated, a wrath of which not even Pyrrhus himself was unaware, as Proxenus the historian relates and as Pyrrhus himself records in his own memoirs.'[10]

The news of Pyrrhus' return had caused consternation in Rome. The previous year had been an inauspicious one. A series of plagues had struck Rome. One targeted pregnant women in particular. Another almost wiped out the Roman cattle herds. The same year the statue of Jupiter on the Capitol Hill had been struck by lightning and the head sheared off. This was seen as an omen of defeat by many. The constant warfare and the plague had caused many deaths. Livy's census figures for the years 279 and 271 show that the number of citizens had fallen by 16,000.[11] Despite their victories over the past three years the Romans appear to have been almost as war weary as their Italian enemies. The thought of another war against the previously-victorious Pyrrhus was too much for many. When the consuls tried to raise two new consular armies for 275, many of those conscripted refused to enlist. The senate was forced to take harsh measures. The draft dodgers were threatened with having all their property confiscated and themselves being sold into slavery. Such was the low state of morale that even this threat was insufficient to compel enlistment. It was not until the penalty was actually enforced on one unlucky individual that the remainder conceded and joined the colours.

While Pyrrhus had been campaigning in the south of Italy, the two new Roman consuls had also been active. Manius Curius Dentatus had led an army into Samnia, while his colleague Cornelius had invaded Lucania. His Italian allies, once again under Roman attack, now called on Pyrrhus for assistance. He advanced north from Tarentum with the force he had brought back from Sicily, plus the troops he had raised from Tarentum, perhaps 40,000 men. Pyrrhus would have been expecting to receive reinforcements from his Italian allies, but the Samnites were no longer keen to fight. They had suffered severely from Roman attacks during Pyrrhus' absence and deeply resented him because of this. Few came forward to join his army. After three years of constant defeats by the Romans they were exhausted. Plutarch claims that 'the power of the Samnites had been shattered, and their spirits were broken, in consequence of many defeats at the hands of the Romans.'[12]

Pyrrhus' rapid advance into central Italy appears to have caught the Roman consuls off guard, and they had not yet united their forces. Learning that the Roman armies were still operating separately, Pyrrhus decided to defeat them in detail. He split his army, sending a detachment to Lucania. These were to unite with any Lucanian forces they could find and prevent Cornelius from marching to unite with Curius. Pyrrhus then confronted Curius at Maleventum (Benevento) in Samnia. The consul's army was most likely the usual two legions, about 10,000 men, plus an equal or larger contingent of allies, possibly 20-25,000 men in total. Pyrrhus would have received some limited reinforcements from Samnites, but had detached part of his army to Lucania. Orosius claims his army totaled 86,000 men. Dionysius says it outnumbered the Romans by three to one, perhaps 60-70,000 in total.[13] Both are certainly exaggerations. Dionysius' lower figure, however, may be close to the truth if it also includes the detached force in Lucania. Pyrrhus' army at Maleventum, therefore, would have totalled somewhere between 30,000 and 50,000 men, with 40,000 being a likely figure.

This would have given Pyrrhus a substantial numerical advantage over Curius, and he hastened to take advantage of it before Cornelius could arrive. Curius was a skilled and experienced opponent, who had already been awarded three triumphs. He encamped in a strong position on a hill and awaited reinforcements. Curius wisely refused battle, claiming, either honestly or artfully, that the omens were unfavourable.

Pyrrhus, short of funds, needed a quick and decisive victory before the Roman armies could unite. He therefore devised a desperate plan. Pyrrhus decided to split his army, leading a specially selected force of strike troops around the Roman camp by a night march. This force would then launch a surprise attack on the Roman camp from an unexpected direction and under the cover of darkness. Meanwhile, the main army would divert the Roman's attention by supporting the attack from the front. This plan was, however, dangerous for two reasons. Splitting one's army in the face of the enemy risked having each section defeated separately.

To add to the danger, night attacks were always dangerous. Troops could easily get lost, or even attack their own side in the dark. Thucydides claims that the Athenian attack on the Syracusan counter-wall in 413 was the only night engagement during the entire thirty years of the war. As such it caught the Syracusans totally by surprise and resulted in early Athenian successes. Nonetheless, despite the fact it was a well moonlit night the Athenians soon:

> Fell into great disorder ... taking all in front of them to be enemies ... and ended by coming into collision with each other in many parts of the field, friend with friend ... actually fighting hand to hand, and could only be parted with difficulty.[14]

Pyrrhus' attack was a daring but extremely perilous tactic.

Supposedly, prior to launching his attack, Pyrrhus was subjected to nightmares where most of his teeth fell out and he bled from the mouth. He was disturbed by these visions and feared that a disaster would occur. On a previous occasion, when Pyrrhus had a similar dream, a misfortune had followed. Taking his dream as a bad omen, he wished to delay the battle, but was persuaded by his advisors not to let the current favourable opportunity slip from his grasp.

Pyrrhus, leading the pick of his men and best-trained elephants, set out on the march around the Roman camp. The route of the march followed a long circuit through densely-wooded country, 'by long trails that were not even used by people but were mere goat-paths through woods and crags.'[15] The length of the march and the hostile terrain caused unexpected interruptions, and the troops' lights went out. As a result they lost their way and straggled. This inevitably caused delay and the vanguard of the assault force did not arrive until after daybreak, in full view of the enemy camp. Their appearance still startled the Romans, but the element of surprise had been lost. Curius, with the omens suddenly propitious, was able to lead out a force and make an immediate attack. The Romans caught Pyrrhus' force while it was still strung out and exhausted from marching all night. Curius' attack routed the Epirots and captured a number of the elephants. Pyrrhus, with a few cavalry, was able to escape the disaster and rejoin the main force.

Curius, now confident from his success, led his army down from its camp on the hill and formed up, offering battle. The two armies now faced each other on the open plain before the Roman camp, although if Frontinus is to be believed the fight took place 'in confined quarters, where the phalanx, being massed together, would embarrass itself.'[16] Curius, most likely, had selected a narrow battle front where his flanks would be protected. The Romans attacked and drove back parts of Pyrrhus' line. Once again, however, Pyrrhus was able to turn the situation around with the use of his elephant reserve. They routed part of the Roman line and drove the refugees back to their camp.

The Roman camp was, however, well guarded with fresh troops. From their parapets they were able pelt the elephants with showers of javelins. One of the younger animals was wounded and wandered about in search of its mother. Its cries of distress panicked the other elephants. They stampeded back through their own lines, scattering them in confusion. This was the main danger of fielding elephants: when panicked they could be a greater danger to their own side than to the enemy. The rout of the elephants proved decisive. The Romans counter-attacked and drove the disorganized Epirot army from the field.

Although writing about the Battle of Panormus, twenty five years later, Polybius' description of such an action could equally apply to that of Pyrrhus' attack on the Roman camp.

> When the elephants charged the trench and began to be wounded by those who were shooting from the wall, while at the same time a rapid shower of javelins and spears fell on them from the fresh troops drawn up before the trench, they very soon, finding themselves hit and hurt in many places, were thrown into confusion and turned on their own troops trampling down and killing the men and disturbing and breaking the ranks.

On seeing this, the Roman commander 'made a vigorous sally and – caused a severe rout among them, killing many and compelling the rest to quit the field in headlong flight.'[17]

There are, however, different versions of the rout of the elephants at Maleventum. Aelian claims the Romans used the stratagem of coating pigs with tar, setting them on fire and releasing them in the direction of the elephants. Their dying squeals apparently panic elephants. Another source claims that the Romans had used flaming missiles, as they had at Asculum.[18] Whatever the reason, it is clear that it was the rout of the elephants that was the decisive moment of the battle.

The historians writing during the time of the Roman Empire are united in claiming that the battle was an overwhelming Roman victory. Dionysius alleges that the Romans killed two elephants, captured eight and 'wrought great slaughter among the soldiers.' Zonaras asserts that they captured eight elephants, occupied the enemy's camp, and that Pyrrhus escaped with only a few cavalry. Eutropius claims that they took Pyrrhus' camp, killed 23,000 of the enemy and that Curius displayed four captured elephants at his triumph. Orosius records 33,000 Epirot dead.[19] All are agreed that this victory led directly to Pyrrhus quitting Italy.

These are, nevertheless, all pro-Roman and not totally reliable sources. Against this prevailing view is Polybius' statement, that none of the battles between Pyrrhus and the Romans had ended with a decisive victory to either. Justin claims that the Romans had never defeated Pyrrhus in battle.[20] Polybius' more sober assessment is perhaps the closest to the truth. The most likely result of the battle is a Roman victory, but not as decisive as the later Roman propagandists would like to portray. Nor did the defeat lead immediately to Pyrrhus abandoning Italy. On this occasion it appears that the battle may have been a 'Cadmean victory' for the Romans. The Romans certainly claimed a victory, as they renamed the city Beneventum, meaning 'good result', as opposed to its original name, which meant 'evil result'.

Whatever the tactical result of the battle, it was, once again, clearly a strategic victory for the Romans. Curius' victory was matched by that of his fellow consul Cornelius, who had defeated the Lucanians. Both were granted triumphs for the year 275. Pyrrhus had suffered heavy losses, particularly among his best troops and his elephants. His allies had suffered further setbacks and he was still short of money. Pyrrhus sent out further requests to his fellow kings, Antigonus, Antiochus and Ptolemy Philadelphus but no aid was forthcoming. According to both Polyaenus and Justin, Pyrrhus concealed their replies from his Italian allies.[21] With no army and no funds, Pyrrhus decided that his only course of action was to return to Epirus and try to resurrect his fortunes there.

Despite the claims of the later Roman historians, Pyrrhus did not, however, appear to have totally relinquished his hopes for a western empire. He left a strong garrison in Tarentum under his son Helenus and his commander Milon, 'inasmuch as he expected to come back again.' Some time in the autumn of 275, or spring of 274, Pyrrhus embarked 8,000 infantry and 500 cavalry, less than half the force he had brought, and returned to Epirus. According to Plutarch, he left 'after squandering six years time in his wars there, and after being worsted in his undertakings – but he kept his brave spirit unconquered in the midst of his defeats.'[22] In keeping with the true spirit of his nature, and of the age, Pyrrhus now looked about for another war by which he could resurrect his fortunes.

The Romans spent the next three years in finally subduing the Samnites. Once this was completed, in 272, Roman consul Papirius marched on Tarentum. The Tarentines, after they learnt of Pyrrhus' death in Argos that same year, rose up against his garrison and its commander Milon. They called for support from the Carthaginians, who sent a fleet. Milon, besieged by the Romans from the land and the Carthaginians from the sea, surrendered the city to the Romans on the condition that he and his troops were allowed to depart unharmed and with all their possessions intact. The Carthaginians, still being allies of the Romans, sailed away. Papirius then forced the Tarentines to surrender their arms and ships, demolish their walls and to pay tribute to the Romans. Thirty thousand of the Greek inhabitants were sold as slaves and the city was pillaged of its artwork, which was carried off to Rome.

Two years later, the Romans turned their attention towards their rebel garrison in Rhegium and captured the city after a siege. They returned the city to its surviving inhabitants. The 4,500 survivors of the rebel garrison were taken to Rome and brutally executed in batches of 300. Due to the nature of their treason they were not even allowed proper burial but 'were dragged out of the Forum into an open space before the city, where they were torn asunder by birds and dogs.'[23] Five years after Pyrrhus' withdrawal, the Romans had successfully completed their conquest of the Greek cites of southern Italy.

Chapter IX

Greece

'Pyrrhus was away entertaining one hope after another, and since he made one success but the starting point for a new one, while he was determined to make good each disaster by a fresh undertaking, he suffered neither defeat nor victory to put a limit to his troubling himself and troubling others.'
- Plutarch, *Pyrrhus*, 30.

Pyrrhus returned to an Epirus that appears to have avoided the destruction that had engulfed Macedonia and much of Greece, following the Galatian invasion. There is a hint in Appian that there had been some unrest amongst the Epirots during his absence.[1] This may account for his son and regent, Ptolemy, being unable to supply him with reinforcements of money and men. Despite returning with less than half the army he had taken to Italy six years ago, Pyrrhus was, nonetheless, full of his usual burning ambition. Unfortunately, for the realization of his ambitions, he was, as he had been on his return to Italy, extremely short of money. The first problem was easily solved. He was able to reinforce his army with the garrison he had left behind and by recruiting a large number of Galatian mercenaries. The second problem was, as it had been in Italy, more difficult to resolve.

The major dilemma for Pyrrhus was, as has already been discussed, that the two problems were inexorably interlinked. In order for Pyrrhus to defend and, more importantly to him, increase his domains, armed forces were necessary. These had to be paid for. The most obvious way for a general to raise money was to invade enemy territory and ransack it. The obvious target was the Macedonian territory of his rival king, Antigonus Gonatas.

In 278 Antigonus had won a great victory against one of the three Galatian bands that had been ravaging Greece and Macedonia. At Lysimacheia, on the shores of the Chersonese, he had induced the Celts into attacking his abandoned camp. Once they were laden with plunder he trapped their army, reputedly 18,000 strong, between his fleet and army, and won a bloody victory[2].

This feat brought Antigonus the prestige he needed in order to recapture his father's kingdom of Macedonia. The country was in anarchy, the so called 'Dog-days', with the last effective commander, Sosthenes, dead. Pretenders were, however, still numerous. Antigonus could not rely on the capricious Macedonian army, which had previously betrayed his father. He therefore took the dangerous step of enlisting a number of Galatian mercenaries. They had the advantages of not only being courageous but cheap. A band of them enrolled for the sum of twenty-four drachmai each for an entire campaign, whereas a Greek mercenary would have asked for double this sum for a month.[3] Over the next two years Antigonus had eliminated his rivals. In 276 he invaded and recovered Thessaly.

Antigonus' position was, however, not yet secure. His campaigning had been done by mercenary forces and these had to be paid. His exactations on his various 'allies' in Greece had made him unpopular there and, most likely, also in Macedonia. The kingdom was still divided into factions, including, no doubt, one still sympathetic to Pyrrhus.

Plutarch claims that Pyrrhus' motive was simply that 'since he had no money he sought for a war by which he could maintain his army.'[4] Pausanias states that Pyrrhus attacked Antigonus for a number of reasons, but that the main one was his refusal to send aid to him in Italy.[5] Pyrrhus had already threatened to take retribution over this matter. Here Plutarch is probably correct, and Pyrrhus simply created a number of pretexts to justify his raid into Antigonus' territory.

In addition to the motives of raising money and punishing Antigonus, Pyrrhus did have a prior claim to the Macedonian throne, having ruled half of the country from 288 to 284. Plutarch, however, explicitly states that his initial concern was to acquire money, and only after he had had initial success did he then attack Antigonus. This follows a similar pattern to Pyrrhus' invasion of Demetrius' Macedonia in 289. The plundering of territory, however, was generally seen as relinquishing one's claims to the area. Commenting on Demetrius' plundering of Babylonia, Plutarch asserts that 'his action only left Seleucus more firmly established in possession of his kingdom than before, for by ravaging the country he appeared to admit that it no longer belonged to him and his father.'[6] Pyrrhus' destruction of the Macedonian countryside will not have helped any claim he had to the throne. These actions demonstrate just how desperate his shortage of funds must have been.

Justin states that on returning to Epirus, Pyrrhus immediately invaded Macedonia. Pausanias claims that he first rested his army. Both could be correct if Pyrrhus had departed Italy at the end of autumn 275 rather than the spring of 274. He could have rested his veterans from Italy over the winter of 275/4, then embarked on his campaign as soon as the weather allowed in the spring of 274.[7]

Pyrrhus' campaign met with considerable success. He captured a number of towns and as a result 2,000 Macedonian soldiers came over to him. Made confident by his victories, Pyrrhus now decided to march against Antigonus and challenge him for the right to rule over the Macedonians. Antigonus, seeing that Pyrrhus' campaign was now a direct challenge, rather than a nuisance, decided to march west and block the passes into Macedonia. The ensuing battle took place in a narrow defile, probably in one of the gorges of the River Aous. Pyrrhus' army had the best of the initial fighting and drove the Macedonians back in confusion. This, and the earlier desertion, suggests that morale among the Macedonian troops was not high. Antigonus' Galatian mercenaries formed a rearguard that attempted to hold back Pyrrhus' advance. The Celts fought with their usual courage, making 'a sturdy resistance, but after a fierce battle most of them were cut to pieces.'[8] The Macedonian retreat had left their elephants isolated. Their handlers surrendered themselves and their animals to the Epirots.

The rearguard fight of the Galatians had allowed the Macedonian phalanx to reform. Again the low morale of the Macedonians was evident. They were 'filled with confusion and fear because of their previous defeat.'[9] Seeing the hesitation in the Macedonian phalanx, Pyrrhus decided on a bold course of action. He raised his right arm to them and called on their officers to surrender to him. As they had on a number of earlier occasions, the fickle Macedonian phalanx deserted *en masse*. His fellow countrywoman Olympias had succeeded with the same appeal forty years earlier. Antigonus and a few of his cavalry fled the field to the city of Thessalonica.

Pyrrhus was exulted by his victory. He believed that his destruction of the Galatians added enormously to his glory and reputation. He therefore dedicated the most splendid of his spoils to a temple of Athena in Thessaly with the inscription, 'Pyrrhus the Molossian hangs long shields to Athena Itonis taken from the Galatians, and the hosts of Antigonus say that the Aecidae are soldiers.' He also remembered to celebrate his victory over the Macedonians at home in Epirus. At the sanctuary of Zeus at Dodona he hung circular, Macedonian shields, inscribed, 'this metal destroyed Asia rich in gold, this metal made slaves of the Greeks, this metal is lying fatherless by the pillars of Zeus of water streams, the spoil of proud-voiced Macedonia.'[10] In making these two separate offerings Pyrrhus was playing to his different audiences. The Epirots would be impressed by a victory over their long-time enemies the Macedonians. They, in turn, would be impressed by a massacre of their recent oppressors the Celts. Even more to the point, a victory over the Galatians would emulate the deed of his rival Antigonus.

Perhaps the most remarkable result of the battle was the capitulation of the Macedonian infantry to Pyrrhus. This most likely was the result of a combination of factors. The lasting popularity of Pyrrhus' previous rule and his reputation as a general would have greatly impressed the Macedonian infantry. This would have been compared to the unpopularity of Antigonus' father Demetrius, who had been driven out by his own subjects. Although Antigonus would reveal himself to be of a completely different character to his father – stoic and conservative as opposed to flashy and grandiose – he had been on the throne for less than four years, giving little opportunity to demonstrate his qualities and to build his own power base.

Pyrrhus followed up his victory by overrunning all of Thessaly and most of Macedonia. Antigonus managed to hang on to some of the coastal cities. He had inherited a strong fleet from his father, and taking these cities from him without a comparable navy would be extremely difficult. Yet again though, Pyrrhus had failed to follow up a victory on the battle field by finishing off his opponent and consolidating his gains.

Antigonus then waited and watched for a chance to reclaim his throne. At some stage he raised an army, mostly of Galatian mercenaries, and attempted to resurrect his fortunes with a sortie into Macedonia. Ptolemy, son of Pyrrhus, inflicted another defeat on him, forcing him to flee back to his coastal enclaves. According to Plutarch, Pyrrhus, incensed at Antigonus' continued resistance, but unable to do anything about it due to Antigonus' naval superiority, 'railed at Antigonus and called him a shameless man for not laying aside the purple and wearing a common robe.'[11] True to his nature, the philosophical Antigonus ignored this impotent ranting.

The important city of Aegae, the centre of the tombs of the Macedonian kings, also held out against Pyrrhus. He eventually took it and chose to punish the inhabitants for their opposition. Among other measures he left a garrison of Galatians within the city. The Celts had a reputation for rapaciousness. As soon as they had control of the city they began to dig up the royal tombs, steal the treasure and, more outrageously, scatter the bones. The Macedonians unsurprisingly complained to their new king, Pyrrhus. He ignored their petitions, treating them with indifference. Pyrrhus was still busy with his campaign of conquest and the Galatians had proved to be an invaluable part of his army. He may also have remembered the desecration of the Epirot tombs by Lysimachus and been in a less than sympathetic mood. This lack of concern did not endear Pyrrhus to his new subjects.

Frustrated by Antigonus' continued existence, Pyrrhus, true to his nature, again began to look around for new schemes to expand his power, before his control of Macedonia was securely and firmly established. As Justin puts it, Pyrrhus 'not content with what had once been the object of his wishes, began to contemplate the subjugation of Greece and Asia. He had no greater delight in ruling than in warfare.'[12] In the endless, fratricidal politics of the Greek cities such an opportunity was not slow in coming. At some stage between his conquest of Macedonia and the commencement of his new campaign, Pyrrhus recalled his son Helenus and part of his garrison from Tarentum. His commander Milon was left to maintain his interests. With his success in Macedonia and the opportunities it had opened, Pyrrhus' ambitions in Italy were now firmly placed in the background.

Cleonymus, the same member of the Spartan royal family who had earlier campaigned in Italy, soon came to him with an offer. The Spartans had chosen his nephew Areus as king, over the claims of Cleonymus, due to his violent and irrational behaviour. His dissolute character had been amply demonstrated during that time.

The disappointment of being overlooked for the throne by the Spartans had festered within Cleonymus for years. The situation came to a head over marital intrigues. In his later life Cleonymus had married a beautiful young woman, Chilonis, a member of the other Spartan royal family. The marriage was certainly a political one, made by him to increase his prestige and acquire influential allies. Chilonis, however, was disappointed by her marriage to a much older husband, and she fell desperately in love with a younger man, Acrotatus. To make matters worse for Cleonymus, Acrotatus was the son of King Areus, the cause of his resentment. It also did not help Cleonymus' cause that the affair was common gossip within Sparta.

Cleonymus appears to have already joined Pyrrhus' court. He is reported to have led a successful assault during Pyrrhus' siege of Aegae. Cleonymus now approached Pyrrhus with a scheme to overthrow Areus and place himself on the throne, while the king was away from Sparta and campaigning on Crete. Pyrrhus was of course immediately interested. The chance of placing his own puppet king on one of the Spartan thrones was too good to be ignored. Control of Sparta would also give him a strong base for the conquest of Antigonus' remaining strongholds in the south of Greece.

Pyrrhus invaded the Peloponnesus with an army of 25,000 infantry, 2,000 cavalry and 24 elephants.[13] The majority of the army would have consisted of Epirots and Macedonians, supplemented by Thessalian cavalry and Galatian mercenaries. Along the way Pyrrhus was approached by embassies from the Athenians, Achaeans, and Messenians. They were all hoping that Pyrrhus would overthrow Antigonus' garrisons and break his power in southern Greece. Antigonus' rule was not popular. Like his father before him, he had abandoned his grandfather's policy of 'freedom for the Greeks'. Antigonus the One-eyed had followed a policy of supporting democratic governments and of not imposing garrisons on the Greek cities. His grandson ruled by imposing garrisons at strategic points, the most important being Corinth. Most of the cities 'had tyrants imposed on them by the latter, who planted more monarchs in Greece than any other king.'[14]

With the Isthmus of Corinth, the land gateway to the Peloponnesus, held by Antigonus' garrison, Pyrrhus probably crossed the Gulf of Corinth by sea. The Spartan ambassadors met Pyrrhus at the Messenian city of Megalopolis. He artfully assured them that he had come into the Peloponnesus only to attack Antigonus' forces and to liberate the Greek cities from his rule. He also claimed that he wished to send his younger sons to Sparta, if allowed, so that they might get a Spartan, military education. Surprisingly, the Spartans are said to have believed him.

Pyrrhus then betrayed the Spartans and marched on their city. Rather than take the direct road from Megalopolis down the Eurotas valley he appears to have taken a more indirect route in order to surprise the Spartans. The most likely path would have been to march south, through the friendly territory of Messenia. By keeping to the west of the Taiyetos Mountains this route would have concealed his movement from the Spartans. Pyrrhus would have then crossed the mountains via the passes to the east of Messene and arrived in Sparta to the south of the city. Evidence for this proposed course is the existence of two sites in Sparta where Pyrrhus is recorded to have built camps - one to the south of the city and one to the north. As Pyrrhus would later retire north to Argos, it is probable that his original assault on the city came from the south. It was here that Pyrrhus built his camp, no more than three kilometres from the city.[15]

Pyrrhus had outmanoeuvred the Spartans and achieved complete surprise. Immediately on reaching the Spartan lands he began to ravage and plunder the countryside. The Spartans sent envoys to complain about this breach of faith, and an attack without a declaration of war. Pyrrhus simply replied that, 'when you Spartans have decided on a war, it is your habit not to inform your enemy of it. Therefore do not complain of unfair treatment, if I have used a Spartan stratagem against the Spartans.'[16] One of the Spartan ambassadors retorted that 'if you are indeed a god, we shall suffer no harm at your hands, for we have done you no wrong, but if you are a man, another will be found who is even stronger than you.'[17]

The Spartans quickly raised an army and marched out to defend their lands. If Pausanias is to be believed they were also joined by allied contingents of Argives and Messenians.[18] The former is possible, as there were two factions within the city, one supporting Antigonus. The second would appear unlikely, as the Messenians were inveterate enemies of the Spartans and had already allowed Pyrrhus into their city. Perhaps the realities of his policies of domination had already alienated them. Sparta was, at this time, probably capable of fielding an army of about 15,000 men.[19] If they had received assistance from their allies the total strength of their army may have reached 25,000. Whatever their numbers the Greek troops proved no match for Pyrrhus' army. According to both Pausanias and Polyaenus a battle was fought outside of Sparta and 'Pyrrhus, king of

Epirus, defeated the Lacedaemonians in a bloody battle, and marched against their city.'[20] Unfortunately, no other details of the battle survive.

Pyrrhus quickly followed up his victory and marched directly on the city of Sparta. He arrived in the evening and found the town's defences unprepared. Their defeat had shaken the Spartans' confidence. The situation was not helped by their best commander, Areus, being away in Crete. So confident in his return were the supporters of Cleonymus that they had his slaves prepare a feast for the two kings. Panic seems to have overtaken the rest of the city. The Spartan council held an urgent meeting. They decided to send their woman and children away to safety in Crete. When their decision became known, the women vigorously opposed it. One, Archidamia by name, came with sword in hand to the council and rebuked them. She said that they had no wish to live on if Sparta had perished. Their resolve strengthened by the courage of their women, the council now began to take measures for the defence of the city.

The Spartans had always prided themselves on having no walls around their city. Their fourth century king, Agesilaus, had explained 'when somebody had asked why Sparta lacked fortification walls, he pointed to the citizens under arms and said, "these are the Spartans' walls".' Another time he stated that the only fortifications a city needed were the valour of its inhabitants.[21] The new balance of power in the Hellenistic period had, however, forced the Spartans to alter this policy. As early as Cassander's attack in 317, the Spartans 'distrusting their power in arms enclosed their city (which they had always defended, not with walls, but with their swords) with works of defence, in disregard – of the ancient glory of their forefathers.' Justin saw this as decision as a sign of degeneration, rather than the sensible policy that it was. The Spartans continued this policy during Demetrius' invasion of 294. Not only did they throw up temporary fortifications, they also built stone walls to cover the likeliest avenues of attack.[22]

The council ordered these defences to be repaired and strengthened. By attacking from the south Pyrrhus appears to have avoided the Spartan walls, as they are not recorded as playing any role in the coming battle. In response, the Spartan command decided to run a trench parallel to the Epirot camp and reinforce the ends with half-buried wagons. The latter was done in order to make it difficult for the elephants to cross. When the Spartan men began their task of digging the women came up and relieved them. They ordered the fighting men to rest for the following day's battle. The trench was reported to be about 270 metres long, slightly more than 2.5 metres wide and nearly 2 metres deep. In the emergency, the Spartans also called up those under the usual military age of eighteen along with the elderly.

Meanwhile, Pyrrhus held his own council of war. Cleonymus urged him to make the assault immediately, but Pyrrhus delayed. He claimed that if he attacked at night he would lose control of his troops and they would plunder the city unmercifully. Polybius claims that since the time of Alexander, kings

> down to Pyrrhus had – always been ready to give battle to each other in the open field and had done all in their power to overcome each other by force of arms, but they had spared cities, so that whoever conquered might be supreme in them and be honoured by his subjects.[23]

Pyrrhus hoped to place Cleonymus upon the throne of Sparta as an ally, and therefore would not have wished to damage the city too severely. He was probably also influenced by the high, almost awestruck, esteem in which Sparta was still held by the other Greeks. They were still revered as the saviours of Greece, those who had lead the defence against Xerxes' invasion. Plutarch also claims that the Spartans' weakness and lack of preparations made Pyrrhus overconfident.[24] He camped for the night outside of the city, most likely expecting to take it against minimal opposition the next day.

As the day broke, the women handed the soldiers their armour and delivered the fortifications into their charge. In the true tradition of Spartan women they told their husbands and sons that 'it was sweet to conquer before the eyes of their fatherland, and glorious to die in the arms of their mothers and wives, after a fall that was worthy of Sparta.'[25] Cleonymus' estranged wife, Chilonis, withdrew from the rest and placed a noose around her neck, preparing to kill herself rather than to surrender to her husband.

Pyrrhus led the first assault in person but was repulsed. The freshly turned earth, and the trench itself, gave no firm footing to his troops and proved to be impassable. This was, mostly likely, a diversionary attack as Pyrrhus had also sent his son Ptolemy, with a contingent of 2,000 Galatian and Epirot infantry, around one end of the trench. At first the dug-in wagons and the Spartan defenders held their line. The Galatians were able to dig up some of the wagons and force a gap in the defences. Ptolemy was able to push his way through the breach and into the city. The young Spartan prince Acrotatus saw the danger and lead a contingent of 300 men against him. With local knowledge of the terrain, he was able to approach Ptolemy from behind by the use of hollows in the ground. He attacked the enemy rear and forced them to turn and fight. His surprise attack drove the Galatians back against the trench and wagons, crowding them together in confusion. The Spartans slaughtered Ptolemy's force where it stood. Only a small number of survivors managed to flee back across the ditch.

Acrotatus' feat was witnessed by many spectators in the city. As he returned to his post, covered in enemy blood and the glow of victory, the other Spartan women were reputedly envious of Chilonis for having such a heroic lover. The crowd, in the usual, ribald Spartan fashion, exhorted him to rest and make love to Chilonis, in order to produce brave sons for Sparta. It would be interesting to know, however, what Acrotatus' father Areus thought of the affair. He is recorded as denouncing adultery, 'by Heaven, there ought to be no random talk about fair and noble women, and their characters ought to be totally unknown save only to their consorts.'[26]

Pyrrhus continued to make fierce assaults on the main Spartan entrenchment but was repeatedly beaten back. Only nightfall brought an end to the fighting. That night Pyrrhus supposedly had another of his symbolic visions. He dreamed that he had destroyed Sparta with thunderbolts, thrown Zeus-like from his own hands. Pyrrhus was convinced that the dream foretold his capture of the city. As usual with such visions, however, there was always a Jeremiah around to foretell disaster instead. One of his officers claimed that places struck by thunderbolts were to be kept free of the footsteps of men. He re-interpreted the dream to mean that Pyrrhus should not enter the city. Such characters were useful to the ancient writers, as no matter what the eventual outcome, the omens had foretold it. Pyrrhus, in his usual confident manner, declared this to be nonsense. He stated that 'one of the best of all omens is to fight in defence of Pyrrhus.'[27]

As soon as the day broke Pyrrhus again led his army to attack the Spartan defences. His troops tried to fill in the trench by throwing into it any of the battlefield debris lying around. The Spartans sortied out to prevent this. While the enemy was occupied at the trench, Pyrrhus once again tried to turn the position, this time leading the outflanking troops himself. The Epirots, for a second time, forced a way through the wagons. The Spartans again raised the alarm to bring reinforcements. At the crucial moment Pyrrhus' horse was brought down by a javelin thrown by a Cretan, either an ally or mercenary, fighting for the Spartans. Pyrrhus was flung to the ground and his fall threw the attackers into disarray. The Spartans counterattacked, using missile fire to good effect, and drove the attackers back once again.

Pyrrhus called off his attacks and attempted to negotiate with the Spartans, hoping that their losses would force them to come to terms. According to Plutarch, the goddess Fortune now aided the Spartans, 'either because she was satisfied with the bravery of its men', or because of their illustrious past.[28] Ameinas, one of Antigonus' generals, had sent a relief force to assist the Spartans. Just as he arrived in the city, King Areus arrived back from Crete with another 2,000 men. The reinforcements allowed the Spartans to dismiss from their ranks the elderly and the young. They also sent home their women, who had played an important role in the fighting by bringing up supplies and carrying away the wounded.

Pyrrhus, his overtures rebuffed, renewed his attacks. The reinforced Spartans now easily drove back the assaults, inflicting heavy casualties on the attackers. Pyrrhus finally despaired of taking the city. Instead, he proposed to spend the winter in Sparta, building a new camp to the north of the city, ravaging the countryside and starving the population into surrender. Fortune once again intervened and offered Pyrrhus opportunities elsewhere. He changed his plans and marched on Argos instead. Justin, moralizing unconvincingly, claims that 'such a number of women assembled to defend their birth-place that he retreated, overcome not more by bravery on their part than shame on his own.' More realistically he infers that Pyrrhus' heavy losses led to his retreat.[29] As at Lilybaeum earlier, Pyrrhus appears to have had little patience for a long, drawn-out siege. Once the initial assaults on a city had failed, his restless nature seems to have made him search for less painstaking operations.

The new opportunity offered to Pyrrhus once again came about due to the usual internal conflicts within the Greek cities. In Argos there was a feud between two politicians, Aristeas and Aristippus. As Aristippus was an ally of Antigonus, Aristeas naturally sought aid from Pyrrhus. The rival factions of Greek cities had a long history of seeking aid from foreign powers. The only thing that appeared more important than autonomy was destroying one's domestic political opponents. As Plutarch sagely observes, Pyrrhus always saw success 'as but the starting point for a new one, while he was determined to make good each disaster by a fresh undertaking, he suffered neither defeat nor victory to put a limit to his troubling himself and troubling others.'[30]

Immediately, he received Aristeas' offer, Pyrrhus broke off his Spartan campaign and marched against Argos. The Spartans, however, were not prepared to let him leave so easily. Areus and his troops harassed the Epirots while they were on the march, setting frequent ambushes and constantly attacking his rearguard.

One of Pyrrhus' seers had predicted that, due to a series of ill-omened sacrifices, the king would lose a family member. While Pyrrhus was leading his army through a narrow defile, the Spartans made yet another attack on his rearguard. In the excitement of the moment Pyrrhus reputedly forgot this warning. He ordered his son Ptolemy, along with a force of cavalry, to drive off the Spartan attackers.

Ptolemy had a reputation for daring bravery almost equal to that of his father. Justin relates that Ptolemy was:

> Said to have been so brave and enterprising that he took the city of Corcyra with only sixty men. In a naval engagement, too, he is reported to have leaped from a boat, with seven men, into a fifty-oared galley, and to have taken and kept possession of it.[31]

In keeping with his character, Ptolemy threw himself into the fighting. The

Spartans recognized the prince and a picked band attacked him. One of the Cretan mercenaries brought back by Areus, 'a man of stout arm and swift foot – ran up on one side of the prince as he was fighting spiritedly, struck him, and laid him low.'[32]

Ptolemy's death demoralized his troops and they were driven off by the Spartans. Elated by their success, the Spartans pursued the fleeing Epirots, cutting down many. Their commanders appear to have lost control of their troops, for, like Pyrrhus, the Spartans did not normally pursue a beaten enemy too far or too hard. They advanced through the pass and onto the open plain beyond. Here they were, in turn, ambushed and cut off by Pyrrhus' infantry.

Pyrrhus had just learned of the death of his son. In torment at his death, and at his own role in it, he led the charge against the killers himself. His grief supposedly made him invincible and terrible beyond all previous feats of arms. In his blood rage he killed the Spartan commander and his entire bodyguard until he had 'sated himself with Spartan blood.'[33] These losses caused the Spartans to break off their attacks, and Pyrrhus was able to complete the rest of his march unmolested.

When Ptolemy's body was brought to Pyrrhus, he was supposed to have said, with a grim fortitude worthy of a Spartan mother, that 'he had not been killed so soon as he had feared, or his own rashness deserved.'[34] Pyrrhus celebrated his son's funeral with great fanfare and the usual athletic contests. With these rites performed, he continued his march on Argos.

On arrival before the city, Pyrrhus found that Antigonus had occupied the heights above the plain. The following day he sent a message to Antigonus, calling him a robber, and challenging him to come down onto the plain and fight him for the kingdom. Such challenges were not unusual; Alexander had issued one to Darius on the night before the Battle of Gaugamela. The winner of such a battle could then legitimize his rule over 'spear-won' land. This concept was the underlying validation of all the Successor kingdoms.

Antigonus was a much more cautious and less vainglorious character than Pyrrhus. He was more inclined to settle differences by other methods than force of arms. After his defeats in Macedonia, his army was certainly much smaller than that of Pyrrhus. He therefore declined Pyrrhus' challenge, informing him that 'many roads to death lay open to Pyrrhus if he was tired of life.'[35]

While the two armies confronted each other, the Argives sent ambassadors to both kings. They requested that they withdraw and allow the city to become neutral. Antigonus agreed and handed over one of his sons to the Argives as a hostage. Pyrrhus also agreed to retire but made no firm pledge. Both the Argives and Antigonus, naturally enough, suspected his good faith.

A number of omens had encouraged Pyrrhus to attack the city. He was, more realistically, also encouraged by his allies within the city. They had agreed to betray it by opening one of the gates during the night. Once Antigonus had retreated, Pyrrhus put his plan into effect. Whatever the considerations that lead to Pyrrhus postponing a night attack on Sparta were, they do not appear to have applied to Argos. Perhaps the active participation of a fifth column made the chance too good to refuse.

During the night, Pyrrhus was able to infiltrate his Galatians into the city, through the opened gate, and take possession of the market place. The gate was, however, too small to allow the elephants to enter with their towers on. Their handlers were forced to take the towers off and then put them back on once the animals were inside. The darkness, and the confusion this entailed, caused considerable delay.

The Argives, learning of the attack, sounded the alarm. They rushed to secure the strong points within the city, and sent messages to Antigonus. Due to his suspicions of Pyrrhus' good faith, Antigonus had not withdrawn far, and had obviously kept his army on alert. Antigonus quickly marched back to the city. Prudently, he remained outside the walls, sending a relief force under one of his sons into the city. Areus also came with a force of 1,000 lightly-armed Spartans and Cretans. The Argives, assisted by their allies, launched an assault on the Galatians. Pyrrhus, meanwhile, had forced a way into the city by way of one of the gymnasiums. His men gave their battle-cry, but received only a weak response from the hard-pressed Celts.

Pyrrhus realized that they must be in difficulties and pressed his force forward faster, pushing the cavalry out in front. The city was full of water channels, and these proved to be dangerous traps in the dark. Pyrrhus' troops had once again been thrown into confusion during a night attack. The soldiers misinterpreted their orders, straggled and lost their way. Command and control broke down completely on both sides due to the darkness and confusion. As a consequence, the fighting died down and the adversaries separated until daybreak. The hiatus in the fighting allowed all sides to re-organize their forces.

When the light of dawn began to illuminate the situation, Pyrrhus was surprised and concerned by the numbers of the enemy under arms within the city. He was also disturbed by the sight of one of the offerings in the market, a bronze statue of a wolf and a bull in combat. This caused him to remember an ancient oracle that had declared that he was destined to die when he saw a wolf fighting a bull. The image was apparently a common one in Argos and dated back to their founding mythology.

Depressed by both the portent and the course of the fighting, Pyrrhus decide to retreat, but was worried by the narrowness of the gates. He sent a messenger to his son Helenus, with an order to tear down part of the city wall and to cover the retreat. Due to the noise of the fighting inside the city the courier misheard the command and instead delivered an order for Helenus to march to his father's assistance. Helenus entered the city with the rest of the elephants and the pick of his troops. Pyrrhus was, however, already in full retreat. His soldiers clashed head on with Helenus' relief force. Pyrrhus ordered them to turn around and withdraw. Their leaders attempted to do so but were blocked by their comrades still entering the city.

To make a bad situation worse the largest of the elephants had become stuck in the narrow gateway. It lay there roaring out its distress and blocking the retreat. Another of the elephants that had entered the city had lost its handler. It managed to find its dead rider, and taking him up across his tusks, ran amok through the crowded streets. In its crazed rampage it trampled many of its own side. These naturally enough panicked and bolted in every direction. The Argives took this opportunity to attack the invaders. The Epirots were packed tightly together, unable to defend themselves, and were massacred by the Argives. Those that were able to flee were also so pressed together that they inflicted accidental wounds on each other.

Pyrrhus, observing the disaster, took the distinguishing wreath off his helmet and gave it to one of his bodyguards. He turned to face those pursuing him. One of his attackers was one of the hastily-enrolled poor of the city. He managed to wound Pyrrhus slightly with a spear through his breastplate. Pyrrhus turned on his attacker in his usual battle rage. The Argive's mother was watching the battle from the rooftops. When she saw her son confronted by such a dangerous foe, she hurled a tile at him in desperation. With the strength and accuracy born of despair, the tile hit Pyrrhus on his neck, just below his helmet.

The wound caused Pyrrhus' vision to blur and he dropped his reins. He then fell from his horse near to the tomb of Licymnius, one of the companions of Hercules. Without his royal insignia he was unrecognizable to most of the combatants. A certain Zophyrus, one of Antigonus' soldiers, recognized him and dragged him into a doorway just as he was beginning to recover from his wound. As Zophyrus drew his sword to strike the fatal blow, Pyrrhus fixed him with a ferocious stare. Overcome with fear at the enormity of his task Zophyrus froze for a moment and his hands trembled. He quickly recovered his courage and struck at Pyrrhus, but his trembling hand missed the neck and sliced into Pyrrhus' mouth and chin. He struck repeatedly and eventually succeeded in chopping off the king's head.

News of Pyrrhus' death soon spread. One of Antigonus' sons, Alcyoneus, took the head and rode away to his father. When he arrived into his father's presence he cast the head down before him and his commanders. Antigonus, however, when he recognized the head, rather than being elated, flew into a rage. He struck his son repeatedly with his staff, calling him impious and barbarous, and drove him away. Antigonus covered his face in mourning and burst into tears of sorrow. The death of his foe reminded him of the great reversals of fortune of both his grandfather, Antigonus, and his father, Demetrius.

Such was the fate of most of the Successor kings. Many of those who had built great kingdoms had been similarly brought down by fortune. Antigonus, Lysimachus, and Ptolemy Ceraunus had all been struck down in battle. Perdiccas and Seleucus had been murdered at the height of their powers. His own father Demetrius had been deserted by his troops, captured by Seleucus, and drank himself to death while in captivity. Of the kings, only Ptolemy and Cassander had died of natural causes, and if the sources are to be believed, the latter extremely painfully due to divine retribution.

Antigonus and the Argives were successful in the battle. Antigonus followed up his victory by capturing Pyrrhus' camp and his son Helenus. He also recovered the body of Pyrrhus, which he adorned in a manner suitable for burial and had it cremated. Alcyoneus brought Helenus, dressed in his mourning garb, to his father. Antigonus was pleased with his son's more humble manner and told him that 'this is better, my son, than what you did before, but even now you have not done well in allowing this clothing to remain, which is a disgrace to us who are held to be the victors.'[36] He gave Helenus the bones of his father to carry home with him to Epirus for burial.

With this one victory Antigonus, in a manner common to the era of the Successors, completely reversed his fortunes. Although he treated Helenus and the captured Epirot army well, he was able to impose harsh peace conditions for their release. Helenus was forced to cede all of Macedonia and Thessaly to Antigonus in order to obtain their freedom. His victory had also ensured his continued domination of the Peloponnesus.

Antigonus later learnt, however, that his victory in Greece was not sufficient to overcome the aura of Pyrrhus. Alexander II, the son of Pyrrhus and his successor as king of Epirus, invaded Macedonia soon after. Once again, the fickle Macedonian infantry deserted to the Epirot king. Alexander's conquest did not last long. Demetrius, son of Antigonus, drove him out of Macedonia, and for a time out of Epirus itself. Alexander was able to reconquer his kingdom, with the aid of the Acarnanians and the Aetolians. He continued to rule the country, but could not return the country to the power it had been under his father.

The final campaigns of Pyrrhus in many ways epitomize the criticism of his leadership that is a constant theme of the ancient historians, that he could win victories but not turn them into permanent gains. This attitude is perhaps best summed up by Antigonus Gonatas who claimed that he was like 'a player with dice who makes many fine throws but does not understand how to use them when they are made.'[37] Pyrrhus had won impressive victories in battle over both the Spartans and Antigonus, but had singularly failed to follow them up by knocking either completely out of the war. Instead, Pyrrhus moved on to look for easier victories. Both his foes would continue to fight and lend crucial assistance to Argos in its victory over Pyrrhus. On this occasion Pyrrhus' failings had proved fatal.

It is, perhaps, because of these flaws that Pyrrhus failed in his attempts to build a substantial empire. A more meaningful assessment of his life and achievements would be, however, to consider the role he was born to, that as king of Epirus. Pyrrhus had come to the throne when the kingship of Epirus was divided between two feuding branches of the royal family. The kings had, thereby, become largely puppets of foreign powers. This division meant that the kingdom was under constant threat of attack by its neighbours. By the end of his reign, Pyrrhus had both united Epirus under a single king and increased both the size and wealth of his kingdom. He left his son Alexander a kingdom strong enough to continue to challenge for the control of Macedonia. As Justin claims, Pyrrhus had 'rendered his country, which was before but mean and obscure, renowned throughout the world by the fame of his exploits and the glory of his name.'[38] By the standards of his time, his rule over Epirus must be seen as a success.

Pyrrhus' successors were unable to maintain this position. Epirus would return to its previous obscurity. Pyrrhus' family would continue to reign in Epirus until overthrown by a democratic revolution in 232. The Epirot alliance then became the Epirot League, with a federal council.

The Epirots tried to maintain neutrality during the conflicts between Rome and Macedonia, but in 170, during the Third Macedonian War (171–168), the league split apart. The Molossians supported Macedonia, while the Chaonians and Thesprotians allied with Rome. The Romans conquered Molossia in 167 and remorselessly pillaged the country; 150,000 of its inhabitants were enslaved. Central Epirus was devastated and de-populated. It did not recover until the medieval Byzantine period. The Romans believed in nothing if not vengeance. This was even more so when it came to punishing those who had the temerity to challenge their domination of Italy. Despite waiting over a century, the Romans had, as they also would with Carthage, finally exacted their revenge on Pyrrhus' kingdom.

Notes

Preface

1. Plutarch, *Demetrius*, 30.
2. Curtius, 4.11. Curtius wrote a history of Alexander the Great, most likely in the first century AD.
3. Plutarch, *Flamininus*, 21, *Pyrrhus*, 8; Appian, *Syrian Wars*, 10; Livy, 35.14.
4. Plutarch, *Alexander*, 1. For a slightly more detailed discussion of Plutarch and his methods of composition see Chapter 2.

Chapter 1

1. Strabo, 7.75.
2. Hammond, NGL, *Epirus: the geography, the ancient remains, the history and topography of Epirus and adjacent areas* (Oxford, 1967), pp. 340-5.
3. Herodotus, 2.54-7; Homer, *Iliad*, 16:233. Herodotus (c. 484-425) wrote a history of the Greek and Persian Wars of the fifth century. He is alternately known as 'the father of history' or, largely unjustly, as the 'father of lies'.
4. Hammond, pp. 552-4.
5. Thucydides, 2.80. Thucydides was a commander in and wrote a history of the Peloponnesian War (431-411), he died in 395 before he could complete his work.
6. Hammond, p. 423.
7. Pausanias, 1.11.
8. See Hammond, pp. 557-61.
9. Pausanias 8.7; Plutarch, *Alexander*, 10. Pausanias wrote a geographic guide to Greece in the second century AD.
10. Strabo, 6.3.4.
11. Justin, 12.2. Justin's critics claimed his work was an anthology, excerpted from the earlier work of the historian Pompeius Trogus, omitting all that was not pleasurable to read or did not supply a moral lesson. The date of composition is hotly disputed with the period AD 144-230 being the most likely. Justin appears to have been extraordinarily careless in his method of composition and has a poor reputation as an historian.
12. Aristotle, F 614.
13. Livy 8.24. Livy wrote a long history of Rome from its foundations until his own time. Although it cannot be certain, he probably lived from 59 BC until AD 17.
14. Livy, 8.24; Justin, 12.2; Strabo, 6.15.

15. Hammond, p. 558.

16. Diodorus, 18.22. Diodorus wrote a history covering events from the legendary Trojan War until Caesar's campaigns in Gaul. He was a citizen of the town of Agyrios in Sicily and probably wrote his history between the years 56-26 BC.

17. For a full discussion see Hammond, pp. 560-2.

18. Diodorus, 19.11.

19. Diodorus, 19.36.

20. Plutarch, *Pyrrhus*, 2.

21. Diodorus, 19.88; Pausanias, 1.11.

Chapter 2

1. Justin, 17.3

2. Plutarch, *Demetrius*, 28.

3. Plutarch, *Demetrius*, 29.

4. Plutarch, *Demetrius*, 29.

5. Frontinus, *Stratagems*, 2.4.13. Frontinus was a Roman general and writer in the first century AD.

6. Plutarch, *Demetrius*, 30.

7. Plutarch, *Demetrius*, 30.

8. Plutarch, *Pyrrhus*, 5.

9. Plutarch, *Pyrrhus*, 3.

10. Plutarch, *Pyrrhus*, 4.

11. Plutarch, *Pyrrhus*, 8.

12. Plutarch, *Pyrrhus*, 13; Homer, *Iliad*, 1.491ff.

13. Plutarch, *Pyrrhus*, 3.

14. Arrian, *Anabasis*, 7.8; Hypereides, *Funeral Speech*, 31. Arrian (*c.* 86-146 AD) was a native Greek but served as a Roman general and public servant. Among other works he wrote the *Anabasis*, a history of Alexander the Great's campaigns.

15. Plutarch, *Marius*, 2.45.

16. Porphyry of Tyre, *Fragment* 260 F42, F43; Diodorus, 17.71.1; Curtius, 5.6.11. A talent was approximately 27 kg of silver unless stated otherwise.

17. Cassius Dio, 42.49. Cassius Dio was a native of Bithynia. He wrote a history of Rome from the legendary landing of Aeneas until his own time of AD 229. The sections dealing with Pyrrhus' campaigns exist mostly in fragments or in the summary of the twelfth century AD chronicler John Zonaras. Dio's viewpoint is thoroughly pro-Roman and generally shows a contempt for the common people.

18. Plutarch, *Pyrrhus*, 14; *Anthologia Palatina*, 9.518.

19. Thucydides, 2.81.

20. Polyaenus, 4.2.10; Theophrastus, *Historia Plantarum*, 3.12. Polyaenus was a Macedonian by birth. He wrote for and dedicated his book on the stratagems of war to the emperor Marcus Aurelius (AD 161-180).

21. Diodorus, 16.3.
22. Diodorus, 16.53.
23. Polyaenus, 2.29.2.
24. Plutarch, *Aemilius Paulus*, 20.
25. Garoufalias, p. 268, n. 50; other estimates vary from 10-20,000, but see p. 39.

Chapter 3

1. Justin, 16.1.
2. Plutarch, *Pyrrhus*, 6.
3. Plutarch, *Demetrius*, 36.
4. Justin, 16.1.
5. Josephus, 17.168-9.
6. Plutarch, *Pyrrhus*, 9.
7. Pausanias, 10.20; Diodorus, 18.38.
8. Plutarch, *Demetrius*, 41.
9. Plutarch, *Demetrius*, 33, 40; Diodorus, 20.52.
10. Plutarch, *Demetrius*, 43, *Pyrrhus*, 10.
11. Plutarch, *Pyrrhus*, 11.
12. Arrian, *Anabasis*, 4.11.
13. Plutarch, *Demetrius*, 42, 44.
14. Plutarch, *Pyrrhus*, 12. A similar claim about the Macedonians is made in Plutarch, *Demetrius*, 41.
15. Plutarch, *Pyrrhus*, 12.
16. Plutarch, *Pyrrhus*, 12.
17. Pausanias, 1.7.
18. Pausanias, 1.7.
19. Frontinus, *Stratagems*, 3.6.3; Justin, 25.5.
20. Pliny, *Natural History*, 3.101.
21. Garoufalias, p. 297.
22. Thucydides, 2.13.

Chapter 4

1. Diodorus, 20.104.
2. Livy, 10.2.
3. Appian, *Samnite Wars,* 15. Appian (*c*. 95-165 AD) was a native of Alexandria in Egypt. He wrote a series of books on Rome's early wars.

4. Polybius, 3.22-3. Polybius was a Greek general and historian of the first century BC. While a hostage of the Romans he wrote a history to explain the rise of Rome to his fellow Greeks.

5. Harris, WV, *War and Imperialism in Republican Rome 327-70* (Oxford, 1979), p.10.

6. Thucydides, 5.105.

7. Polybius, 1.37.

8. Polybius, 1.6.

9. Diodorus, 19.72.

10. Cassius Dio, 9.39.

11. Dionysius, 1.5. Dionysius wrote a history of Rome from its foundation until the First Punic War in the first century BC. The purpose of his work was to reconcile the Greeks to the rule of the Romans by describing the good qualities of their conquerors.

12. Dionysius, 19.7.

13. Zonaras, 8.2.

14. Appian, *Samnite Wars*, 17.

15. Plutarch, *Pyrrhus* 13; Dionysius, 19.8.

16. Thucydides, 1.108.4.

17. Plutarch, *Pyrrhus*, 13

18. Garoufalias, p.305-6; Plutarch, *Pyrrhus*, 13

19. See Champion, J, 'The Causes of the Third Diadoch War 315-311 B.C.' in *Slingshot* 213 (2001), pp 4-6.

20. Justin, *Prologues*, 17

21. Billows, RA, *Antigonos the One-eyed and the creation of the Hellenistic state* (Berkeley, 1990), pp. 350-1.

22. Cassius Dio, 40.6; Garoufalias, p. 66.

23. Justin, 17.2.

24. Ammanius, 24.6. Ammanius was a Roman general and historian of the fourth century AD.

25. Arrian, *Anabasis*, 5.16-17.

26. Arrian, *Anabasis*, 5.17.

27. Diodorus, 18.34.

28. Polybius, 3.46.

29. Polybius, 3.46.

30. Zonaras, 8.2.

31. Plutarch, *Pyrrhus*, 16.

32. Polyaenus, 6.6.3.

33. Dionysius, 19.9.

34. Xenophon, *Hellenica*, 5.1.31.

35. Dionysius, 19.10.

Chapter 5

1. Dionyisius 20.11: 'Those who fight in close combat with cavalry spears grasped by the middle with both hands and who usually save the day in battles are called *principes* by the Romans.'
2. Livy, 8.8.
3. For a full discussion, see Goldsworthy, *Roman Warfare*, (London, 2000), pp. 49-55.
4. Livy, 8.8.
5. Polybius, 18.30.
6. Polybius, 18.26.
7. Plutarch, *Aemilius Paulus*, 20.
8. Florus, 1.13.
9. Diodorus, 20.104.
10. Garoufalias, pp. 337-9. Modern estimates of the numbers of troops present vary from 20,000-50,000 for the Romans and 25,000-35,000 for Pyrrhus' army.
11. Chaniotis, *War in the Hellenistic World*, (Malden, 2005) p.21.
12. Frontinus, 4.1.13; Plutarch, *Pyrrhus*, 16.
13. Herodotus, 7.146.
14. Dionysius, 19.12; Plutarch, *Pyrrhus*, 17.
15. Plutarch, *Pyrrhus*, 17.
16. Zonaras, 8.3.
17. Zonaras, 8.3.
18. Frontinus, 2.6.10.
19. http://en.wikipedia.org/wiki/Archilochus
20. Plato, *Symposium*, 221b-c. For a full discussion of the behaviour of routed Greek armies see Hanson, VD, *The Western Way of War: Infantry Battle in Classical Greece* (Oxford, 1989), pp. 177-184.
21. Plutarch, *Pyrrhus*, 17.
22. Zonaras, 8.3.
23. Livy, *Periochae*, 13.1.
24. Garoufalias, p. 76.
25. Plutarch, *Pyrrhus*, 18.
26. Livy, *Periochae*, 13.1.
27. Zonaras, 8.4; Plutarch, *Pyrrhus*, 18
28. Appian, *Samnite Wars*, 22; Plutarch, *Pyrrhus*, 18.
29. Plutarch, *Pyrrhus*, 18; Zonaras, 8.4.
30. Plutarch, *Pyrrhus*, 19.
31. Plutarch, *Pyrrhus*, 19.
32. Diodorus, 16.54.

33. Harris, p. 44.

34. Plutarch, *Sulla*, 32.

35. Cassius Dio, 9.40.

36. Dionysius, 19.15.

37. Plutarch, *Pyrrhus*, 20.

38. Plutarch, *Pyrrhus*, 20.

39. Dionysius, 1.5.

40. Thucydides, 1.22.

Chapter 6

1. Dionysius, 20.1–2.

2. Frontinus, 2.3.21.

3. Livy, 7.37, 10.38, 24.2; Polybius, 2.26.

4. Zonaras, 8.5.

5. Livy, 8.9.

6. Zonaras, 8.5.

7. Zonaras, 8.5.

8. Zonaras, 8.5.

9. Dionysius, 20.1.

10. The references for the different accounts of the battle are: Dionysius, 20.1-3; Plutarch, *Pyrrhus*, 21; Zonaras, 8.5.

11. Plutarch, *Pyrrhus*, 21.

12. Frontinus, 2.2.1.

13. Plutarch, *Pyrrhus*, 21.

14. Dionysius, 20.1.

15. Frontinus, 2.3.21.

16. Livy, 10.27.

17. Livy, 10.14.

18. Livy, 8.27; Justin, 23.2.

19. Polybius, 18.28.

20. Dionysius, 20.1.

21. Dionysius, 20.2.

22. Thucydides, 6.70.

23. Dionysius, 20.3.

24. Dionysius, 20.3.

25. Plutarch, *Pyrrhus*, 21; Dionysius, 20.3.

26. Zonaras, 10.5.

27. Plutarch, *Pyrrhus*, 21.

28. Plutarch, *Pyrrhus*, 21.

29. Garoufalias, pp. 92-3.

30. This is neatly portrayed by the Spartan king, Agesilaus. When he was criticized by his allies for not providing enough soldiers he responded by ordering the army to separate by occupation. Only the Spartans claimed to be soldiers by profession (Plutarch, *Agesilaus*, 26).

31. Curtius, 4.13.40; Arrian, 3.12.

32. Zonaras, 10.5.

33. Plutarch, *Pyrrhus*, 21.

34. Polybius, 1.11.

35. Plutarch, *Pyrrhus*, 21.

Chapter 7

1. Plutarch, *Pyrrhus*, 22.

2. Justin, 24.4.

3. Justin, 24.5.

4. Herodotus, 1.166.

5. Herodotus, 7.158.

6. Herodotus, 7.65; Diodorus, 11.20.

7. Diodorus, 11.21.

8. Not to be confused with the historian, Dionysius of Halicarnassus.

9. Diodorus, 14.47.

10. Diodorus, 14.51.

11. Diodorus, 15.13.

12. Plutarch, *Pyrrhus*, 22.

13. Justin, 18.2.

14. Polybius, 3.25.

15. Justin, 18.2.

16. Appian, *Samnite Wars*, 28

17. Garoufalias, p. 392.

18. Diodorus, 22.8.

19. Polybius, 6.25.

20. Plutarch, *Pyrrhus*, 22. Diodorus, 22.9, records only 1,500 cavalry.

21. Justin, 23.3.

22. Goldsworthy, *The Punic Wars* (London, 2000), p. 82.

23. Diodorus, 22.10; Plutarch, *Pyrrhus*, 22.

24. Plutarch, *Pyrrhus*, 22.

25. Curtius, 8.13.

26. Polybius, 1.56.

27. Justin, 23.3; Polybius, 7.4.

28. Diodorus, 22.10, 24.1.

29. Plutarch, *Pyrrhus*, 23.

30. Garoufalias, p.108.

31. Plutarch, *Pyrrhus*, 26.

32. Plutarch, *Pyrrhus*, 23.

33. Dionysius, 20.8.

34. Plutarch, *Pyrrhus*, 23. Most historians follow Plutarch's narrative and place this battle prior to the siege of Lilybauem. Plutarch's text here is, however, muddled. Nor can he be relied upon for accurate chronology. For example, earlier in his life of Pyrrhus he places the plot to kill the king after the Battle of Heraclea, whereas all the other sources relate it as occurring after the Battle of Asculum. For Pyrrhus to delay the siege of Lilybaeum and march right across the length of Sicily in order to defeat the Mamertines would appear to be unlikely.

35. Plutarch, *Pyrrhus*, 23.

36. Zonaras, 10.6.

37. Justin, 23.3.

38. Plutarch, *Pyrrhus*, 23.

39. Plutarch, *Pyrrhus*, 23.

Chapter 8

1.   Zonaras, 10.6.

2.   Appian, *Samnite Wars*, 29; Diodorus, 27.4; Zonaras, 10.6.

3.   Appian, *Samnite Wars*, 29; Justin 25.3.

4.   Plutarch, *Pyrrhus*, 24.

5.   Plutarch, *Pyrrhus*, 24.

6.   Plutarch, *Pyrrhus*, 24.

7.   Justin, 25.3.

8.   Dionysius, 20.9.

9.   Dionysius, 20.9.

10. Dionysius, 20.10.

11. Livy, *Periochae*, 13-14.

12. Plutarch, *Pyrrhus*, 25.

13. Dionysius. 20.10; Garoufalias, p.118.

14. Thucydides, 7.43-4.

15. Dionysius, 20.11.

16. Frontinus, 2.2.1.

17. Polybius, 1.40.

18. Aelian, *de Natura Animalium,* 16.36; Orosius, 4.2.5; Scullard, *The Elephant in the Greek and Roman World* (London, 1974) p.112.

19. Dionysius, 20.12; Zonaras, 10.6; Garoufalias, p.120.

20. Polybius, 18.28; Justin, 25.5.

21. Polyaenus, 6.6.1; Justin, 25.3.

22. Plutarch, *Pyrrhus,* 26.

23. Dionysius, 20.16.

Chapter 9

1. Appian, *Samnite Wars,* 27.

2. Justin, 25.1-2.

3. Tarn, WW, *Antigonos Gonatas* (Chicago, 1969), pp. 169-170.

4. Plutarch, *Pyrrhus,* 26.

5. Pausanias, 1.13.2.

6. Plutarch, *Demetrius,* 7.

7. Justin, 25.3; Pausanias, 1.13.2.

8. Plutarch, *Pyrrhus,* 26.

9. Plutarch, *Pyrrhus,* 26.

10. Pausanias, 1.13.2.

11. Plutarch, *Pyrrhus,* 26.

12. Justin, 25.4.

13. Plutarch, *Pyrrhus,* 26.

14. Polybius, 2.41.

15. Polybius, 5.19.

16. Polyaenus, 6.6.2.

17. Plutarch, *Pyrrhus,* 26.

18. Pausanias, 1.13.3.

19. Garoufalias, p. 449.

20. Polyaenus, 8.49.

21. Plutarch, *Sayings of Spartans,* Agesilaus, 29, 30.

22. Justin, 14.5; Pausanias, 1.13.3.

23. Polybius, 18.3.

24. Plutarch, *Pyrrhus,* 27.

25. Plutarch, *Pyrrhus,* 27.

26. Plutarch, *Sayings of Spartans,* Areus 1.

27. Plutarch *Pyrrhus,* 29, a paraphrase of Homer's *Iliad,* 12.243.

28. Plutarch, *Pyrrhus,* 29.

29. Justin, 25.4.

30. Plutarch, *Pyrrhus*, 30.
31. Justin, 25.4.
32. Plutarch, *Pyrrhus*, 30.
33. Plutarch, *Pyrrhus*,, 30.
34. Justin, 25.4.
35. Plutarch, *Pyrrhus*, 31.
36. Plutarch, *Pyrrhus*, 34.
37. Plutarch, *Pyrrhus* ,26.
38. Justin, 25.5.

Bibliography

Billows, RA, *Antigonos the One-eyed and the creation of the Hellenistic state* (Berkeley, 1990).

Bosworth, AB, *The legacy of Alexander: politics, warfare, and propaganda under the successors* (Oxford, 2002).

Burn, AR, *Persia & the Greeks* (London, 1984).

Champion, J, 'The Causes of the Third Diadoch War 315-311 BC', in *Slingshot*, 213 (2001), pp 3-6.

Chaniotis, *War in the Hellenistic World*, (Malden, 2005).

Garoufalias, P, *Pyrrhus, King of Epirus* (London, 1979).

Goldsworthy, A, *Roman Warfare*, (London, 2000).

Goldsworthy, A, *The Punic Wars* (London, 2000).

Graves, R, *Greek Myths* (London, 1981).

Hammond, NGL, *Epirus: the geography, the ancient remains, the history and topography of Epirus and adjacent areas* (Oxford, 1967).

Hanson, VD, *The Western Way of War: Infantry Battle in Classical Greece* (Oxford, 1989).

Harris, WV, *War and Imperialism in Republican Rome 327-70* (Oxford, 1987).

Head, D, *The Armies of the Macedonian and Punic Wars 359 BC to 146 BC* (Goring-by-Sea, 1982).

Kincaid, CA, *Successors of Alexander the Great* (Chicago, 1985).

Lund, HS, *Lysimachus: a study in early Hellenistic Kingship* (London, 1992).

Markle, MM, 'The Macedonian sarissa, spear, and related armor', in *American Journal of Archaeology* 81 (1977), p 323.

Markle, MM, 'Use of the sarissa by Philip and Alexander of Macedonia', in *American Journal of Archaeology* 82 (1978), p 483.

Mommsen, T, *The History of Rome* vol. 2 (London, 1908).

Picard, GC & C, *Carthage* (London, 1987).

Scullard, HH, *The Elephant in the Greek and Roman World* (London, 1974).

Tarn, WW, *Antigonos Gonatas* (Chicago, 1969).

The following translations of the ancient sources were used:

Arrian, *The Campaigns of Alexander,* translated by A de Selincourt (Harmondsworth 1958).

Appian, *The Samnite Wars,* translated by H White, http://www.livius.org/ap-ark/appian/appian_samnite_1.html

Cassius Dio, *Roman History,* translated by E Cary, http://penelope.uchicago.edu/Thayer/E/Roman/Texts/Cassius_Dio/ home. html

Curtius, *The History of Alexander,* translated by J Yardley (Harmondsworth, 1984).

Diodorus Siculus, *The Library of History IV*, translated by C H Oldfather (London and Cambridge, Massachusetts, 1946).

Diodorus Siculus, *The Library of History VI*, translated by C H Oldfather (London and Cambridge, Massachusetts, 1954).

Diodorus Siculus, *The Library of History VII*, translated by C L Sherman (London and Cambridge, Massachusetts, 1952).

Diodorus Siculus, *The Library of History VIII*, translated by C Bradford Wells (London and Cambridge, Massachusetts, 1963).

Diodorus Siculus, *The Library of History IX*, translated by R M Geer

(London and Cambridge, Massachusetts, 1947).

Diodorus Siculus, *The Library of History X*, translated by R M Geer

(London and Cambridge, Massachusetts, 1954).

Diodorus Siculus, *The Library of History XI*, translated by F R Walton

(London and Cambridge, Massachusetts, 1957).

Dionysius of Halicarnassus, *Roman Antiquities*, translated by E Cary,
http.//penelope.uchicago.edu/Thayer/E/Texts/Dionysius_of_
Halicarnassus/home/html

Frontinus, *The Stratagemata*, translated by C E Bennet,
http://penelope.uchicago.edu/Thayer/E/Roman/Texts/Frontinus/
Stratagematahome.html

Herodotus, *The Histories*, translated by A de Selincourt (Harmondsworth, 1954).

Justin, *Epitome of the Philippic History of Pompeius Trogus*, translated by J S Watson,
http://www.forumromanum.org/literature/justin/english/index.html

Livy, *The History of Rome*, translated by Rev. C Roberts,
http://www.forumromanum.org/literature/liviusx.html

Pausanias, *Guide to Greece, volume 1: Central Greece*, translated by P Levi (Harmondsworth 1979).

Guide to Greece, volume 2: Southern Greece, translated by P Levi (Harmondsworth 1971).

Plutarch, *Parallel Lives*, translated by B Perrin,
http://penelope.uchicago.edu/Thayer/E/Roman/Texts/Plutarch/ Lives/ home.html

- *Sayings of the Spartans*, translated by B Perrin,
http://penelope.uchicago.edu/Thayer/E/Roman/Texts/Plutarch/Moralia/Sayings_of_S
partans*/main.html

Polyaenus, *Stratagems*, translated by R Shepherd,
http://www.attalus.org/translate/polyaenus.html

Polybius, *The Histories*, translated by W R Paton,
http://penelope.uchicago.edu/Thayer/E/Roman/Texts/Polybius/ home.html

Strabo, *The Geography of Strabo*, translated by H L Jones (London, 1917).

Thucydides, *The Landmark Thucydides*, translated by R Crawley (New York, 1998).

Zonaras (Cassius Dio), translated by E Cary,
http://Penelope.uchicago.edu/Thayer/E/Roman/Texts/Cassius_Dio/ Home.html

Index

152